# THE ATLANTIC OCEAN

# The Atlantic Ocean

*Reports from Britain and America*

## ANDREW O'HAGAN

MARINER BOOKS
HOUGHTON MIFFLIN HARCOURT
BOSTON • NEW YORK
2013

First published in the UK in different form as *The Atlantic Ocean: Essays on Britain and America*

*Library of Congress Cataloging-in-Publication Data*
O'Hagan, Andrew, date.
The Atlantic Ocean : reports from Britain and America /
Andrew O'Hagan. — 1st U.S. ed.
p. cm.
"First published as The Atlantic Ocean: Essays on Britain and America in 2008 by Faber and Faber Limited" — T.p. verso.
ISBN 978-0-15-101378-4
1. United States — Relations — Great Britain. 2. Great Britain
— Relations — United States. 3. United States — Foreign public opinion, British.
4. Public opinion — Great Britain. 5. Popular culture — Great Britain.
6. Popular culture — United States.
I. Title.
E183.8.G70445 2013
327.73041—dc23        2012016365

Book design by Brian Moore

Printed in the United States of America
DOC 10 9 8 7 6 5 4 3 2 1

"The Killing of James Bulger," "On Begging," "The American Dream of Lee Harvey Oswald," "Many Andies," "Good Fibs," "Saint Marilyn," "7/7," "On the End of British Farming," "On Lad Magazines," "Four Funerals and a Wedding," "After Hurricane Katrina," "Guilt: A Memoir," and "The Boy Who Mistook His Life for a Crime" first appeared in the *London Review of Books.* "England's Flowers" first appeared in the *Guardian Weekend.* "The Glasgow Sludge Boat" first appeared in *Granta.* "Introduction to *Go Tell It on the Mountain*" first appeared in the 2001 Penguin UK edition. "England and the Beatles," "Racing Against Reality," "E. M. Forster: The Story of Affection," and "Styron's Choice" first appeared in the *New York Review of Books.*

The author is grateful to John Fuller for permission to quote the poem "1948" by Roy Fuller.

*For my daughter Nell*

# Contents

# THE ATLANTIC OCEAN

# The Killing of James Bulger

THE ABDUCTION AND MURDER of James Bulger, a two-year-old boy from Liverpool, has caused unprecedented grief and anger. Hours before the two ten-year-old boys accused of the crime arrived at South Sefton Magistrates' Court, a large, baying crowd had formed outside. As a pair of blue vans drew up, the crowd surged forward, bawling and screaming. A number of men tried to reach the vehicles, to get at the youths inside, and scuffles spilled onto the road. Some leapt over crash barriers and burst through police cordons, lobbing rocks and banging on the sides of the vans. Many in the crowd — sick with condemnation — howled and spat and wept.

Home Secretary Kenneth Clarke has promised measures to deal with "nasty, persistent juvenile little offenders." Those two little offenders — if they were the offenders, the childish child murderers from Walton — were caught on camera twice. First on the security camera at the shopping precinct in Bootle where they lifted James, and again by the camera of a security firm on Breeze Hill as they dragged James past — the child clearly in some distress.

Watching those boys on camera brought into my head a

flurry of pictures from my own boyhood. At that age, we were brimming with nastiness. I grew up in the last of Scotland's new-town developments. There were lots of children, lots of dogs and lots of building sites. Torture among our kind was fairly commonplace. I remember two furious old teachers driving me and my six-year-old girlfriend, Heather Watt, home early one morning. In recent weeks we had been walking the mile to school in the company of a boy, smaller and younger than ourselves, a fragile boy with ginger hair called David. I think we thought of him as "our boy." We bossed him. Occasionally, when he didn't walk straight or carry our bags or speak when we wanted him to, we'd slap him or hit his hands with a ruler. We had to pass through fields to get to school, with diggers going and "workies" taking little notice of us, though from time to time they'd bring over empty lemonade bottles which we could exchange for money or sweets at the chip shop. We must have looked innocent enough, holding hands, Heather and I, walking the younger boy to school.

Over time, we started to hit the boy hard. Our way to the school was dotted with new trees, freshly planted and bound to supporting stalks with rubber belts. We got into the habit of removing belts every day: we began to punish David with them whenever we thought he'd "been bad." Just a few hits at first on top of his shorts, not so's you'd notice. It got worse, though, and on the last morning, when we were caught by the two old lady teachers, we were beating his bare legs with the coiled-up straps. Though we'd set out on time that morning, we were late, having spent the best part of half an hour on top of an out-of-the-way railway bridge practically skinning the screaming boy's legs.

That incident caused a scandal in our square. My mother was employed as a cleaner in another local primary school with

David's mother, and—although I remember crying and being confused and not quite knowing what we'd done wrong—I could see that we'd caused a lot of embarrassment. Up until the age of ten, I'd both taken part in and witnessed many such incidents. Some of my brothers had reputations for being a bit wild; other boys said they'd "do anything." I watched them do any number of crazy things to other kids around the squares, and I watched the other kids do some brutal things in return. One time, the family had to sit in front of a children's panel. That's what happens in Scotland if a child under sixteen commits an offense: the social work department calls in the whole family in an effort to assess what the real problem is and decide whether the child should be in care—which in my brother's case would have meant a residential, List D school. In the event, that didn't happen, but it took a long time for the community—especially our teachers—to forget what he did. With a friend, he'd burnt down a wing of our local Catholic secondary school.

It's not that any of us were evil; even the more bookish and shy among us were given to a bit of destructive boredom and stupid imagining. Now and then it got out of hand. The boys I hung around with in my preteen years were always losing their heads. During the good weather, the light nights, what started off as a game of rounders or crazy golf would end up as a game of clubbing the neighbor's cat to death. A night of camping on the playing fields could usually be turned into an opportunity for the wrecking of vegetable gardens, or the killing of frogs and people's pet rabbits. Mindless stuff. Yet now and again people would get into things that you sensed were about to go over the edge, or were already over it. My memory tells me that that point was much more difficult to judge than I'd now like to think.

My friend Moggie began taking music lessons at the house of a woman who lived in the next square. She started going out when she was supposed to be teaching him, leaving him to baby-sit her child, who was not yet a year old. Moggie would have been about seven or eight. One day I was in with him, bashing uselessly on her old piano, when he shouted me to the front of the living room.

"I'm biting the baby," he said. "D'you want to?"

The baby was lying on a white toweling nappy and Moggie was bent over her, biting her arms and then her legs and then the cheeks of her face. He said he did it all the time and that the baby liked it. He said it was like tickling. I didn't want to do it but said I'd stay and watch. Another game he played was to put on a record, hoist the baby onto her legs and shake her in time to the music. She obviously wasn't walking yet, but he would jostle her and jam her legs on the carpet. Her head would jerk about and she would cry. Some time later, the bite marks were discovered and Moggie was barred from the house, although everyone — including the baby's parents — said that she had been bitten by the dog. I got to stay, since the woman reckoned I was sensible. Another boy who came to that house used to swallow handfuls of the woman's pills (she always had a great variety lying around, so much so that her daughter was eventually rushed to hospital after eating a load). Moggie joined the navy, and the pill swallower was at the edge of a mob of boys who killed someone at a local ATM ten years later. In the years that I hung around it, that house (and there were many others like it) had been the site of a large number of life-threatening games, solvent abuses and youthful experiments gone wrong.

Something happened when we all got together, even though we were that young. We were competitive, deluded and full of our own small powers. And, of course, we spoke our own language. We had our own way of walking — which wasn't unlike that of the two boys on the video — dragging our feet, hands in our pockets, heads always lolling towards the shoulder. That culpable tilt gave the full measure of our arrogant, untelling ways. As only dependents can be, we were full of our own independence. The approval that really mattered was that of the wee Moggies and Bennas and Caesars we ran around with. There were times when I'm sure we could've led each other into just about anything.

*Just William*-type adventures — earning pocket money or looking for fun — would more often than not end in nastiness or threats to each other or danger to other people, especially to girls our own age and younger boys. There was badness in it, a form of delinquency that most of us have left behind. The girls with whom I read books and colored-in, with whom I regularly played office, were the victims of verbal taunting, harassment and gang violence when I ran around with boys. We all carried sticks and were all of us baby arsonists who could never get enough matches. We stole them from our houses, stole money out of our mothers' purses with which to buy them and begged them from construction workers. I can remember pleading with my mother to buy me a Little Big Man action doll from Woolworth's and then burning it in a field with my pals. Most of our games, when I think of it, were predicated on someone else's humiliation or eventual pain. It made us feel strong and untouchable.

If all of this sounds uncommonly horrific, then I can only say that it did not seem so then; it was the main way that most of the boys I knew used up their spare time. There was no steady regression towards the juvenile barbarism famously characterized in *Lord of the Flies*. We lived two lives at once: while most of the stuff detailed above went on, we all made our first communions, sang in the school choir, did our homework, became altar boys and some went to matches or played brilliantly at football. We didn't stop to think, nor did our parents, that something dire might result from the darker of our extracurricular activities. Except when that murky side took over, and your bad-bastard-ness became obvious to everyone.

Bullies who had no aptitude for classwork—who always got "easily distracted" scribbled in red ink on report cards that never made it home—had unbelievable concentration when it came to torturing minors, in the playground or on the way home. For many of the pupils bullying was a serious game. It involved strategies, points scored for and against, and not a little detailed planning. It was scary, competitive and brought out the very worst in those who had anything to do with it. Kids who were targeted over a long period we thought deviant in some way, by which I mean that they were in some way out of it—maybe serious, bright, quiet, keeping themselves to themselves. When I was nine, there was a particular boy who lived two squares up. For years I'd listened to boys telling of how they'd love to do him in. I sort of liked him, but even so, I joined in the chase when we pursued him in and out of the development and across fields. This stood high in our repertoire of time fillers. "Where's Broon?"—the boy's name was Alan Brown—took its place in a list of nasty games that included snipes (skinning each other's knuckles with cards after each lost game), kiss, cuddle and torture (with girls), blue murder (the same, but sorer) and that kind of thing. If anyone came to the door when these games had gone too far, our mothers and fathers went ape. Belted and sent to bed, many of us would get up after dark and stare out the window, over the square, into each other's bedrooms. We grinned and flashed our torches, trying to pass messages. The message, I remember, was always quite clear: it meant, see you tomorrow.

Even the youths who came from happy homes enjoyed the childish ritual of running away. When parents, sick with anxiety, came to the door or to school looking for their children, we'd never let on. We'd help eleven-year-old absconders get together the bus fare to a bigger place, all of us filling a bag with stolen tins and chipping in coppers for some hero's running-away fund. Of course, they'd always be caught and brought back, but not before we'd enjoyed the parental worry and the police presence in the classroom while the drama lasted. We all took and assigned roles in cruel little dramas of our own devising. Our talk would be full of new and interesting ways to worry or harass our parents, especially our fathers, whom we all hated. Stealing his fags or drink brought a great, often awesome feeling of quid pro quo.

I found many girls to be the same in that respect: I had a twelve-year-old table-tennis friend, Alison, who told us she'd been crushing old light bulbs in a bowl and sprinkling them into her father's porridge. We thought that was great. Some of us knew how to stop it, though, while others just kept it up. A couple of my boyhood friends assiduously built bridges between their mindless, childish venom—their bad-boyish misdemeanors—and adult crime. Not many, but some.

Around the time of our cruelty to the boy David, the local news was full of the disappearance of a three-year-old boy called Sandy Davidson, who'd last been seen playing on one of the town's many open construction sites. Guesses were that he'd either fallen into a pipe trench and been covered, or that he'd been abducted. He was never found. We thought about him, in class we prayed for him, and when we weren't out looking for something to get into, we tried to figure out what had happened to him.

Our mothers' warnings to stay clear of the dumps taught us that Sandy's fate could easily have been our own. And in silent, instinctive ways I'm sure we understood something of Sandy's other possible end, the one that wasn't an accident. We knew something of children's fearsome cruelty to children, and we lived with our own passion for misadventure. Though we knew it neither as cruelty nor as misadventure. No one believed that Sandy was playing alone at the building site that day. We didn't know it then, but as many of us grew older we came to think it not inconceivable that Sandy had come to grief at the hands of boys not a lot older than himself, playing in a makeshift sand-pit. All of these things have returned with the news of James Bulger's murder. More than once this week, a single image has floated into my head: a grainy Strathclyde Police picture of a sandy-haired boy, with its caption "Have You Seen Sandy?"

*March 1993*

# On Begging

G EORGE BAROLI AND I were soaked to the skin. We sat on a wooden bench in the rain; a green bottle of sherry sat between us. George stared straight ahead most of the time, tilting the bottle up to his mouth with both hands, getting it into position, holding it there and breathing through his nose. I tried to roll him a cigarette inside my jacket while he spoke of Newcastle, of how he thought he'd never leave it, and then telling me stories of his life now, as a beggar in London. He tapped my arm. "Times's bad," he said, "but good times is just around the corner."

George talked a lot about time; mainly he spoke of how it went too slow. He was seventy, sleeping most nights at the Bondway emergency night shelter in Vauxhall. When he turned to me, I noticed how mottled the irises of his eyes were, how patches of white and light gray jostled for space on them in such a way as to give him a look of shock and bewilderment. He wore one of the longest coats I've ever seen; it went all the way down, ending on top of a yellowish pair of sand shoes. His face was full of crevices and shelves, shallow nicks and lines of confusion, and his lips were dark and scorched-looking. He said he was schizophrenic, that years ago, in Newcastle, he'd had injections, but that that had all stopped. He said he needed medicine, tablets, something other than what he was given now and again for "bowel-opening." Lunchers marched across the gardens, crouched under umbrellas, eating bananas. He puffed at my damp roll-up.

"Do ye believe Christ is the Son of God?" he asked casually.

"Sometimes," I said, wiping the bottle. He then did something which is quite unusual between beggars: he asked me for money. I gave him some change and the rest of the Golden Virginia. He stood up, nodded, slid his arms into the long coat and walked off. An attendant, patrolling the path, strode up and told me to get rid of the bottle. And he hoped I wasn't begging: "This isn't the place." I pulled my hood up and made off, slipping between the charging umbrellas, thinking to find a decent spot over the Thames.

The railway bridge by Charing Cross, I thought, might make a good begging pitch, what with all those mauve scarves and coats making their way over to the South Bank Center. I found a plastic breadboard and, placing it upside down, sat on it at the top of the stairs on the Embankment side. I stared at the ground, soaking dirt covered with fag stubs and tickets, lifting my head just occasionally to see who was looking. Then I'd ask them for money. I'd put a hand out and ask for spare change.

This matter of sitting on the ground begging was as far from my normal point of view as any I can properly imagine. It wasn't my life and, previous to this, I knew nothing of it. Yet as soon as I folded my legs on that bridge, the moment I looked up to address some stranger with my bogus little request, I felt I was no longer part of the places I knew. I felt I'd been here for years; already I burned with resentments that normally take time to kindle. I had never been among the walkers-past, I was sure—though, in fact, I had never been anywhere but among them. Without quite knowing why, I forgot all about the conditions of journalism and the vantage points of my own life, and felt at once that I was genuinely and irrevocably under some-one else's feet. In this frame of mind, you begin to notice things about passersby that you would never, when following your normal routines, notice about yourself.

Searching for signs of pity, I see only embarrassment. In the seconds of eye contact, some people evidently wish the ground would swallow them up. Others, newly elevated, puffed-up and tight, looked as if they wished the ground would swallow me. In my new way of thinking I began to detect contempt and fear in the faces of most who passed. I obviously looked—and the thought made me uneasy—like I'd meant to look; people responded in the ways I knew they'd respond, in the ways I responded myself when passing a lone, wet beggar on a bridge. There were signs of sadness and disappointment in some faces, as if the promise of a pleasant evening were somehow blighted at the sight of me. There are those who tell you to get a job, to piss off or to leave them alone. And others—with their "Sorry, mate," "No change, pal" or "I'm in the same boat" patter—return you to yourself a bit, speaking to you in ways you'd thought suspended by the rules of the game. But perhaps not, perhaps they're just the kind of people who can return a glance with a glance of their own, and who prefer to speak when spoken to.

People say that they hate the way beggars publicly expose themselves, expose their need and their need to expose their need. The walkers-past, on the other hand, with their mad-dened eyes and embarrassed shoes, their twitches and blushes and grunts, expose just about everything a beggar would wish to know about who they are. In waves of the hand and the words they choose to spit, in haughty tut-tutting and superior giggling, a great number of those who pass by express their dislike of beggars and their general scorn of any sort of in-your-face poverty. Or that's how it looked from where I sat.

The money I was given that afternoon I got in different ways. Usually, it arrived in my lap after falling through four feet of air. I'd chase coins from the flying givers all but into the Thames itself; a few coins bounced beside me and leapt through the bars of the railing, vanishing into the water. The trains might rattle in and out behind me for an hour without my gaining a penny. Then someone would appear at the top of the stairs — usually a woman — and over she'd come with a disquieted expression, a look of concern. She'd ask, was I OK, hungry? "You look very tired . . . I'm sorry," she'd say. She'd hand over a pound or 50p and leave with a glance backwards. I'd wonder who she was. A beggar's relationship with strangers (i.e., anyone who isn't a policeman or another beggar) is always the same: a request made and usually ignored, though occasionally met. I tried begging at different spots along the bridge and was glared at by beggars who had their own territory marked out with bin liners, cardboard and sleeping bags. With the light fading and the tourists elsewhere, I leaned against the railing and looked at my hand, separating the coins to count what I'd made. It came to £2.86.

In the last ten years, street begging in Britain has become visible in ways unseen since the early nineteenth century. This has coincided, of course, with the Thatcher years, in which the idea of society as a non-thing, as a fruitless misnomer, has come into its own — with the time it has taken the word "dispossession" to become wholly familiar to anyone who dwelled anywhere near the wrong side of the tracks. To many, the large-scale return of begging — like rises in unemployment, house repossessions and the closure of hospitals — was a sure sign that things were not going well. But the most powerful mediators in this non-society have chosen to prove it a sign of something else: that the chosen profession of scroungers and layabouts, of wasters and filthy idlers, is on the move. Such voices boom loudly these days. It's not about economic ruin, they say, it's about idleness; it's not to be called poverty, it's to be called sponging.

"Beggars were once a rare sight on Britain's streets and provoked more sympathy than disgust. But all that has changed over the last few years as the streets of our major cities have become hunting grounds — not for penniless unfortunates, but for a new breed of professional beggars. Many of them are not in need at all." This, from a July report in the *Daily Express,* was headlined "Scandal of the Bogus Beggars." Two months earlier, the *Mail on Sunday* had spoken of "a sinister and violent new phenomenon which threatens to engulf the capital and, if police fears prove correct, could break out into open warfare as the tourist season reaches its peak: aggravated begging." It went on: "More and more respectable people are having to run the gauntlet of intimidating beggars, blocking their path, being abusive, spitting and threatening to infect them with Aids." According to which report you read, beggars are making so much ("Benefit cheats who gang up on victims net £1,000 a week," roared the *Daily Mail*) that jewelers, brickies and bankers are giving up their jobs in favor of begging. "Scruffy Dave Naylor," according to the *Daily Star,* "has got it made. He can earn up to £85 a day — doing nothing. He just haunts a tube station looking pathetic, and people drop their hard-earned cash into his plastic cup. For dirty, greasy-haired Dave, 19, is king of the hard-faced professional beggars working Central London."

These reports — with their penny-dreadful conflation of begging with theft, Social Security fraud and gang violence — have taken their toll in public wariness. People are increasingly suspicious of anyone who's asking for money. London Underground pasted up thousands of posters warning customers not to give, warning them to avoid being exploited by the increasing number of "professional" beggars. Opposition comes from unexpected as well as extremely predictable places. Churches, once the final and surest refuge of the needy, are turning people away; some have their own poster campaigns. Father Ken Hewitt, of St. Augustine's Church in South Kensington, thinks beggars are, in the main, liars and cheats: "They're all professionals, they know what they're doing. They've actually got homes, most of them . . . I'm not aware of any part of the Gospel which suggests that Jesus casually gave money away to anyone who asked." Hewitt claims to know of a family of beggars seen wheeling a supermarket trolley full of alcohol. He earns £12,000 a year and reckons some beggars must make around £200 a week.

Intolerance of this kind may be striking, but it is not new. Unlike, say, dramatists, beggars have never had a break from being one of the subgroups of the great British underclass. With bards, vagabonds, rhymers, minstrels, fencers, wastrels, robbers, cripples, rioters, barrators, ribalds, sloths, rag-and-bone men, COs, Gypsies, dole scroungers, poll-tax dodgers and Avon ladies, they are more or less permanent fixtures on the mythical list of great British degenerates. Whatever was happening in British history, you can be sure that there or thereabouts was some supposed counterfeiting hedge-creeper, lying by the road with his clack dish.

In 1362, Langland was writing about the "loller's way of life," about beggars "filling their bags and stomachs by lies, sitting by night over a hot fire, where they untie their legs, which have been bound up in the daytime, and lying at ease, roasting themselves over the coals, and turning their back to the heat, drinking gallantly and deep, after which they then draw to bed, and rise when they are in the humour . . . and contrive to live in idleness, and ease, by the labours of other men." Acts and proclamations sprouted over time, sympathetic to the idea that beggary was in most cases the favored trade of the impotent lush and thieving bawd. Henry VIII's statute against vagrancy proclaimed that "vacabundes and Beggers have of longe tyme increased & dayly do increase" and allowed that justices of the peace should provide the true poor with limited licenses to beg; anyone begging outside these limits would be set in stocks; beggars caught without a license would be stripped and whipped; compulsive beggars-without-a-license would be whipped, pilloried and have an ear cut off for each of their two subsequent offenses. The idea of "licensed" begging caught on. Holinshed's chronicles tell of a proclamation of the City of London which demanded "that all vagabondes depart the city within five days." Some beggars, deemed truly to be in need, were given badges to wear so that they might beg legally and be allowed to buy from grocers.

Today's equivalent of these licenses are the cards given to the homeless vendors of the *Big Issue*. Launched in September 1991 with backing from the Body Shop organization, the magazine's stated objective is "to help the homeless help themselves." There are more than 3,000 registered vendors selling around 90,000 copies a week, in Manchester and Brighton as well as in London. A separate edition is published in Scotland—launched last June—with weekly sales of 60,000. The licensees buy stock from the *Big Issue*'s distributor for 20p and then sell them at the cover price of 50p. Most of the regular vendors I spoke to shifted around 30 copies a day. Charismatic, friendly showmen sold a lot more; those who drank or looked dirty sold fewer. An old vendor I spoke to at Oxford Circus said the secret was to "smile a bit more than usual."

The *Big Issue* seems a very nineties way of making begging a little more respectable; with its entrepreneurial benevolence, its "feelgoodishness," it can at times look like the acceptable face of destitution. (In the same way, the Youth Opportunities Scheme and the Job Club were intended to make unemployment more respectable while keeping the figures down.) There's a lot of suitable talk about giving people confidence, adding to their self-esteem, helping them to "reintegrate," to raise their heads from the ground-staring position. Someone involved with the magazine told me that selling the paper taught the vendors how to become "like tele-sales people." It's an independent thing, though, and it shouldn't be blamed for doing what it can (and can't). So long as homelessness and poverty are not the big issue, the *Big Issue* will provide a small earning option for those who can't make the money anywhere else. The real difficulty is for those who, for one reason or another, do not sell the magazine. For, in line with historical precedent, the benefits accruing to the licensed are simultaneously deemed undeserved by the unlicensed, the illegitimates. People think they're a fraud.

Londoners have always been worried about being exploited by those posing as needy. A writer to the *Gentleman's Magazine* for December 1796:

> In my late walks about London and its environs, I have observed with some concern the multiplied swarms of beggars of every description . . . Impressed with the idea that more of these miserable objects are beggars by choice than by neces-

sity, I leave them with the wish that our laws, or magistrates, would at least endeavour to lessen their numbers, or by some badge or other enable kind-hearted Christians to discern their proper objects.

Visitors to the Spitalfields Benevolent Society in 1802 were exhorted to take note of the society's newly adopted maxim "that street-beggars are, with very few exceptions, so utterly worthless and incorrigible, as to be undeserving the attention of such a Society." The general fear was that London workhouses were attracting scroungers from all over the country. J. C. Ribton Turner, a nineteenth-century beggarologist, recorded the graffiti on the walls of the vagrant wards of various workhouses and relayed them to a Victorian public eager for confirmation of their views on the great unwashed: "Private notice—Saucy Harry and his moll will be at Chester to eat their Christmas dinner, when they hope Sarcer and the rest of the fraternity will meet them at the union—14 Nov. 1865"; "Wild Scoty, the celebrated king of the cadgers, is in Newgate, in London, going to be hanged by the kneck till he is dead, this is a great fact—written by his mate."

Sellers of brass rings, rotten cotton and fake Windsor soap, ballad singers, china menders, smashers (who dealt in counterfeit money), mushroom fakers (umbrella repairers), fraters (licensed beggars who preyed on women) and begging-letter writers vied for the attentions of a London public increasingly ambivalent about the Christian duty of giving. Lurid tales of advanced conmanship filled the papers: "Many beggars," Francis Grose reported, "extort charities by practising Faquir-like voluntary austerities and cruelties on themselves"; and, in *London Labour and the London Poor,* Henry Mayhew offered a chart of prices:

| | |
|---|---|
| Loan of child, without grub | 0s. 9d. |
| Two ditto | 1s. 2d. |
| Ditto, with grub and Godfreys Cordial | 1s. 9d. |
| If out after twelve at night for each child, extra | 0s. 2d. |
| For a school of children, say half a dozen | 2s. 6d. |
| Loan of any garment, per day | 0s. 6d. |
| Going as a pal to vindicate any statement | 1s. 0d. |

Extortion stories, tales of self-mutilation and child-hiring, serial dramas of beggars hiding vast quantities of money, growing rich and sailing for Jamaica; some running gangs, stashing hundreds and throwing colossal, gin-sodden orgies for all their begging pals and their molls: it was all part of the smoggy legend of Victorian London. And that smog, long since vanished from other quarters, has never quite unfurled from around the ankles of the British beggar.

I sat on a bleached-out walkway near London Bridge, staring into a gigantic billboard: "Pepsi Max: Max the Taste, Axe the Sugar." The concrete walkway sloped down from a modern block of offices labeled Colechurch House. It was the middle of the morning, cold, with hardly anyone around. I sat cross-legged with a torn piece of cardboard in front of me covered with loose change. Passersby caught sight of me as they came round the bend; most would cross over to the other side of the slope, aiming to give me a wide berth. After an hour or so of being avoided, an elderly man came near. When I asked him if he had any spare change, he fixed me with a look of boiling contempt. Almost everything he had on was tan-colored. His shoes, his jacket, his scarf—all tan. He came right up to me. "You should do something about this," he said, digging a hand into trousers that were slightly darker than the rest. He pulled out three coins, tutted and threw them on the card. "Sitting there," he muttered as he walked away, "sitting there like that!"

The tan man's 42p was what I made all morning. I was, by that time, stiff with sitting, so I walked over London Bridge, stopping here and there to look into the river. It was choppy, the air was choppy, with sirens and horns going off everywhere. I was about to start begging when I noticed a guy sitting on the other side. He looked over: this was clearly his pitch. It turned out that he was seventeen, from Leeds, and had begged around town every other day for a month. Today was bad, he was saying, only 60p the whole morning. When I said 42p, he laughed. He'd come to London looking for family he'd never seen and now couldn't find. He was a bag of nerves, and wearing a T-shirt without a jacket, clearly very cold: he'd left some clothes with someone somewhere and, he insisted, would get them soon.

I walked into the City and begged through lunchtime outside a building on the corner of Cannon and Friday streets, in the shadow of St. Paul's. A lot of suits went past, a lot of bad looks, seemingly hundreds of them, perhaps thousands of shoes, all clicking, all nipping off somewhere. None of them gave. Tourist buses kept stopping at the lights across from me. I felt their eyes. I laughed, imagining the guy in the bus with the microphone, the tour operator, pointing to Sir Christopher Wren's construction, on the left, and on the right, pointing to me, Baroness Thatcher's. I felt edgy at that corner, though; it was too open; I was getting a lot of looks, and the City is notoriously tight with beggars, indeed with everyone. I pulled my hood up and waited. It came at about 2:40. A lone policeman carrying a raincoat.

"Are you begging, sir?" he asked.

"No, just looking," I said, pulling the zip up further.

"I must ask you to move on . . . on you go, go on." I went back across the bridge, noticing that the guy from Leeds had moved on too, though he'd left his cardboard behind.

There are around thirty-five drop-in centers for the homeless in London. Mostly run by volunteers, they each have their own target groups and range of facilities. They aim to serve not only those living on the streets (not all beggars are homeless, just as not all homeless are beggars) but those living in unstable, temporary accommodation such as night shelters, hostels and DSS-funded bed-and-breakfast places. Almost every beggar you speak to has just come from or is just on his way to one of these places. Day centers, soup runs and night shelters give some structure to the average vagrant's day: a simple version of the structure (morning mail, breakfast, car, office, phone, lunch, shopping, dinner, date, telly, bed) those with possessions take for granted, even on days when nothing's going on.

Over the eleven years of its existence, The Passage, a day center for over-twenty-fives in Carlisle Place, near Victoria, has provided hundreds of (mainly) vagrant men—many with alcohol or mental health problems—with access to food, toilets, showers, washing tubs and dryers. Other in-house services include specialists' advice on DSS and housing matters as well as the offer of help from detox and drug rehabilitation agencies. The London Connection in Westminster tries to attract young people aged between sixteen and twenty-six; it has television, a pool table, provides free razors and cheap lunches. The Kaleidoscope Project in Kingston upon Thames aims to serve heroin users in need of treatment. They house a medical team that runs a methadone program and needle exchange. A few of the existing drop-in centers grew out of Victorian soup kitchens or Christian missions of the 1930s, but most sprang up in the 1980s to meet a sudden need.

I stood for a bit outside the Southwark drop-in center in Paradise Street. There were Christian posters on Day-Glo paper behind the windows, behind wire. It looked like the youth clubs I remembered from Ayrshire, like freestanding public toilets or an old-style dole office stranded at the end of a street full of small houses. It was one of the poorer centers: really just a charity hall run by a few people who believed in God. It wasn't full of dryers and free condoms like some of the others. I walked in, returning the nods of some men playing dominoes at a folding table by the door. A man with red hair beckoned me over to a table in the corner, behind which he stood fixing sandwiches and sorting mugs. A giant tea urn sat on the table, drips falling rapidly from the nozzle. A bucket on the floor caught them as they dropped; the milk had been added in the urn and there was about three inches of milky—almost white—tea quivering in the bucket. I took a mug and sat down.

The sandwich maker came over and started telling me about the mission, how it was used by a lot of unemployed people just looking for somewhere to sit down. They do two meals a week, on Tuesday and Thursday afternoons, just simple things. The tea was as sweet as it was white. While we talked, a guy over by the window—a skinhead wearing a hooded sweater, with a bangle on his wrist—kept looking up as if he wanted to come into the conversation. I asked the boss if they say prayers. "There are services," he said, "but only for those who want it." Then the skinhead got up. "You from Glasgow?" he asked with a Glaswegian accent. "I thought that as soon as I heard you talking." He sat across from me and went on about how he used to live on the street. Homeless, but not a beggar, he insisted: "No, I could never hack that. If you're hungry later, there's this place in New Cross that gives out dinners, sandwiches and that, from the stuff the supermarkets don't sell. I still go up there myself sometimes, sling a few in a carrier bag, you know, does me a couple of days."

He'd been resettled, as they say, out of Spur House, an all-male DSS hostel in Lewisham. He'd been there six months when he was given a local-authority flat. He said it was great at Spur, "brilliant . . . a magic laugh . . . bevvying, smoking hash and fucking about. It was a party." I asked him what it was like having his own place. "Shite," he said, "the rent's only two quid a week, 'cause I'm on the broo, but I don't even pay that. To me it's just a squat. It's a right fuckin' dump." He tells me to go to Spur House: "You'll get in there, no sweat." The boss goes back to tend the sandwiches and the dripping urn.

On my way out, I stopped to talk to a guy with a radio held to his ear; there was shouting and booing coming out of it. He asked for a cigarette, placing the radio on the step. We squatted down.

"Some mess," he said. The booing had crackled into a report: "Leaders of the main political parties joined forces today in denouncing last night's victory"—it was the day after the Isle of Dogs council election—"Derek Beackon of the BNP won the seat, opponents say, by appealing to outrage among the local white community over the allocation of council . . . Dr. George Carey, the archbish—" The owner of the radio was shaking his head, twisting the aerial. "This'll be the start of it," he said. "They'll all be at each other's throats." We sat smoking, listening to the reaction of the archbishop and the news of how Home Secretary Michael Howard deplores the event.

The tube to Victoria cost more than double what I had made all day. There was a girl at the top of the stairs when I got there. The place was packed; it was a good spot. After talking to me warily a while, she told me she'd made a tenner begging over the last three hours. She looked very pale. From Bradford, she'd come to London with nothing but a pair of tights, some knickers, and a couple of CDs in a plastic bag that she hoped to sell. She was pregnant by a guy she hated; her parents hated her and she them. She was five months gone. "I've been here five weeks and still no dole money," she said. Sleeping in a B & B in Holborn — rent paid by the DSS — she had to be out by 9:30 in the morning. She had started begging "to pass the time."

Victoria is full of police, blue shirts flitting past on every side. I stood with a group of dossers outside the station, at a bus stop across from the theater where the musical *Starlight Express* plays. The group was constantly separating and coming together, splitting and gathering, like a flock of pigeons, each man going off to beg and returning, moments later, with nothing in his expression to indicate success or failure. We sat on a low wall, two cans of Special Brew circulating. Some kept hold of their own; drinking, as it were, privately. One of them — younger than the rest — was drunk and agitated and kept spinning around and hassling passersby in a loud voice. A couple of coppers walked up to him. They began to argue. As it hotted up, the others got up off the wall, pointing and shouting. I stepped around them at this point, switching on the tape recorder in my pocket. "Don't start all that," says one of the cops to the jumpy one, who's trying to pull away from his grasp.

"I've been here longer than you, mate. I live around here. Piss off."

They got on either side of him and pushed him towards a police van parked outside the station. Then they came back, moving quickly through the group, prodding and shouting. "Beat it. Move on. Get." A very fat woman, her face painfully red and bloated with drink, sat on the ground beside the wall, bawling. She had no socks or shoes on, and the soles of her feet were filthy. She held on to a can of lager, crying her head off, while everyone around her dispersed. One of the cops flicked her arm, trying to get her attention. "On your feet, on your feet," he tells her over and over again. Her face stays crumpled and red, she's gripping the can, she doesn't move.

I walked towards Vincent's Square, speaking, on the way, to a girl at the corner selling copies of the *Big Issue*. She'd sold twenty copies all day; it was late afternoon. "Everybody's in such a big rush, you know. I haven't had any lunch," she said. In London for four months, she'd come from Canada and couldn't get back. "I'm here now," she said, "and I've been trying to get a regular job. Sometimes I sleep in a hostel, and other times I just crash down somewhere or with people I meet. I don't do very well. Some of them selling this are, like, experienced hustlers, but I'm not that good."

Round the corner, on a door of Westminster Cathedral, someone had put up a poster warning people not to give to beggars: "If you want to give, please donate to a recognised charity." A security guard had been taken on to keep beggars away. I folded my jacket over my arm, flattened down my hair and walked in. The smell of incense and candle wax hit me immediately, making me feel sick. I could hear the sound of a communion bell, a bell I used to ring myself, coming from an altar at the far end of the church. I almost swooned. I swiped a copy of the *Catholic Herald* and made back for the door; I dipped my hand in the holy-water font and looked out at the square. A man was lying, full-stretch, beside a bench where a number of drinkers had gathered. I stepped out with the stolen paper and unfolded it in the square, glad to have stolen something and vaguely wondering if there would be a queue for the confessionals. On the front page was an article headlined "Cardinal Attacks Western

Values." It was a report on Cardinal Hume's address to a Prague symposium entitled "Living the Gospel in Liberty and Solidarity." The cardinal warned against "the consumer culture" of Europe and suggested that "the key tasks facing the Church are the need for economic justice, the moral imperative to help migrants and refugees, and the importance of combating nationalist pressures." I dried the remaining moisture on my fingers by mussing up my hair.

Laurie McGlone lay in a doorway in Victoria Street, next to an Oddbins off-license. His face was coarse as sackcloth and his eyes were puffy and wet, blinking eagerly over the passing crowds like a pair of old salmon struggling to shoot the rapids. The bristles on his face were gray, and around his hairline ran an angry red rash. He spoke with a strong but soft Irish accent: "I make very, very little money, just enough for a . . ." He nods to Oddbins. "How long have you been from Scotland, then . . . all your life you say, all your life. Well it's a wild, wild life." I asked him if they gave him dole money.

"If I puts roots down," he said. "But I don't, you see, I just keep going from place to place. I've been on the trawlers now, I've been in Iceland, and in Germany, all over the fuckin' world. I'm very, very bad. I just drift from place to place. You see, I've got a drink problem, and sometimes I get nothing for a drink. Now, I've worked with Gypsies and everything . . . One day a tall, a very tall man comes walking down here — down Victoria Street there — and hit me right on the head with an umbrella. He got me right here, cut me, and called me a bastard, a lazy-fuckin'-bastard-cunt. This is a dangerous, dangerous job."

He had tattoos all the way up his arm, which he'd got, he said, in Trieste in 1946.

"I worked with me brother, we worked with horses. We ran

them and we took bets. I did that, and then I drank. A wee girl in The Passage, from Roscommon, she said if I wanted to get off the drink she'd put me in a place, a house in Clapham for drinkers. If I came back tomorrow she'd help me. She was talking to me just like you're talking to me now. What did I do? I met a guy from Liverpool round the back of the church, the cathedral there, and he gave me a couple of cans. So I was fucked, I couldn't go to her."

Two women went past wearing fancy hats, as if they were going to a wedding. Laurie grinned: "Which one's yours?" We laughed.

"Where will you sleep tonight?" I asked.

"I couldn't care less, Jock. I really couldn't care less."

Begging is a criminal offense in Britain. Ears are no longer cut off for it: the usual penalty is a £50 fine or three days' imprisonment. In the Charing Cross area of London, between January and June of this year, 708 people were arrested for suspected begging offenses. Over the same period last year, 487 were arrested. Of those arrested this year, 205 were charged and 477 were let off with a caution. In 1991 there was an energetic campaign, known as Operation Taurus, to rid the area of beggars. Constable Brent Hyatt, a member of the Homeless Unit based at Charing Cross police station, seems pretty certain that the younger beggars, at least, often live on the street by choice; that arresting beggars stops them from reoffending.

A beggar I met in Leicester Square told of being arrested three times. Twice he'd been fined. Each time, he said, he had spent a few days begging in order to make up the fine. In one month this year (May) the number of begging arrests tripled. The protestations of those who oppose begging, those — including many churches, newspapers and charity organizations — who believe it has nothing to do with poverty and the ways of the economy, have had an extremely significant effect on the public perception of begging as a criminal activity. Most of those arrested in Charing Cross were between seventeen and twenty-nine. Many more under-sixteens are arrested than over-sixties. A majority of the younger ones, say the police, have come from "a bad background": from borstals, split families, "abuse situations" or some form of council care. On arrest, this year, the largest proportion of beggars (210) in the Charing Cross area had between £1 and £5 on them; 160 carried between £10 and £50; 130 had between £5 and £10; 95 had less than 99p; and only 10 had more than £50. In other words, a substantial majority had less than £10 to their name.

A man with an acoustic guitar kept climbing on top of the parapet on Westminster Bridge the morning I went down there to beg. As I walked up, I could hear him strumming and singing the Stones' song "Start Me Up." He strummed on as a pleasure boat, the *Chevering,* passed underneath him, going downriver. The people on the boat looked up, many through their cameras. The high-wire guitarist was colored red; he looked like a well-weathered Highlander or someone who'd just finished buzzing a bag of glue. He looked mad and indignant. I closed in as two coppers did the same. "It's beautiful, the water," he said to one of the cops, while shaking his head, refusing to hand over the guitar or be helped down. Someone took a picture as the police brought him down and booked him.

I stood at the opposite end of the bridge, beside St. Thomas's Hospital, asking for money. Almost right away, even before the crowd had fully dispersed from around the minstrel-jumper, a man in a red anorak gave me £1.20. He stuck his hand in his pocket, laughed as he handed the coins over, then sniggered, shuffled and whispered "Good luck." I tried the technique of walking up to people and moving along with them, asking on the trot. They seemed to hate that, to be more than usually offended. I made another 70p before the clock struck one, then I headed off towards Waterloo.

I got 20p off a couple holding hands on a bench down the South Bank. They sat near a slab of gray paving onto which were engraved Wordsworth's lines about the Thames:

> O Glide, fair stream, forever so.
> Thy quiet soul on all bestowing,
> Till all our minds forever flow
> As thy deep waters now are flowing.

Further on, along the side of the Royal Festival Hall, I was moved on; not by the police this time, but by a burly beggar twice my size who owned the pitch, or so he said. I sat down on one of the concrete connecting paths on the way to Waterloo Underground station and put a handkerchief on the ground covered with coppers. People passed by. I pulled my hood up and leaned back against the wall. Battalions of suits became like one suit—the skin of an armored multipede slithering past. I tried to imagine the levels of anxiety involved in having to beg like this almost every day. The handkerchief, for the longest hour, remained undisturbed. Then I got two pound coins in quick succession.

St. Martin-in-the-Fields day center, at Trafalgar Square, was due to open at 6:30 the evening I went. I arrived there just after five and already there were two dozen people waiting around outside. An elderly man in a gray coat, with white hair and beard and no teeth, argued furiously with a stocky woman in front of the church. They pushed each other and swore like mad, each of them looking as if they were about to start throwing punches. Beside me was a teenage guy with a ponytail, his head pulled down so his chin touched his chest; his arms were inside his jacket, the sleeves hanging baggy and empty. Eventually he tapped me for a cigarette. The waiting crowd continued to swell; old ladies wearing numerous coats stood beside women less than a third their age. A boy dropped a puppy and the stocky woman got angry again, saying he wasn't taking good enough care of it. The center was in the church crypt, and by now there was a fat queue of people all the way down to the door.

They opened up at twenty past six. The crowd burst through, some chatting in groups, others very much by themselves. Once inside, we took our places on plastic seats lining the walls of a long corridor with a concrete floor. There was something about that subterranean corridor that made it seem very familiar, as if I'd been there many times before, with the same sort of crowd, not in life but in novels — novels written eighty or ninety years ago. I wondered about the modern journey that brought these people here; the rites of passage from the world of carpets, central heating and pedal bins — of families and furniture and everything-you-know — to the familiarity of this damp, Victorian chamber filled with ugliness and dismay and unknowable sadness.

A volunteer came round with cloakroom tickets, talking briskly with those he recognized. He started down the other end with the first ticket. I was number 76. We stood up and formed a queue down the middle of the corridor. The air was filled with the noises of scraping chair legs and shouting voices. I got to the door, handed over my ticket and gave my name as requested. Once inside, we were offered mugs of tea and a couple of biscuits: quick sugar for those who needed it. When I walked into the main room the first thing I noticed was how the place stank of piss. It was a cavernous space filled with rows of burst armchairs, most of which had people in them, eating soup or steak pie with boiled carrots. A few of them sat on a table at the back, shouting to an old geezer at the front to turn the telly over. Some were shouting for football and others for a Harrison Ford movie. The telly gave out most of the light in the room.

In the toilet, a blethering Mancunian with no socks tried to wash his feet in the sink next to me as I shaved with a razor and soap given to me by the ticket collector at the door. Other people had showers and some tried to wash out some clothes. I asked one of the volunteers if he knew of a place I could get into for the night. He told me to go up St. Martin's Lane, down a certain alley and knock on the only blue door. I stepped out of the crypt, passing a dozen or so people on the steps; one of them was allowed in as I got out.

There was a scuffle going on in front of the blue door. The stocky woman from before was now fighting with a guy she said stole a fiver from her. "It was all I had," she said. "You don't steal from your own kind. It's not right." I followed her inside and sat by a table, across from a guy who was pulling on a pair of trousers that were way too small. The woman told me she slept on the Strand, had done for ten months, and was constantly trying to avoid plainclothes policemen, who were always, she said, picking on beggars. She said she could not get money from the dole because she had no address. Without missing a beat, she told me she was a lesbian who'd been raped five times before she was eighteen. "The Jesus Army always get you," she said, "and I say, 'I'm a lesbian, how about it?' and they say, 'No, God doesn't like that,' and I say, 'God doesn't like that? Well, God liked for me to be raped five times and abused as a kid, so fuck him!'"

A social worker came and took me to a tiny room with two chairs and a small desk that looked like a police interview cell, except for the mysterious presence of a stepladder and an oil painting in a gilt frame. She told me what to do to get income support if I was begging, and how to see a housing officer if homeless. I could speak to the DSS about short-term accommodation. But tonight would be difficult. She gave me a map showing how to get to an emergency night shelter in Camden and brought me out of the room. Through an open door down the hall I could see an old man propped against the wall. He was in the middle of asking someone for gloves and "maybe a jacket."

Over the last two decades, thousands of psychiatric beds have been lost in Britain. The former patients, now decanted into "the community," can be seen on the streets every day in a state of profound confusion, often despair; left like the members of some schizophrenic tribe to wander aimlessly about, without treatment or support. In the first twenty-eight days after discharge from the hospital, mentally ill men are over two hundred times more likely to commit suicide than the ordinary population.

At Bondway's night shelter in Vauxhall, 50 percent of the residents are alcoholic and 20 percent have psychiatric problems. The dormitories I was shown around were crammed with mattresses and sleeping bags, on which men — all of them seemingly over fifty-five — lay sleeping or coughing or staring into space. Many such people, ejected from bed-and-breakfasts first thing in the morning, will eventually drop out of sight. Having no connections, no family and no medical support or supervision, they will simply amble into the stew of the great urban unknown.

On July 2 of this year, a man walking down Cheyne Walk, beside Chelsea Marina, noticed something bobbing in the water. The dead man was thirty, five feet eight inches tall, slightly built, with brown eyes and dark brown collar-length hair. He was clean shaven, with irregular teeth which were otherwise in fairly good nick. He had no tattoos. His face and upper body were discolored and bloated, but he was nowhere near the point at which he would have been difficult to recognize by those who had known him. An odontologist at the Department of Forensic Medicine, Guy's Hospital, prepared a report on the special features of the teeth, for comparison with the dental records of missing persons. When found, he was wearing a navy anorak with a zipper front and distinctive purple buttons, a black T-shirt, blue jeans and black trainers. He wore odd socks. The trainers had ROYAL MAIL stamped on them in red, surrounded by a miniature Union Jack. He had no money, cards or means of identification on him whatsoever. His pockets contained only one thing: a tiny book of biblical quotes, two inches by one, entitled *Golden Words*.

Without a name, the dead man is referred to by Wapping River Police as "DB23": the twenty-third dead body pulled from the Thames this year. Drawings are made of him, posters put up, newspaper reports and advertisements are published. The post office records are trawled to check if a pair of company shoes were ever issued to such a man. Yet nothing: nobody seems to know of him, nobody comes forward. Thought to have been a vagrant, a traveling pauper of unstable personality and no fixed address, he remains unidentified, destined, if no one who knows this man can be traced, to be buried at the expense of the local council and laid in an unmarked grave. As if he'd never existed.

A woman was recovered from the river near Embankment in September; on her middle finger she wore a gold ring with three white stones set in the center. The tide had probably carried her downriver, since bruising on the body suggested she'd bumped against bollards and bridges before being found. She was DB30. Seventy-two missing persons matched her description, and as he talked to me about her, the identification officer began to feel that she might turn out to be a young woman who went missing after being discharged from a psychiatric ward at University College Hospital. I left him in his office at Wapping, surrounded by paper and photographs and dead people's clothes, looking for the name of an attractive, thirty-year-old woman whom nobody seemed to know. There are certain kinds of vanishing which will never attract much interest; disappearances unlikely to stimulate much in the way of shock or curiosity; the byproducts of a society not a society, of a time not of its time, of a country spinning hellishly backwards.

Ray Dickinson does a Salvation Army soup run twice a week. I met him — as a helper rather than a customer — after dark, at the Regent Hall in Oxford Street, on a cold Thursday in September. He was stocking the van with soup, hot drinks and sandwiches. Also in the van was Allan, an ex-homeless guy who helps out from time to time. While Ray was sorting out the hot water, Allan talked of the trouble he was having finding a job. He had worked, years ago, in catering, and he regularly went round to the job center in Mortimer Street (which specializes in kitchen work) to see what there was. "They sent me down for an interview to a place in Cannon Street," he said. "I went into this kitchen, a right mess it was, and the guy tells me to start right away. So I gutted the place, scrubbed the floor, washed up and got the place looking immaculate. Then the guy, he says, 'I don't think there's much more to do, why don't you go home?' And I says, 'Well, when should I come back?' The guy says, 'Look, mate, don't bother coming back, there's no job for you here.' " Allan said he was used to it, that it happened all the time.

We called at the Canadian Muffin Company in Soho, a regular donor to the soup run of unsold stock. The rain was coming down fairly hard when we stopped in some narrow streets by Lincoln's Inn Fields, where a few people lay in doorways and in alcoves by the road. We brought them soup and sandwiches and cakes, whatever we had that they fancied. They were mostly covered in blankets or cardboard and didn't seem to me far in enough to be out of the rain. We drove on. An Indian woman appeared when we stopped in the square, asking for tea and soup and orange juice if we had it. Further up the road, an old man was sipping at empty cups and sorting through wet rubbish lying in the road. He pulled his head down as we came near, putting one hand over his eyes and waving us away with the other.

After a conversation about the various strengths of tea, I asked two guys — one very young, one very old — if they begged during the day. They were lying with blankets under the arches of the Royal Courts of Justice. The older one said there wasn't much in it, it wasn't too safe, but when you had nothing else it sometimes did the trick. They both laughed, telling the story of how, one night as they lay here, the TV game-show host Henry Kelly jumped out of a taxi and gave them a tenner. We left some muffins they could eat in the morning and drove round to Waterloo Bridge. Three men and a woman lay on a raised platform under the bridge. They had sleeping bags, and cardboard boxes to protect their heads. A lamp attached to one of the pillars lit up the area where they lay as well as a fair strip of the river beside them.

On the Strand, an old woman with whiskers came up. She

called herself Mel and slept sometimes on the steps of the Adelphi Theatre. I asked her where she came from. "Oh, the East End, I think," she said. "I've got asthma, it's the damp."

"Couldn't you get into a hostel somewhere?"

"I tried being in a place. I just couldn't get on with it." While we spoke, a youngish woman with long, straight hair drank cup after cup of hot chocolate. She had tears running down her face and screamed intermittently into the middle distance — something hard to make out about husbands and communists.

There are many soup vans in central London. In some places, like the Strand, they very nearly queue up to serve people. But the need is astonishing, and people depend on them. Everyone I saw needed what they were given, and most needed more than that. I recognized many beggars I'd spoken to, some of whom I'd sat beside in the street, but none of them recognized me. Or none of them let on. I left Ray and Allan in the rain at Euston station. It was 2:30 a.m. and they were nearing the end of the run. I turned round before I got to the corner and saw Ray walking down a darkened slope, clutching a cup of hot something or other.

The night I left the advice center with its mystery stepladder and oil painting in a gilt frame, I went to Camden as the woman had suggested. The night shelter is secreted on St. Pancras Way, across the road from the Tropical Diseases Hospital. It was cloudy and inky dark as I walked up the road. The pavement was thick with dust, as if there'd been drilling going on nearby. Nine men stood outside the shelter, all very different-looking, most of them familiar to each other. The building is three stories tall; a light flickered erratically on the second floor.

Pablo, the Talker, was telling the others about his day and

laying out his plans for the future. I'd noticed it before: in groups like this, there's always a stable collection of types: the avid Talker, the eager Listener, the Contradictor (who's sometimes the Talker), the Loner and the Oldie (who's sometimes the Loner). Pablo was the Talker. The Listener was keen to hear the details of some fruit-picking work the Talker had heard of in Kent. "Thirty quid a day plus food; no bed, just sleeping bags on the kitchen floor. I have blankets—many, many blankets—every time you see the Salvation Army, it's blankets. You'll be OK for blankets if you're coming with the fruit." The Listener's eyebrows were knitted.

"How do you get on it?" he asked.

"They have a list at The Passage," said Pablo. There's much talk of dole money: its coming, its going or its being refused. The Loner's never had a giro account to draw on. A couple of the others say they can't get by on it. The Oldie sniggers. Someone, the Talker, says that Friday's the best day to beg if you can do it. If you can do it, you can make a couple of quid. The Contradictor draws his mouth into a frown. "That depends," he says.

The door is opened—we are now about fifteen strong. The two men on duty try, not altogether successfully, to be kind. The one standing in the door holds a clipboard. Those who were in last night get in first. You're allowed to stay for three consecutive nights. About ten men go through the door. The guy with the clipboard then closes it and we wait another fifteen minutes. The Oldie—who's obviously been a bit of a Talker in his time—introduces some disquiet by wondering aloud how likely we are to be let in. The clipboard opens the door and asks for those who've never stayed before to step up. Four of us file in. We are asked to wait in the corridor so that he can speak to us. The second guy on duty comes out of his office and joins the clipboard at the door to help explain to the old man why he's not getting in. It's clear that it's not a matter of space but of some not-forgotten incident. There's a second's disputation in the corridor about whether someone should intervene on the Oldie's behalf. No one moves. The door is closed on the old man and we hear the rules: "No drinking or using drugs . . . leave at eight a.m. . . . be back by ten p.m. tomorrow night . . . must complete a Housing Benefit Form . . . go on downstairs and have some soup and toast and tea if you want it."

Down in the kitchen, there is a non-drip tea urn, plenty of bread to make toast with and a pot of lime-green soup. The chairs round the tables are the same color as the soup. The room smells of overboiled veg and chlorine bleach. Except for the Talker, few talk. Most, like the guy sitting next to me, quietly eat the soup in great, overflowing spoonfuls. Rolling cigarettes and staring at the table, a couple of the first-timers speak of the "liberty" taken with the Oldie. Back upstairs, I completed the Housing Benefit Form. The clipboard told me that, at twenty-five, I was on the border age-wise, so could I show him ID? No, well, I should bring it next time. Then they assigned bed numbers. I was 5B.

When I got up to the dormitory, 5A was already in bed. The room had two beds, was semi-partitioned, with a small closet beside each bed. There wasn't much to it. A massive lamp attached to the wall, like something used to light the pitch in a football stadium, flooded the room. I took my shoes off and lay on the bed's plastic undersheet, listening to the noise of taxis and sirens outside. It was 11:20. You couldn't put the light out: it was controlled, I guessed, by the clipboard. The room felt damp. The other guy was snoring and coughing, sometimes together. I stared at the ceiling and wondered where the taxis were going. Everything went quiet. I turned to face the wall and, just there, written in shaky block letters, was the single word GHOSTS.

I left the night shelter at eight in the morning, nearly tripping over ten loaves of bread and ten pints of milk on the doorstep. I got the tube to Bank and lost myself in the station's connecting tunnels. I carried a card on which I'd written *Hungry, please help*. I squatted in one of the tunnels with my hood up and the sign balanced on my knees. People immediately started turning their heads, in seeming astonishment. Some stop a few feet from me and stare—I can't tell whether their faces show pity or the dull stirrings of verbal abuse. I sat for an hour, and made around £3.50. Then two Underground employees came up—twin flashes of blue trousers and orange bibs—telling me to beat it. I went to Moorgate and pitched myself at the bottom of some stairs leading to the platforms. The air was cool and the ground hard and cold. Hordes of clacking shoes went by, birling and squeaking on the newly renovated floor.

At Moorgate, at least on the day I sat there, two distinct types of givers revealed themselves. One is a giver-despite-himself; he'd Federal Express the coins if he could. The other more often than not is a woman; glad to be of help, and happy to give coins and food and advice. She thinks there's something wrong with a society that keeps people like this; we're losing our way; she's concerned at the way we seem to be going. She will often give a pound or more.

"How long have you been like this?" a woman asked me with a pained expression on her face. I quickly made up a figure. "I wish I could do more," she said, giving me a pound and some coppers and an apple from her bag. A red-faced man with gold-rimmed glasses gave me a banana from his briefcase; a beautiful girl gave me a cheese sandwich in a plastic wrapper and some change; a sick-looking man with liver spots on his hands and face rubbed my head and told me I was young, then he gave me 70p. Thousands of people must have passed over the hours I was there. Most of them, as usual, would ignore me or curse or snigger. But it wasn't a bad pitch at all: the hours of asking and waiting had brought £18.86, an apple, a banana and a sandwich. That was the first day I'd made more than a fiver. And it was my last day.

As I waited for the train that would take me away from there, I remembered being told by a coroner's officer at King's Cross that eighty people this year, in London alone, have died by throwing themselves in front of trains. I waited for my return passage to a world of CDs and aquarium fish and beers in the fridge. The other kind of beggar, the real kind, goes for days without money or proper food. Many are mentally ill and alone in the definitive sense; out of touch with family, social services and the network of names and phone numbers that keeps us going. A tribe of the needy and bewildered, they march – now and then stopping to make a few quid – aimless and unhelped, towards some vanishing point real or imagined.

For me, the surprise at the end of all this was my lack of surprise. Whatever the situation thirty years ago, I'd always felt – sniffling towards adulthood in the 1980s – that my time was one in which the sight of a few people eating out of bins and begging in the street was acceptable. It was something that happened. And it never gave pause with us the way it did with parents or others who spoke of a time when things were not this way. Two weeks after that last day at Moorgate, I stopped outside Warren Street station to buy a paper. A beggar under a blue blanket reclined against the McDonald's window. While we talked, about Scotland and about Wales, he said that he knew me, or used to know me. I joked about the unlikelihood and, itching to be in some other place, found a way to say that I'd never seen him before in my life. I was back among the passersby.

*November 1993*

# The Glasgow Sludge Boat

THE CLYDE USED TO BE one of the noisiest rivers. Thirty or forty years ago you could hear the strike of metal against metal, the riveter's bedlam, down most of the narrow channel from Glasgow and at several other ship-building towns on the estuary. There was a sound of horns on the water, and of engines turning. Chains unfurled and cargoes were lifted; there was chatter on the piers. But it is very quiet now. Seagulls murmur overhead and nip at the banks. You can hear almost nothing. The water might lap a little, or ripple when pushed by the wind. But mostly it sits still.

This quietness is broken, five days a week, by the passage of the two ships which carry one of the Clyde's last cargoes: human effluent, sewage, sludge.

Glaswegians call these ships the sludge boats. Every morning, they sail west down the river to turn, eventually, south into the estuary's mouth, the Firth, where they will drop their load into the sea. By this stage of the voyage, their elderly passengers may be dancing on the deck, or, if the weather is wet or windy, playing bingo in the lounge. Underneath them, a few thousand tons of human sewage (perhaps some of their own, transported from their homes) will be slopping in the holds.

There was a time when passengers and cargo set sail from the Clyde to New York, Montreal, Buenos Aires, Calcutta and Bombay in liners equipped to carry awkward things like railway locomotives and difficult people like tea planters. And now, almost alone on the river, this: tons of shit accompanied by an average complement of seventy old-age pensioners enjoying a grand day out, and traveling free.

This morning it was the ladies — and several gentlemen — of Our Holy Redeemer's Senior Citizens Club of Clydebank who were taking a trip down the river. I'd watched them ambling onto the boat from the wharf at Shieldhall sewage works, each of them with a plastic bag filled with sandwiches and sweets. Now I could hear the party arranging itself on the deck above me, as I stood down below to watch the sludge being loaded into the ship's eight tanks. It came from the wharf through an enormous red pipe, then into a funnel, and then from the funnel into a hopper, which channeled the sludge evenly through the ship's basement. It took about an hour and thirty minutes to load up. As the ship filled — with wakeful passengers and tired sludge — a little fountain of perfume sprinkled silently over the hopper's top.

We were on board the *Garroch Head,* a handsome ship named after the point near the dumping ground forty miles downstream, and built on the Clyde, as was her sister ship, the *Dalmarnock* (named after a sewage works). The *Garroch Head* can carry 3,500 tons of sludge, the *Dalmarnock* 3,000 tons. They are not particularly old ships — both were launched in the 1970s — but neither seems likely to survive the century. After 1998, the process of dumping at sea will be outlawed by a directive from the European Union on grounds of ecology and public health. And yet this quiet disposal, this burial of a city's intimate wastes in ninety fathoms halfway between the islands of Bute and Arran, once seemed such a neat and clean solution.

Until the 1890s, Glasgow's untreated sewage went straight into the river's upper reaches, where it bubbled under the surface and crept ashore as black mud. Civic concern arose with the stench; the population was still growing in a city made by the first industrial revolution and popularly described as "the workshop of the world." In 1889, the city's engineer, Alexander Frew, read a paper on the sewage question to the Glasgow Philosophical Society, and then addressed increasingly heated questions about what was to be done. He opposed dumping at sea, and suggested instead that the sewage be spread along the banks of the Clyde, where it would come to form fine agricultural land. The city rejected this scheme, though a feeling persisted that something *useful* (and profitable) might be done with Glasgow's swelling effluent; in London at that time, the Native Guano Company of Kingston upon Thames appeared to be setting a trend with this sort of thing. Glasgow's own brand, Globe Fertiliser, was popular for a short while. But here, science was ahead of the game — or behind it — with new artificial fertilizers that were more powerful and cheaper than the processed human stuff.

How did other cities arrange their disposal? A delegation went from Glasgow to Paris to find out, and there discovered a great tunnel on either side of the river Seine. Sewage poured out of pipes into these tunnels, which then poured into the Seine some miles from the city. The Seine, however, was clean when compared with the Clyde, because (as the delegation noted) the current carried the effluent away from the city to less fortunate towns further downstream, and then to the sea. The Clyde, on the other hand, was tidal; sewage went with the ebb and came back up with the flood—a mess that, like an unwanted stray dog, could not be shooed away. There was also another reason for the Seine's relative purity, which perversely had to do with Glasgow's greater progress in sanitation. Paris had 600,000 closets, or lavatories, but only a third of them were water closets; the rest were dry, their waste carried away by night-soil carts to fields and dumps. Glasgow, thanks to its climate and municipal reservoirs and pipes, had most of its lavatories flushed by water. It had wet sewage rather than dry, and much more of it to get rid of.

In 1898, nine years after the Paris trip, another delegation traveled south, this time to London, where they were shown the system of sewers, sewage works and, lastly, sewage ships which carried the capital's waste to its destination far out in the Thames estuary. They were impressed, and by 1910 Glasgow had a similar system in place—the second largest (after London's) in the world, with three great sewage works sending their produce down the Clyde in ships.

The passengers came later, just after the First World War, when a benevolent but cost-conscious Glasgow city council (then called the Glasgow Corporation) decided that convalescing servicemen would benefit from a day out on the Clyde. Cruising on pleasure steamers up and down the estuary and across to its islands was then Glasgow's great summer pastime; the sludge boats offered the city council the prospect of killing two birds with one stone. Their voyages were already paid for out of the rates. The servicemen could travel free. It was seen as an expression of socialist goodwill—allied with the enlightened Victorian municipalism that had given Glasgow its lavish water supply and so many public parks. The vessels were rebuilt to carry passengers, fitted out with more lifeboats and saloons, equipped with deck quoits. By and by, their traffic in convalescing servicemen died away, to be replaced, thanks to the charitable offices of the Glasgow Corporation, by old people who couldn't afford cruises on the regular steamships, but who may have been encouraged by the doctor to take the air.

And so it was, in the summer of 1995, that I came to be traveling with the Clydebank Holy Redeemer's club on top of 3,500 tons of sludge.

Everything — or everything visible to the passenger — on the *Garroch Head* was scrupulously clean. The wooden table and chairs in the lounge shone with polish; the urinals gleamed; the deck was as free of dirt as any deck could be. The haphazard filth and toxic stews of Glasgow were kept well out of sight. There was a sense among the crew that it was this opposition of cleanliness to filth that carried them and their ship forward on each voyage.

We sailed past the grass and rubble where the shipyards used to be — Connell's and Blythswood to starboard, Simons and Lobnitz to port — and I talked to a woman who was leaning on the ship's rail and enjoying the breeze. She was called Mary Kay McRory, she was eighty, and she had a big green cardigan pulled across her chest. Her eyes ran, but she laughed a lot as she spoke. She said the first time she had sailed on the Clyde was in 1921, when she had traveled as a six-year-old with her family on the steamer that took cattle and people from Derry in Ireland to Glasgow, and very seldom took the same ones back again. Mary Kay's father was escaping some bother in Donegal; he'd heard of work in Glasgow, came over and was employed right away as a lamplighter. Then he summoned his wife and the six children. "We came away from Donegal with biscuits," Mary Kay said. "Everybody would throw biscuits over the wall to you. They were good biscuits. The food over there was good."

She had worked as a waitress, when the city was still full

of tea rooms, and then on the Glasgow trams for twenty-five years. I asked her if Glasgow had changed much, and she got me by the arm. "Ye can say what ye like," she said, "but there's no poverty now, none." She talked a lot about sanitation, about toilets and baths, in the way many old Glaswegians do. Those who remember lavatories shared with neighbors and trips to the public bathhouse tend to talk more about these matters than people like me who grew up thinking it was nothing special to have porcelain bits at the top of the stairs stamped ARMITAGE SHANKS.

Plastic bags were being rustled in the lounge. Out of them came the day's supplies: sandwiches of white bread cut into quarters and filled variously with slates of corned beef, chicken breast, shiny squares of gammon, salmon paste and cheese spreads. And then the treats to follow: Paris buns, Blue Riband biscuits, Tunnock's teacakes, Bourbon creams. Some of the women dropped sweeteners into their tea and stirred melodically for a long time after. Others placed ginger snaps at the edge of their saucers, or unwrapped tight wads of shortbread, ready for distribution. Neat stacks of white bread and sweet acres of treats stretched on the table, in front of every passenger. All the mouths were going—shredding meat and sloshing tea—like washing machines on a full load.

This was not lunch for the Holy Redeemer's club; merely elevenses.

Sludge, in the particular sense of our sludge boat's cargo, comes about like this. The sewage pumped into Glasgow's three sewage works is twice screened. The first screening takes out large objects—lumps of wood, rags, metal—that somehow find their way into the sewers. The second screening extracts smaller, abrasive materials such as glass and sand. Then comes the first separation process, designed to make the organic component of the sewage sink to the bottom of the tank ( just as sediment will settle in a bottle of wine). They call this the stage of primary settlement. The heavy stuff at the bottom is called raw sludge; the clearer liquid above is settled sewage.

The raw sludge is not ready to dispose of; it needs further modification and is subject to biochemical breakdown. Some of it goes through a process called digestion. Bacteria are allowed into the holding chambers, where they feed energetically on the proteins and carbohydrates, diminishing the organic matter until the sludge is fit to be spread on farmland or made ready for dumping at sea. Then, at the works near the wharf at Shieldhall, the sludge is "settled" one last time, to increase the content of sinkable solids in the watery mix. The stuff in the hold has passed through many systems—biological and mechanical—and it will have no final rest from the biological, even at the bottom of the sea. It degrades there to feed marine life (the fishing near the dumping ground is said to be fairly good) and continue its journey through the ecosystem.

There has, however, been an awful lot of it dumped, and all in the same place. In the first year of the sludge boats, 213,867 tons were carried down the Clyde. In 1995, the figure was 1.8 million tons. The total for the century is 82.6 million tons. The seabed at the dump's center is said to be damaged, its organisms contaminated. The EU has delivered its verdict. Glasgow needs a new venue for the sludge, and old ideas are being reexamined. Fertilizer, for example. Sludge is rich in nitrates (4 percent), phosphate (3 percent) and potassium (1 percent), and full of nutrients—it could do a good job on the land, and farmers seem willing to try it for free. It is also well suited to growing grass and is already being spread on derelict industrial sites to prepare them for reclamation. A new product range—sludge cakes, sludge pellets—will be tried on the waste ground that was once the Ravenscraig steelworks, the largest and last of Scotland's steel plants, where the soil has been poisoned by decades of metal wastes. Sludge used there could make a meadow grow.

We passed Greenock, which used to make ships and sugar, and then veered left into the Firth proper. The *Garroch Head* was going at a fair pelt now, and most of the passengers had their eyes down, playing a restive round or two of bingo. Some were nibbling still at the corners of buns and sandwiches. From the saloon porthole the water looked silver, as if some giant shoal of mackerel swam just beneath the surface. The islands of Great and Little Cumbrae stood out, like two large boulders only recently dropped into the sea.

We passed them. Up on the bridge, the crew were slowing the vessel down, ready to discharge their load. We had reached the dumping ground, and as soon as the position was right a crewman on the bridge flicked a switch and I heard a little rumble. The valves were opening. I thought I could feel the cargo starting to be pulled by gravity from its tanks.

I went down from the bridge to the deck nearest the water and saw the first of the billowing columns. Fierce puffs, great Turner clouds of wayward brown matter, rose and spread in an instant over the surface. The waters of the Firth were all at once rusty and thick, and the boat was an island in a sea of sludge. This was all in the first few minutes.

We moved off, leaning to port, aiming to complete a full circle as the sludge descended. A group of pensioners stood in a row looking out, covering their mouths and noses with white hankies. All the worst odor of a modern city, until now stored and battened down, was released in this time-stopping, comical stench. I looked up at the coast and wondered for a second where it had all begun, because this was an ending, and the sense of an ending was as palpable and strong as the brew in the sea before us.

The ship turned about and headed home. Its emptying had taken ten minutes. Back in the saloon, the pensioners were dancing to a song called "Campbeltown Loch, I Wish Ye Were Whisky." My tea sat just where I'd left it, and I was happy to notice it was still quite warm.

*December 1995*

# The American Dream of
# Lee Harvey Oswald

W HEN GARY GILMORE faced his executioners one cold morning in 1977, there was a serious, anxious, bearded reporter-type standing only a few feet away. Before the hood was placed over Gilmore's head, the man walked over to the chair and took both of the killer's hands into his own. "I don't know why I'm here," he said. Gilmore looked up and replied sweetly: "You're going to help me escape."

The man's name was Lawrence Schiller. And he did help Gilmore escape: he took him to the world, over the tops of the Mormon hills and the mobile homes of Utah; he flew with the story of Gary Gilmore. He produced the television film, sold the interviews, oversaw pictures, advised on chat shows and specials, became the reporter's reporter, the producer's producer, and he later brought in Norman Mailer to write the book. He showed himself to be the king dealmaker and media broker, the chief documenter, of grand-scale American tragedy. Wherever there has been sensational news in America over the last thirty years, there you will invariably find Lawrence Schiller.

Schiller has helped all manner of American figures escape in this way, through the portals of recorded history, into legend.

Marilyn Monroe, during the filming of a bathing scene in her last, unfinished film, *Something's Got to Give,* suddenly disrobed on the set, at the studios of Twentieth Century Fox. Just as she did so, there appeared a young man with a camera. He was on assignment for *Life* (expecting to take some pretty pictures of the actress in performance), and his eyes nearly popped out of his head. Marilyn, he was alert enough to know, had not been photographed naked since the late 1940s, when she accepted fifty dollars to pose nude for a calendar. Schiller's exclusive photographs were syndicated around the world. And Norman Mailer later wrote the book.

When O. J. Simpson wanted to tell the world of his innocence, and the globe's media scratched at the door, there was only one man with the skill to breeze into his cell. Lawrence Schiller came in with his beard, his anxiety and his notepad, and he helped Simpson write a book called *I Want to Tell You,* a book that had nothing to do with Norman Mailer, but which sold uncontrollably during the Simpson trial. Schiller has had one of the strangest — and most strangely necessary — jobs in America. He understood the power of syndication in a way no one else did; he felt the need for made-for-TV movies while others still haggled over cinema releases and back catalogues; he saw the point of cable; he knows how to cut up a story, how to apportion it and how to pin down exclusivity. And he has, from time to time, introduced himself as a new sort of figure in the world of books. The Producer.

So it was with a certain inevitability, as the KGB archives were opened up to the West in 1992, that Lawrence Schiller would find himself in Moscow. The new documents would bear on many things, but Schiller, as usual anything but slow on the uptake, knew they might tell us something we needed to know about Lee Harvey Oswald, perhaps the most mysterious and most tragic American figure in the age of Schiller. If the gods of reason were attentive, it would make sense for him to be reunited with his sparring partner and sometime mate, Norman Mailer. Surely, if he was to help Lee Harvey Oswald to "escape," there was only one writer in America who could reliably meet the task.

But there were problems to be overcome. Schiller and Mailer—odd partners in the worlds of show and tell—had not always got on. "When it comes to lying," Mailer warbled to gossip columnist Liz Smith of the *New York Daily News* in the mid-1980s, "Larry Schiller makes Baron von Munchausen look like George Washington." Yet at the beginning of this new book there is an appreciation: "To Larry Schiller, my skilled and wily colleague in interview and investigation, for the six months we labored side by side in Minsk and Moscow, and then again in Dallas, feeling as close as family (and occasionally as contentious)."

In a way, Norman Mailer has been staring for most of his life into the face of Lee Harvey Oswald. Mailer's characters have always been parts of himself, and part and parcel of the America of his time. If Marilyn Monroe was his dream lover—"every man's love affair with America"—and Ernest Hemingway his idea of a self-like literary champ, it might also be said that his astronauts, his boxers, his single-minded karmic killers, his existential heroes, Greenwich Village idiots, his political ogres and saints, his high-minded Trillings, turncoat Podhoretzes, his self-authenticating graffiti artists and his cursed, totalitarian generals were also travelers in Mailer's inner cosmos.

It could be said to be natural, Mailer's interest in Lee Harvey Oswald. "Natural" in the sense that he has always, as a writer, been interested in people who broke rules and took chances, who lived urgently and died violently. He has also set himself the task of shadowing those who, like himself, were greedy for action and who forged their celebrity in the heat of extreme activity. But his relation to Oswald is even more proximate than that. Oswald may have killed the president, and Mailer, much more than any writer of his generation, has always tended to see himself as an American president manqué. In 1959, in his *Advertisements for Myself,* he wrote that "like many another vain, empty, and bullying body of our time, I have been running for President these last ten years in the privacy of my mind, and it occurs to me that I am less close now than when I began."

In the summer of 1960, the year after he wrote that, he visited John F. Kennedy at home in Hyannisport. He was there on behalf of *Esquire* magazine, to interview the young Catholic who sought the Democratic nomination, and Kennedy took him very seriously. In fact, he had mugged up before meeting the novelist. He knew that Mailer was hurt over the critical mauling he'd received for *The Deer Park,* and so, on meeting him, Kennedy named that novel as his favorite book of Mailer's. The *Esquire* piece came out, very much in favor of Kennedy, and was called "Superman Comes to the Supermart." *Esquire,* at that time, was not without influence, especially among the young, especially among the young of New York. When Kennedy scraped home in that state, and so won the nomination, Mailer claimed that he was the cause of the victory, and later claimed to have inadvertently won him the presidency.

So you might well say that Mailer had a bit of a vested interest in President Kennedy, and another sort of vested interest in the mind of an outsider like Oswald. He has the good novelist's sense of correspondence, the inventor's joy at the magic of possibility, and he looks into Oswald's eyes with the thrill of one who imagines those eyes to have fixed on his one-time subject, JFK — very probably through the telescopic sights of a bolt-action Mannlicher-Carcano. *Oswald's Tale* is many things, but it is not another framing of the question "Who Shot Kennedy?" Mailer wants to know what sort of person Oswald was: "Before we understand a murderer — if he is one — we must first discover his motive. But to find the motive, we do well to encounter the man. In Oswald's case, that could be no simple task. How many young men are as timid and bold as Lee Harvey Oswald? . . . To understand a person is to comprehend his reasons for action. The conceit arose that one understood Oswald."

The understanding of Oswald begins in Moscow, and it is a good place to start. He traveled there in 1959 on an Intourist visa, and almost immediately tried to cut himself free of America. He wanted to relinquish his American citizenship, but the consul refused him, and he spent his first weeks there in a state of utter frustration. He tried, a little halfheartedly, to commit suicide in his bathroom at the Berlin Hotel, but was saved by Rimma, the first of several uncertain Russian girlfriends. The authorities eventually decided he could stay, but he remained under KGB surveillance and was moved to Minsk, to work in a radio factory.

Minsk in the late 1950s looked quite new: its stately apartment buildings of yellow stone, its wide avenues, were all built on top of the earlier Minsk, which had been destroyed by the Germans twice — once when they came in, and again when they retreated back to Poland three years later. Mailer draws an intimate picture of family life: there are a great many women — women keen on men who were cultured and kind and not cheap — messing around in shared kitchens, trying to keep things clean, making things to eat, worrying over illness and injury.

Marina Prusakova worked in a pharmacy. She had come from Leningrad, and she'd had a few boyfriends, some of whom remember her with affection, some of whom say she was a good-time girl. What is clear about Marina — even before she met Oswald — is that she was no good at housework or cooking. She lived with her aunt and uncle, and they would sometimes despair over her messiness, her lateness and her lack of direction. On March 17, 1961, Marina went to a trade-union dance with her friends from the Medical Institute. She wore a red dress and white slippers. She was asked to dance by an American — at first she thought he might come from one of the Baltic countries — who called himself Alik. She liked him; he was very polite, sweet and reserved. He was well dressed. She took him to meet her aunt, who liked men to be polite; and soon enough Marina and Alik were married. At the wedding they all sang "Chattanooga Choo Choo."

Mailer recognizes the virtue in attempting to understand Oswald through his marriage. He is not the first to have done so: he acknowledges and borrows from Priscilla Johnson McMillan's *Marina and Lee,* though he is able to add to that mostly American account, thanks to the KGB transcripts. The newly married couple's apartment was bugged, and their early married life, their frequent strife and their makings-up are documented here. Mailer and Schiller interviewed everyone they could find who knew them. Oswald was a lazy worker, and was much resented at the radio factory, not only for putting his feet up on the desk, but for the special treatment he received as a foreigner. He hated the job, but he didn't seem to notice that his apartment was bigger than anyone else's.

The surveillance reports on Oswald make poor reading. If he was an American agent (as many suspect), we can only assume from these reports that he was no more effective in this capacity than he was as a builder of radios. He walked around, looked into shops, picked up a book, failed to buy it, walked back home. Oswald was a dissipater; he was not a great student in Russia, an ideologue or a planner. He was a ditherer; he wasn't at all sure who he was or what he wanted to do. Furthermore, he was dyslexic. "His orthography is so bad at times," Mailer points out, "that the man is not revealed but concealed — in the worst of his letters he seems stupid and illiterate." But Mailer argues that this should not be allowed to hide something else about him: "Considering that he was still in his very early twenties, it is . . . not inaccurate to speak of him as a young intellectual." Mailer is keen, keener than any writer has been before, to reveal the nuances of Oswald's character and the reach of his mind. He serves notice on the common way of seeing Oswald — as an incompetent, shifty, stupid and impotent rat — and encourages us to think of him not only as having intelligence, but as having other qualities that might cause him to be liked here and there, and to be loved, as he sometimes was.

The stuff gained by Mailer and Schiller in their Russian interviews is more interesting than the stuff emerging from the lifeless files of the KGB. The absence of revelations in the KGB documents is more than made up for by Mailer's imaginative use of the new detail they contain. He uses it to fill out Oswald's time in Minsk, to give word of his troubles, and the changing shape of his mind. Cold War Berlin seemed dank and sinister in Mailer's novel *Harlot's Ghost;* the Minsk of *Oswald's Tale* seems bright and tells us quite a bit. The Cold War antics are vaguely comic. The interviews with older Russians bleed lavishly into the story: we feel we know Oswald better, and are newly acquainted with some possible motivations, by seeing the world he lived in during those confused years. It gives us clues, and deep background, to the hows and whys of Oswald's state of mind as he plunges forward — or backward — to his American end.

Russia was his bid for the solvent, invisible life. When Russia failed him, something seems to have died in him; something new was born. He eventually wrote to the American embassy, looking to have his passport back. It took many agonies, much red tape, but eventually it was returned. He'd fought the bureaucracies of America and Russia in turn, and he'd beaten them, but he'd left himself with no open roads after all that. He took a reluctant Marina and child back to Texas, with a head full of scrap, and perhaps some ideas we can't yet speak of. Mailer ends the Russian part of his book — the firmer and slower-paced part — having provided a portrait of a man in crisis, a man unsure of his next big move. But let us leave Lee Harvey Oswald for the time being, crossing the ocean and scribbling some lines on Holland America Line notepaper: "I wonder what would happen if someone would stand up and say he was utterly opposed not only to the government, but to the people, to the entire land and complete foundation of society." You might say that shards of motivation were coming together, to make a window of opportunity.

On May 4, 1901, at about eight o'clock in the evening, the building that stood at 411 Elm Street in Dallas was struck by lightning. It burned all night, and the Southern Rock Island Plow Company, which owned the property, was forced to abandon it. The owners built a new seven-story building on the same site, of modern design, with arched windows on the sixth floor. In 1963, the building was being leased by the Texas School Book Depository Company, a private textbook-brokerage firm.

I walked along in the too hot afternoon, in the summer of 1995, and kept thinking how inordinately white the pavement was. The streets around Dealey Plaza looked like they'd only recently been scrubbed. The former Book Depository stood there like a warning, like a symbol of something not too bright or happy-making. It was one of those buildings that one knew something about; it sat in the memory, though I, for one, had never been to Dallas before. But I knew this building very well. It looked like it hadn't changed at all since 1901, though many things had changed around it. It stood up, blank and indifferent, in the hot afternoon, and I thought of Bates's hilltop house in *Psycho*.

The building is owned now by Dallas County; they use it as an administration building. It is full of offices and workspaces, except on the sixth floor, which is reserved for something special. The whole floor is kept for what is called, by those who keep it, "the memory of a nation." It is known, by those who don't keep it, as Oswaldworld. But the places that make up Oswaldworld are more than one: they include the houses he rented in Dallas, the streets along which he supposedly made his escape, the place where he shot Tippett, the police officer, and the area of the cinema where he was arrested. It also encompasses the police garage where Oswald was shot; the post office across the road where Jack Ruby mailed his postal order minutes before; the spot where Ruby's Carousel Club stood. It is a whole bunch of bricks and sticks and marks on the ground, but it is even more than that. It is also a place in the mind—perhaps a place in the mind of everyone in America. Oswaldworld is the place where national chaos is; it's the place where good presidents get shot by nobodies. It's also the place where certainties break down, or fail to hold, and where absurdity and unknowable violence are unleashed from the margins. In the mind of just about everyone alive in America—and in places beyond America—there is a little corner marked Oswaldworld. There in Dallas, I could see it plainly in front of me. It had been appropriately housed.

Just a few streets over from the old Book Depository build-ing there is a place called the Conspiracy Museum. The guys working there are weird: experts in who-did-what-to-whom-and-why in 1963; twentysomethings with an amateur grasp of ballistics; muggers-up on the constituent parts of the CIA, the internal workings of the FBI, the gripes of the Mafia; young men with strong views on the presence of shadows on the grassy knoll. They charge seven dollars for the lowdown on who re-ally shot Kennedy. A guy with a baseball cap and a mustache is speaking to tourists: he edits a fanzine for "dudes obsessed with the case." I hear him speaking to a bunch of tourists from Pennsylvania, emitting a sort of mantra—an Oliver Stone–like loop of verbal fact and fiction—that seeks to pound his guests out of their confusion. He even has theories about the people who run the Book Depository museum, the thing on the sixth floor, round the corner. "They don't know what they're doing," he says. "It's all a whitewash. The people over there aren't even qualified to speak of this thing."

There are other guys, perhaps related, who sell conspiracy mags and buttons on the grassy knoll. They sell maps and plans, too, and speak like born-again Christians. They have a way of saying the word "truth" that makes you feel like a liar, or a believer in lies. They walk up and down in shorts: they seem to like being there, so close to something big, and you're almost surprised to see them stowing away dollar bills. They look up at the windows of the former Book Depository, counting up to the corner window of the sixth floor, and they look at you quizzi-cally, saying, "No . . . no, it couldn't have been." As one of them says this, I notice there are tracks on his arms.

When you come out of the lift at the sixth floor you're imme-diately confronted by a giant photograph of what the floor was like on November 22, 1963. The roof beams are the same as the ones you see above your head, but the place in the photograph is not all corporate and red, as the space is now — it looks grimy, and is covered with boxes of books. I hear a voice beside me say, "He was a real people-person." There is a display on the wall of things-from-1963: a poster for *Psycho,* a program for a new musical starring Richard Burton and Julie Andrews called *Camelot,* an advertisement for *Who's Afraid of Virginia Woolf?* There is a row of books from the time: Barbara Tuchman's *The Guns of August,* Betty Friedan's *The Feminine Mystique, The Rise and Fall of the Third Reich* by William Shirer. On every side you can hear Kennedy's voice: "Let the word go forth . . . that the torch has been passed to a new generation of Americans." It is repeated over and over.

There are panels of pictures, with text, all around. This must be what is meant by a multimedia presentation, for there are videos going, radios blaring, and looped bits of speeches and snatches of the inaugural address. As I walk past, I catch a spread from *Life* about racial turbulence in Birmingham, Alabama. The headline says, "They Fight a Fire That Won't Go Out." I take a few steps and hear JFK's voice grow louder, drowning out a previous speech of his: "I look forward to an America that will not be afraid of grace and beauty."

As you make your way from panel to panel, you notice a sense of dread in yourself. Like station stops on a terrible journey (dare I say it, like Stations of the Cross), each of these displays, with their separate titles — "The Kennedy White House," "Turmoil at Home," "The Trip to Texas," "Reception in Dallas" — increases that dread. I looked at pictures of them arriving in Dallas, moving through the streets; I saw Jackie in her famous outfit, waving to people, the children smiling back. The Texas Book Depository building emerges in the corner of the next screen; the cars move slowly, you can hear the voices of radio announcers and snatches of Kennedy's speech wafting from the front of the room, from the earlier part of the exhibition. You know that when you turn the next corner and see the next panel, it will show the assassination. As you turn the corner you can already hear the shots, you can hear Walter Cronkite announce the death of the president at a panel some way in front of that, and distantly, down the far end of the sixth floor, you can hear the "Funeral March" as recorded in Washington. As I turn, I see everything is dark. There are flickering pictures on a TV screen of the president's Lincoln turning into Elm Street and running past the front of the building I'm standing in myself. I see him lurch in his seat, and feel it might all be happening now, outside, on this sunny day.

This clamor of memorial sounds, this crosscurrent of hard images and bits of life, this blend of recorded seconds in the unfolding of a prime historic moment—they are all part of what they call the "Memory of a Nation." And being a nation that knows how to harness and punish verisimilitude, and tease out bitter emotion, this exhibition is astonishingly unlike anything of its kind I've ever seen. There is, in fact, nothing of its kind. It is a pure exercise in the heightening of reality, in the Disneyfying of a cataclysmic moment in real life, a moment full of mystery and importance but also full of banality and pointlessness and stupidity. The sixth floor offers visitors the thrill of presidential assassination, the thrill of communal mourning, the thrill of whodunit, the thrill of revenge, the thrill of national pride, the thrill of having been there and the gloom of being none the wiser. As I stood by the corner window of the sixth floor, beside the sniper's nest, looking through the window, down through the trees, I almost expected a motorcade to appear beneath the leaves. You can't help but feel you are momentarily at the center of another sort of universe. I stood at the window alone. It was like a movie set, smaller than I'd thought, and maybe like a model. It must all have looked so possible from here, so terribly likely. It was hard to think of it. On November 22, 1963, Lee Harvey Oswald crouched here, lifted his rifle, peered through a telescopic sight stamped HOLLYWOOD — a detail seldom referred to — and shot the president. Everybody in the world would know where they were.

*December 1995*

# Many Andies

ALL HIS LIFE Andy Warhol looked like death. He came into the world that way: blank, rheumy-eyed, sick as the day was long. An unmerry child with St. Vitus' dance, the young Warhol lay twitching in his bed under a blanket of fan magazines, the source of all his imaginary friendships — with Errol Flynn and Louella Parsons, Hedda Hopper and Gary Cooper — and the only thing he craved in those Pittsburgh days was the chance to be as lovable as Shirley Temple. The adult Warhol looked as much like death and lived as much by desire. A mobile presentation of twentieth-century estrangement. A man in a wig in a season in hell. "A sphinx without a secret," said Truman Capote; "the Ecce Homo of modern exhibitionism," said Stephen Spender. For his own part, Warhol was intensely reasonable: "I just want to be a machine," he said.

There were many Andies: the Andy who brought cruelty back into art; the Andy who worried about "boy trouble"; the Andy who saw to the heart of advertising and who fashioned the media that fashioned him; the Andy who knew how to use the delinquent energies of those around him but who was scared of getting close to folk in case they got ill; the Andy who was bored like an old stuffed aunt; the Andy who went to mass at St. Patrick's every Sunday; the Andy who made new things fabulous and fashionable and more interesting than they were; the Andy who sucked up to Imelda Marcos and took tea with the Shah of Iran; the Andy who knew how the Bomb had maimed us, how television had made us, how money was everything, and everything was glorious. Warhol became a virtual-reality show starring himself: Andrew Warhola playing "Andy" better than Norma Jeane Baker ever played "Marilyn." In 1968, while Soviet tanks prepared to roll into the Czechoslovakia of Andy's origins, Warhol was writhing in agony on the floor of his New York studio, shot by Valerie Solanas, a funny woman who had appeared in one of his movies. By that time Warhol had come to represent what Don DeLillo has called "the revenge of popular culture on those who take it too seriously."

Warhol outlined a new sort of wanting. America is there in his paintings, and the things people wanted—a Coke, a perfection, a quick end—are documented in a manner which suggests both the campiness and the terror of mass production. For all his dazzling befuddlement, Warhol had a clear notion of what was happening in his time on that continent of big wishes, and he made stuff out of it—pictures and movies and boxes and versions of himself—that will always say something of what it was like to be alive in those specimen days, those bright-eyed years running to madness after the war. His weird albino mentality stands behind the notions we have today about the value of disposable objects and the meaningfulness of celebrity, and it is Warhol's signature that sits on the lips of that ironic smirker, the contemporary Artist-Personality, with his vast narcissism, his love of being cool, his pose of knowing nothing you couldn't know yourself if only you weren't so knowing. Warhol's thinking is everywhere now: his rinky-dink voice is trapped in the general formaldehyde.

But the career started in shoes. Warhol caused a bit of bother at college with some George Grosz–like drawings of little boys with their fingers stuck up their noses. Grosz's notion of Dada—the organized use of insanity to express contempt for a bankrupt world—was evidently Warhol's for a minute or two, but the American boy was not the type to bandy words with a world that was bankrupt, and in time he'd find better uses for insanity. But first he wanted to be rich. Warhol's attitude towards money was a cross between Jay Gatsby's and Holly Golightly's—he yearned for the world where money allowed you to be whoever you wanted to be, where money was confidence and confidence was character, and where each day was a promise of diamonds as big as the Ritz. Carmel Snow, who edited *Harper's Bazaar* during the fifties, told a story about Warhol turning up at her New York office, and when he opened his portfolio, a cockroach crawled out from beneath the folds. The art director of *Glamour* magazine asked him to draw some shoes, and he brought her a whole load the next day. Warhol's shoe drawings were an original and sexy mixture—bang-on for the time and the venue, with their cool lines and blurred edges and stylishly camp gold leaf and delicate watercolors. Warhol started doing shoes for a weekly advert in the *New York Times*. *Shoes, Shoes, Shoes* brings together some of the best of those commercial drawings, which were collected once before in an equally delightful portfolio called *A la Recherche du Shoe Perdu.*

Warhol's pretty shoes, we gather from our sources, may in fact be inky revelations of something fairly robust in the artist's character. He was a foot fetishist. The New York poet John Giorno, an old boyfriend of the bewigged one, gave an account several years ago of what his pal liked to do on his nights in. Just to get you in the mood, here's his account of what he and Andy did on the day John Kennedy was shot.

> We heard Walter Cronkite say "President Kennedy died at 2 p.m. on November 22nd, 1963." We started hugging each other, pressing our bodies together and trembling. I started crying and Andy started crying. We wept big fat tears. It was a symbol of the catastrophe of our own lives. We kissed and Andy sucked my tongue. It was the first time we kissed. It has the sweet taste of kissing death. It was all exhilarating, like when you get kicked in the head and see stars.

But this was only the beginning of the ways in which this nimble pair would express the catastrophe of their own lives. They grew in fact to quite like their catastrophe. And Andy was never one to take his mind off his work: "There was Andy Warhol on his hands and knees, licking my shoes with his little red tongue. Too good to be believed! I thought, with a rush, 'He's sucking my shoes!' It was hot. My shoes were covered with saliva. I got some poppers to make it better."

Warhol took his first faltering steps out of the commercial market with his *Foot Book*, a collection of drawings of his friends' feet, and then he broke through with a show called *Crazy Golden Slippers*, a bunch of lacquered shoe drawings in which each shoe was called Mae West or James Dean or Elvis Presley or Julie Andrews.

As a strictly commercial artist, Warhol not only knew how to make things pretty, he had the knack — the *New Yorker*-ish knack — of making style a matter of poise and clarity and simplicity and self-concealment. He learned what he could from the great fashion illustrators, the society cartoonists, Aubrey Beardsley and Max Beerbohm, but he got most of what is fresh in his drawings from a New-York-in-the-fifties world of homosexual felicity, a literary world of gentle other-persuasion, whose emergent prince was Truman Capote. In *Style, Style, Style,* beside a drawing of a portly lady in a yellow dress and a pink umbrella and a green fan, it says: "Fashion wasn't what you wore someplace anymore; it was the whole reason for going." And this was the first of Warhol's very good perceptions: fashion is about event and situation and attitude. It is about how people are in a given moment. Warhol realized that personality was as natural as a pair of polka-dot Chanel gloves. For him, everything that was interesting and stylish, everything involving taste, had to do with artifice. And so, in his way, Warhol predated all the pink thinkers on Camp sensibility. It would be 1964 before Susan Sontag emerged with her "Notes on Camp," which reads nowadays, in its arch solemnity, like some kind of ambush on the tendency itself, and which must be among the least effectively stylized pronouncements on the virtues of American stylization. However, I'd sooner, by a thousand times, have Sontag's notion of how "one is drawn to Camp when one realizes that 'sincerity' is not enough," or Warhol's sense that throwing on a dress is never bad for a laugh, than have to put up with one more word on the subject from the contributors to *Who Is Andy Warhol?,* a book so deeply off you wouldn't feed it to Oscar de la Renta's dogs.

Here's Matthew Tinkcom: "Camp is the alibi for gay-infected labor to be caught in the chain of value-coding within capitalist political economies . . . I would suggest that Camp is more productively seen in relation to what it says about bourgeois representation (and its tendency to exclude gays) than in whatever help it lends in the formation of identities." This is just one of the papers presented at the opening of the Andy Warhol Museum in April 1995. I'm sure everybody had a nice day out, but why must the speeches then be collected in this way? No good comes of it. Colin MacCabe tells us in his preface that "it is not clear that Warhol's prodigious output has ever been satisfactorily described, still less understood"—which is true enough, and might be a good reason to throw a conference, to commission a proper book or to put together a documentary film. But it's an interest not at all well served by the flinging together of a batch of four-year-old conference papers, some of which might have been funny and erudite from the speaker's platform, but which now lie on the page gasping for breath. The book has an ugly cover, is unevenly set, has poorly reproduced illustrations, is badly proofed and, most depressing of all, is made up of the sort of itchy, perfunctory essays which, in this format, do few of the authors any favors at all.

Mercifully, there is one essay here, by one of the editors, Peter Wollen, which is useful in helping you get the connection between Warhol's commercial drawings and his big silk-screens, between the fashion pages and The Factory, and the role he came to assume there as Svengali-producer and artist-voyeur. Clement Greenberg "saw painting as an activity which existed within the limits of its own world, self-validated and self-contained," says Wollen.

> Warhol, more than anyone else, broke open this enclosed world of "ambitious art," a world in which art had become a kind of substitute religion with its substitute theology and clerisy. The Warholian Renaissance indeed repeated, in miniature, many of the features that Burckhardt saw in the Florentine Renaissance—a breaking-down of cultural barriers, an exuberant neo-Paganism, the rise of the artist as celebrity, a fascination with a certain kind of court culture.

Warhol was to become the most accompanied, the most surrounded, of all contemporary artists. Not only did he like people to give him ideas, and often to do the work, but he had something in him which liked to push people to the furthest extremes of their personality, where he could observe them, and film them.

The director Naomi Levine once said that Warhol "provoked people with his passiveness into becoming freaky." People were attracted to The Factory—dope socialites, beautiful kids, energetic misfits, hip weirdos and the conventionally famous—by Warhol's name, and by his odd ability to create a scene which seemed both open and closed at the same time. A salon of reprobates, it was vaguely countercultural, full of drugs and hurt and paranoia, but still it managed to be a place where work got done. The people who went there were thinking differently—the sixties were truly under way—and they needed a place to explore their energy, a place that could exploit their manic sense of being anything other than their parents, and Warhol maintained the conditions, paid the rent, provided the logo, dominating everything with his few words, his great curiosity, his non-judgment, his ambient coolness, his sadistic glee. One of those nicely deranged kids was Billy Name, who painted the place silver, and who said that The Factory was like "a big box camera—you'd walk into it, expose yourself and develop yourself."

Billy Name used to cut hair at The Factory, and he took a lot of color pictures with his Olympus Pen-F, a smart little camera, before retreating into a darkroom at the back of the studio, where he mumbled happily to himself and never saw a soul for a full year. The pictures have now come to light in *All Tomorrow's Parties,* the best and most intimate photographic record of Warhol's empire there has ever been: the people here have real color (or blusher) on their cheeks; all the purple and yellow of those days is evident on the scratchy, vivid surface of these pictures. They are glorious in a way. David Hickey, in his foreword, speaks of how the pictures "restore that scene to us where its surface shines and wrinkles, in the midst of New York weather and Sixties fashion, in a tactile grunge of downtown Manhattan and the quotidian tumult of quarrels, messy lunches and spilled drinks." Joe Dallesandro in a turtleneck looking at some prints; Brigid Berlin running in with the milkshakes; Susan Bottomly cuddling a stuffed camel; Viva showing off her knickers; Taylor Mead sticking out his tongue in Max's Kansas City; Lou Reed checking his buttonhole at John Cale's wedding. One big silvery moment in the history of Pop Art, or the history of Nothing.

For all Warhol's love of crazy girls in their posh frocks and his growing curiosity about the higher society, his first impulse as an artist was basically democratic. He believed that anybody could be beautiful or interesting — "if everybody's not a beauty, then nobody is" — though he also believed that money made people better people. The older he got, the more he wanted rich people around him, and shopping became his only love. But at the time of his best paintings Warhol was attracted to the idea that consumerism was the great leveler. Buying makes us all free. A pair of jeans is a pair of jeans is a pair of jeans, you can only wear one pair at a time, and that is what Warhol adored about America. He liked to imagine everyone being subjected to the same repetitive imagery — soup tins, Liz Taylors — and imagine that modern iconography made us all the same, all answerable to our desires, all open to the lure of the available, and all capable of becoming a famous image, for fifteen minutes, in a future nobody knows. Such faith in democracy is essentially heartless, and he knew that too. Choice isn't everything. And some people don't have it. Most people could buy a box of Brillo pads, but hardly anybody could buy one of Andy Warhol's *Brillo Boxes*. Warhol's democracy had boring limitations: he trusted to the Art Market, not the supermarket.

Pop Art was, for a time, a good joke at the expense of the more traditional art world, but it also managed to turn a strobe lamp on the wider culture, making all manner of products and personalities go suddenly slow and suddenly stark. In this light, the most familiar contemporary objects seemed alienated and strange, and a sensibility emerged that was all to do with time and place. Fifties domestic inertia — the tyranny of the pedal bin — lay exposed in the vast and gaudy paintings of Campbell's soup and Coca-Cola; and the face of Marilyn Monroe, the most innocent and disconcerting of the fifties fluff, and stone dead, reminded the world how easy it was to be blown away, how certain it seemed that death was the most common currency of them all. Death is cheap and easy to produce. Everybody can afford one.

Someone read out a dreadfully funny thing at Andy Warhol's funeral. "When I die I don't want to leave any leftovers," they quoted Andy as saying. "I'd like to disappear. People wouldn't say he died today, they'd say he disappeared. But I do like the idea of people turning into dust or sand, and it would be very glamorous to be reincarnated as a big ring on Elizabeth Taylor's finger." A decade before Warhol disappeared, he spent his afternoons in business meetings, and his nights at Studio 54. A bedlam of cocaine and orgasms and famous names and quaaludes and tears, Studio 54 was the end zone of the New York world that Warhol had first come in search of — a Stork Club or El Morocco for a new generation looped on *Saturday Night Fever*. The not at all unfeverish Anthony Haden-Guest, in his book *The Last Party*, offers the view that Studio 54 was the apex of everything good and optimistic and various in that famously golden age, the late seventies. To our man, the disco was a libertine harbor of top Rabelaisian fun, a place where Balzacian monsters could frug the night away, hoovering the family fortune up a hole in their faces, and all the happy people could spin through the palace, so pleased, so lucky, allowed at last into the Jacobean masque. Other people say it was just a sweaty dump full of idiots shouting at each other, but Mr. Haden-Guest is a social historian.

Warhol by that time was glazed with celebrity. For someone who never had much to say but who somehow managed to say it, he suddenly didn't have much to say. He had never been right since his brush with death. The crazy people were kept at a distance — and he simply liked to drink a few vodkas and take snaps from the balconies of rubbishy discos. Most of his instincts were gone, but still he liked to look at the dance floor, and the dancing people, with their dancing feet, each little toe there trapped in a golden shoe.

*October 1997*

# *Good Fibs*

NEVER GIVE A WRITER a key to your apartment. Or your office. Never let him talk to your children. If he says he wants to take a bath, tell him the plumbing's knackered. If he makes for the fridge, say everybody just died of food poisoning. Don't encourage him in any way. Never give him your mother's phone number. Keep him away from anything sharp. Tell him nothing you wouldn't tell your worst enemy. Hide from him in the supermarket. Avoid eye contact. Never go out to war with one; never share his drugs. And never, never kiss a writer. Never kiss one no matter what. At the hard core of twentieth-century American writing, these would appear to be the big lessons. And they all crumble down to one thing in the end: never trust a genius who even thinks he might be American.

The great Yankee book editors made themselves great by ignoring this advice. The best of them — Maxwell Perkins, Robert Giroux, Joe Fox, Bennett Cerf — allowed many brilliant young things to roll about on their front lawns, and some days they even took a drink in the company of these writers, or let their dogs loose to lick their fidgety, callused hands. A sad business, this little kindness, but now and then it proved a wise invest-ment of faith or pity. Mr. Cerf, of Random House, was especially good in this way, and was known to give sets of office keys to his "special writers," so that they'd have somewhere to spread their elbows in New York. William Faulkner was never out of there. Always at night. Always drunk. But one morning even Cerf got fed up with the brewery toxins in the office hum. He took back the key. Another of Cerf's specials, Truman Capote, a young goldfish new-swimming into the scene, remembered Faulkner coming over to his place for a party. The elder Southern gentle-man had hoped for a bath. Capote said fine. After fifty minutes he started to worry. What was Faulkner up to? He went into the bathroom and found Faulkner crying in the cold water. Capote said nothing. He just sat on the loo and looked at the older man crying away to himself. And that is one of the other lessons of American literature: Capote and Faulkner in the bathroom.

Truman Capote was too young then, and too successful too quickly, to be expected to give a toss for Life's Big Lessons. Be-sides, he knew quite a bit about life already. Without so much as a full alphabet in his head, nothing of spelling, nothing of math, he had made his own way out of Monroeville, Alabama. He had the blondest hair and a nice red scarf. His ear was pitch-perfect. And out of all the grand mess of things — his sad, flying-away mother, Lillie Mae, his broken-winged father, Arch Persons, his blowzy maiden aunts, Sookie and Callie and Jennie, who brought him up as a nearly-girl — he raced for the glorylands. Capote's young life is a small, operatic cliché, a story of aban-donment in a slow-burning Southern hollow, all the world held at a distance, all of a boy's wonder clouded with local fevers. And out of those tossings and turnings a strange and clear pros-ody was born.

George Plimpton has tripped on a handy way of telling the

story of a life, so long as that life happens to be one like Truman Capote's. In place of an account shaped by Plimpton's sentences, what we have (*Truman Capote: In Which Various Friends, Enemies, Acquaintances, and Detractors Recall His Turbulent Career*) is a birth-to-death narrative made up of the voices of those who knew the subject. It is a fine and busy book, a small marvel of editing and selection, each bit of spoken evidence sitting good and lively in its place. It is a method Plimpton (along with his sometime collaborator Jean Stein) used much less beguilingly in a book about Robert Kennedy, but which they deployed to quite stunning effect in *Edie,* the story of Warhol starlet Edie Sedgwick. "The form is particularly appealing for a number of reasons," Plimpton writes, "not least of which is that the reader is treated to information delivered firsthand, as if one had happened in on a large gathering, perhaps a cocktail party, in this cave of Truman Capote's acquaintances. With a glass in hand (probably a vodka) our reader moves from group to group and listens in on personal reminiscences, opinions, vitriol, and anecdote."

The analogy, I suspect, suits the world of Plimpton as much as it does the world of Capote. And that is one of the book's strengths: Plimpton, like James Boswell, is an enthusiast for the world he is conjuring; he knows it well, knows all the figures in the carpet; the people are for the most part his acquaintances too, and his way of arranging their words is bent by his own understanding of how it all was. Though filled with the noise of coffeehouses and café society, *The Life of Johnson* is an oral biography of a quite different sort — and Boswell a sharper prism than any other biographer — but there is nevertheless something pleasingly Boswellian in Plimpton's arrangements. He, too, has a subject who suits the gossipy method, and whose adult life and achievements give themselves to an endless parade of anecdotalists, filled with all the loquacious wonder of the day. But the party analogy shows a fault, too. People at parties like to talk about other people at parties. The areas of Capote's life which are served well by this compendium of chatterers are all the public parts—his debut, his celebrity, his big party, his success, his open betrayals, his decline—while the more private occasions are mere whispers in the corner of the room. So Plimpton fills thirty-one pages with talk of the night of Truman's Black and White Ball, but only twenty-four pages with his entire childhood. (This is a less happy Boswellian trait.) The party method favors the partygoers, and you'd be better off in the company of Gerald Clarke's biography, published in 1988, if you wanted to know about Capote's more private world or were curious about whom he was sleeping with. What we have here is Plimpton's people speaking for themselves, some for the first time, and very few of them seem shy of the opportunity, or of Plimpton's probable vodkas. They give us the talked-about Truman Capote. Perhaps the only Capote that Capote would have cared for.

In 1944 he started to work as a runner at *The New Yorker*. He arrived on his first Monday in ballet pumps and a little black cape. "What is *that?*" asked Harold Ross. The runner's pencil-sharpening colleagues left the great editor none the wiser. "He was an absolutely gorgeous apparition," said Brendan Gill, "fluttering, flitting up and down the corridors of the magazine. He was indeed tiny. He and Miss Terry, our office manager, were an extraordinary couple. They were both the same size and they got on wonderfully well. He always adored elderly women and he adored Miss Terry, who was quite vicious, and was a bigot about almost everything, which also suited Truman. But he *was* an office boy."

His office-boyishness did not win every time. Those were the days, or so we imagine, when barefaced cheek was not always guaranteed to bring instant promotion: Capote was sacked for insulting Robert Frost. Nobody at *The New Yorker* had spotted him for a writer. A petulant miss, yes. A homosexual villain, maybe. But not a writer. Or not the sort of writer easily carved into nullity by the gentle-minded fiction editors of the time. The proper home for a talent like his — gilt-edged, romantic, dark and stylishly frail — was a fashion magazine like *Harper's Bazaar.* This was a world away from Harold Ross's manly fine-tuning: a place, rather, for womanly fine-tuning, and for subtle new writing by people such as Jean Stafford and Eudora Welty; and beyond that it was one of the robust new advertising venues, like *Mademoiselle,* one of the postwar places devoted to a new sort of self-making. Capote did not reflect a generation, as Fitzgerald had done, or seek to scrub the world new with carbolic silences, like Ernest Hemingway, or to turn things upside down, like James Baldwin. His political triumphs would be in the manner of his small personal displays — seasonal disturbances on the ground where fashion and writing and crime and movies met and clashed by night. And out of all this he would emerge a celebrity, a world-class speaker-up for men and women who thought it modern to have more than one self attached to oneself. In this sense he was a progenitor of the world that *Vanity Fair* now takes for granted.

Capote's first novel, *Other Voices, Other Rooms,* even today reads like something wondrously perverse. It is an unbelievably precocious book, with the bones of the Old South gleaming in its sentences; it's a vivid world of creaky houses that are hot all day, imperfect cousins, crooked trees, and the lickety-split smack of children's feet on decaying floorboards. Old women grow beards in the months before they die; two-headed babies are shown in jars by the men of the traveling fair. The thirteen-year-old boy Joel is called back to an old house — where his dying, bedridden father throws red tennis balls down the stairs to attract attention — and becomes involved with his cousin Randolph, a wasted aesthete of no fixed accent and fathomless disappointments. It is not an original setting, in fact rather standard if one thinks of Faulkner and Carson McCullers and others of the Southern Gothic, with their yellow-eyed mamas and idiot boys. But there is a patience in Capote's novel, a surprising charity, a seamlessly variegated emotion, that would have made it quite remarkable in a very good writer double his age, which was twenty-four.

People tend to blame early success for all the horrors that follow. But that can be only partly true for Truman Capote. Success just made him more himself, more *himselves,* and without it there would have been no real life to speak of. Capote knew what he was doing, and rightly feared it. He pulled the voices of the past down among the present. He made a tender mosaic of previous wrongs. And when he was done, he looked at it and saw his own face, his own salvation, his own sexual nature. And that may be the problem. He saw himself too clearly, settled too many scores with that first book. Too much was fixed in there. Plimpton quotes something he said later on:

> Do you remember the young boy who goes to a crumbling mansion in search of his father and finds an old man who is crippled and can't speak and can communicate only by bouncing red tennis balls down the stairs? . . . The fact that the old man is crippled and mute was my way of transferring my own inability to communicate with my father. I was not only the boy in the story but also the old man.

It seems that Capote's first real moment of clarity about the past, and the dimensions of his personality, was also the moment of an overwhelming international success. Boy and old man were bound together. He would spend the rest of his life, his writing life, trying to lose the knowledge that had brought him to himself and fixed him at that point. That was his horror: too early he lost sight of his own unwisdom.

In *Breakfast at Tiffany's* he tried to show a world where the love of money was both the grandest and the simplest of all loves. Holly Golightly is a delightful creation, camp and light, gruesome and vulnerable, a woman who will fill her life at whatever cost, even if that means emptying her life. Capote's writing became plainer. He honed his verbal sensualities until they became epigrams. Mag Wildwood "was a triumph over ugliness, so often more beguiling than real beauty, if only because it contains paradox."

> DORIS LILLY: There was a lot of wondering about who the original Holly Golightly was. Pamela Drake and I were living in this brownstone walk-up on East 78th Street, exactly the one in *Breakfast at Tiffany's. Exactly.* Truman used to come over all the time and watch me put make-up on before I went out . . . There's an awful lot of me in Holly Golightly. There is much more of me than there is of Carol Marcus and a girl called Bee Dabney, a painter. More of me than either of these two ladies. I know.

You wouldn't especially want to argue with what Doris Lilly knows; she once wrote a book called *How to Marry a Millionaire.* But her words show how keen many people were to be associated with Capote's creations. He was fashionable in a new way for a writer. People felt that he summoned a world of sophistication and superior irony. He had all the social details so prettily laid on the page. But you'd be a fool to miss the shadows that mark these technicolored pictures of America.

If Capote could be thought to have chosen friends who were

idealizations of himself—stunning, long-necked women, in the main, who knew how to surf over other people's smallness—the characters in his books were less ideal, and more hurt, and more afraid. Holly Golightly's dreams only mask her basic despairs (her "mean reds"). She longs for the simple side of herself, the side that "belongs," and calls itself Lulamae Barnes, but something unknown drives her towards a glorious nowhere, a New York, where she might call herself by any name she chooses. That is her small, engaging tragedy. Capote obviously knew girls like that (Carol Marcus, Slim Keith, Marilyn Monroe), but none of them were as much like that as his own mother. It was she who ran away to New York and married a rich Cuban. She who kept the appearance of wealth when all had gone down the Swanee. And she who eventually killed herself in the unbearable glare of a New York afternoon. And perhaps even more than his mother, Holly was merely Truman. Everything he wanted came to him, and yet something refused him, something small, unknowable, something maybe long gone. Holly was not just a cute cupcake with a sassy line who got a bit muddled. She was someone who had grown remote from herself, and who hadn't the peace of mind required to give her cat a name. Capote once asked himself a question: "If you had to live in just one place—without ever leaving—where would it be?" His answer is memorable, and not least because of the hollow sound of it, what you might call the Golightly ring. "Oh, dear," he said. "What a devastating notion. To be grounded in just one place."

Capote's life was a deep fiction. He almost admitted as much himself. There was something in it which was entirely made up, and that was fine, for as long as it was fine. It was his fiction writing that told the truth. And it was agony to him. A family man once asked him what it was like finishing a novel. "It's like taking your firstborn child out onto the lawn and shooting it through the head," he said.

Truman Capote may have taken to writing nonfiction because he was more comfortable with facts than he was with the truth. A good novelist, one who wrote in the Capote manner, could not avoid himself in writing a novel. His method would render that impossible. But he could bring his creative abilities to bear on some facts. Even a whole world of facts. He could let his style roam across the matter of other people's hearts. He could write nonfiction. And decorating those true subjects would be second nature. Nonfiction has changed greatly since then — become interchangeable with the voices in a novel — and in some part that change is due to the seriousness with which writers like Capote turned to it in the sixties. But the nonfiction he wrote was the opposite of personal. If he used the skill of a novelist in writing *In Cold Blood,* it was a kind of novelistic skill that he did not use in the writing of his own novels. He was simply being a very good storyteller in his nonfiction, and telling a kind of story that seemed to have a lot to do with the truth, with being factually accurate, but which really cared far less for truth than it did for narrative drive and surprise. In at least one important sense, *In Cold Blood* is Capote's least truthful book.

But it is a very good one, and it may be the high point of the thing Tom Wolfe called the New Journalism. Capote did not invent it. There were already a fair number of good writers, sound listeners, who were into that sort of concentrated, high-style reportage. Anyhow, the best claim of responsibility for its American trademark is that of Lillian Ross, who in 1952 wrote *Picture,* an arresting, intimate account of the making of John Huston's movie of *The Red Badge of Courage.* But Joseph Mitchell was doing a similar thing; John Hersey used something of the method in writing *Hiroshima,* as did James Agee in *Let Us Now Praise Famous Men.* Since we're presently interested in truth, I have to say, in all truth, that each of these writers, as nonfictionists, was more taken up with questions of factual accuracy than Capote ever was. Capote had found a way of writing well about real-life events — and that was an essential discovery for him — but he was never one to throw away a trick. After all, he'd left behind the truth when he stopped writing his novels. He was now free to make a few things up. Not that he ever admitted as much. He spoke piously in interviews about the wholesome truth of every comma; he made large claims for his all-seeing witnesses.

*In Cold Blood* is a narrative account of the killing of the Clutters, a conservative, agricultural family who were killed at their home outside the town of Holcomb, among the cornfields of Kansas, at the end of the fifties. The Clutter house, the Holcomb community, was not so unlike Capote's own deserted home in Alabama, and he took his childhood friend Harper Lee out to Kansas to help with the murder story. Though Capote did not set out to make a novel of the episode, he did both more than that and less. He did more in the sense that he pounded most of the details out of the ground — his research was pretty stunning — and he brought the case alive with the quality of his observations of true things. And he also did more in the sense that he shaped those terrible events, on the page, in such a way as to show the heartlessness not only of the killers but of the killers' upbringings; he showed pity where the system could not, and the cold blood referred to in his title is not only that of the killers, it is that of the executioners. Capote's own novels depend on truths out of order, deep wells of uncertainty, and amoral sweats. But he was detached enough from the world of

*In Cold Blood* to place order on it. He could invent a comple-
tion for it. The book may not be a record of absolute truth, but
it is a moral artifact, and more than anything a work of beautiful
invention.

The trouble — at least the trouble for some — is that Capote
took liberties. He took liberties for the purpose of moral clarity, something he never did in his fiction. Plimpton's people are
good on this. Harold Nye:

> What he had in the galleys was incorrect. It was a fiction
> thing, and being a young officer, I took offense at the fact that
> he didn't tell the truth. So I refused to approve them. Truman
> and I got into a little bit of a verbal battle and he wound up
> calling me a tyrant. What he did was to take this lady who ran
> the little apartment house in Las Vegas where Perry Smith
> [one of the killers] had been, and fictionalize her way out of
> character. Accuracy was not his point . . . It was probably
> an insignificant thing, except I was under the impression the
> book was going to be factual, and it was not; it was a fiction
> book.

Though not, as I said before, the sort of fiction book normally written by Truman Capote. The sort written by Dickens
maybe, or Hardy. Anyway, the point is that Capote made things
up, and that was something he could do, and had to do, in order
to have the true-to-life book he wanted to publish. He swore it
was all accurate, but it is clear now he invented whole sections:
the business of the lady in Las Vegas, the idea that Detective
Alvin Dewey closed his eyes as the executions took place, the
ending, where Dewey meets a young friend of Nancy, one of the
slain, in a cemetery overlooking the town. None of it happened
as Capote wished it had.

Kenneth Tynan pinned a wriggling Capote to the wall on this delicate point of ethics and *In Cold Blood*. "We are talking," Tynan wrote, "about responsibility. For the first time an influential writer in the front rank has been placed in a privileged intimacy with criminals about to die and, in my view, done less than he might have to save them . . . No piece of prose, however deathless, is worth a human life." And Tynan is joined at Plimpton's party by the composer Ned Rorem, fluttering a letter he once wrote to the *Saturday Review of Literature:* "Capote got two million and his heroes got the rope. That book . . . was completed before the deaths of Smith and Hickock: yet, had they not died, there would have been no book." Rorem was not alone in thinking Capote had garlanded his sad story with a multitude of well-turned falsities.

Capote had, by this point in his life, made himself an emperor of good fibs. He told the most excellent lies, and knew they didn't matter that much, so long as they improved his stories and made people laugh or squirm that extra bit. The pianist and writer Robert Fitzdale remembers Capote regaling a dinner table with the news that he had slept with Garbo. He told another group that all her Picassos were hung upside down. "I notice something about Truman," says the composer Arthur Gold, "whenever he begins to fantasize or tell lies, he looks up. His eyes go heavenward and he doesn't look at you. Just watch, whenever his eyes go up, whatever he is telling you is not the truth. A sort of 17th-century Madonna look."

ROBERT FITZDALE: His lies were better than other people's truths. Much more interesting.

GORE VIDAL: There are different sorts of liars . . . Capote's lies had a double purpose: one was to attract attention to himself and to distract attention from what he looked and sounded like. Second, ultimately they were calculated to destroy other people—these lies were usually sexual anecdotes about famous people that he would improvise as he went along. You could not mention anyone famous to him—"Oh, I know him so well"—and he'd start in . . . Joyce Susskind once said he was responsible for more New York divorces than the most busy of correspondents.

As you would expect in a book of this sort, there is a good deal of bitchiness, much of it pluming from the curled lips of Gore Vidal. But that might be fair enough: Capote himself was a bitch and a snob, elegant virtues he learned at the knee of the master, Cecil Beaton. But at least with Truman Capote it came from a good place. He was sensitive and he wanted to be liked. During his boyhood, as a formidable sissy in small-town Alabama, he would do a nice thing on those many occasions he was confronted by bullies. He would cartwheel around them. Just spin and spin and spin until the frightening ones laughed out loud and slapped his back.

The adult Capote did cartwheels for the rich. He loved those women, his swans—a Paley, an Agnelli, a Guinness, a Radziwill—and he allowed himself a long season as their jester, their girlfriend, their ornament, their pet. It is not easy to understand his fascination with those translucent airheads. He liked the small vegetables they served up, he liked their helicopters to the snow, their yachts to the clear blue yonder. They were his perfect audience, I suppose: beautiful, self-made, with too much time on their hands. He gave them a party they would never forget. But they forgot that his lies were only for living. He kept the truth for his fiction, and when he wrote up their lives in *Answered Prayers,* a half-finished novel serialized in *Esquire,* they dropped him, and left him to break apart, and to drink himself away.

At the close of things, Capote could not live without the love of those he idealized. He'd even lost all self-love, which left him as badly off as his mother, and worse off than Holly Golightly — a character, like him, who had everything and nothing. His last novel took its title from a lament of Saint Theresa's. "More tears are shed over answered prayers than unanswered ones."

*April 1998*

# England's Flowers

OR A LONG TIME, England used to go to bed early. It
was a country then of chimneys and cocoa drinkers. Rich
tea was the favorite dip. In the evening, people would listen to well-spoken liars on the radio; they would polish their
own shoes and go up the stairs early. There were flowers on
the wallpaper, flowers on the carpet. There were flowers on the
china and on the lampshades. The bedspread was usually an
acre of roses, their redness quite faded in the wash.

The people of that country breathed flowers in their
sleep. And, sometimes, their dreams—much like the old bal-
lads—were pastoral dramas shaded in green. The flowerbed
of England was love bower and grave. The typical house in the
typical street: a mouth of flowers, an English garden. How small
the world is in the English memory: everywhere an outpost, a
colony, a dominion; and in every field there was a flower-decked
corner of home, where a soldier's bones made it forever England. Prime ministers and poets have made much of England's
flowers. And the people have, too. Flowers put them in mind of
who they like to be; the old houses, the old soil.

But what is the Elizabethan garden now? The empire is

gone: there's more of the world in England now than there is of England in the world. The supermarket is a global bazaar; the television set is a mobile room with a view. England could never be that old thing again. But the love of flowers has grown somehow. It's as if the people were keen for the scent of that other England, that place of shelter and communal worth, of blooms as symbols of national feeling. It's as if they yearn, from time to time — usually in times of disaster and dismay — for a childish liberty of flowers, like Wordsworth's sacred nurseries of blooming youth:

> *In whose collegiate shelter England's Flowers*
> *Expand, enjoying through their vernal hours*
> *The air of liberty, the light of truth.*

And maybe there's a longing for something more: a runaway sense of popular pride, a more fevered application of Wordsworth's floriation, such as that of Alfred Austin, with his "Who Would Not Die for England!"

> *So across the far-off foam,*
> *Bring him hither, bring him home,*
> *Over avenues of wave, —*
> *English ground, — to English grave;*
> *Where his soldier dust may rest,*
> *England's Flag above his breast,*
> *And, love-tended, long may bloom*
> *English flowers about his tomb.*

England's flowers. What a commodity. Wrapped in plastic at the palace gates. Yet most of those flowers were not English. Most flowers sold in England now are not from this place. They are products of other debatable lands and they have their own stories.

This is the story of one bunch. The flowers' existence began in 1970. They are a breed of the most popular white lily, *Lilium longiflorum*. With lilies, the shortest route from breeding to market is eight years. In 1978 the first of our breed of lilies was produced by Herut Yahel of the Israeli agricultural research group. Nowadays, Israel produces ten to fifteen million of these bulbs every year.

Dudu Efron is a bulb manufacturer. He stood talking under an orange tree, a half year after Princess Diana's death. It was a normal March day in the Israeli desert, and Efron stood fanning himself with a mobile phone. "The Arabs hate everything we produce," he said, "but sometimes business is stronger than politics." He was talking about the fact that many Israeli flowers end up in the Persian Gulf. They go to Holland first. "The flowers, they lose their identity at the market. And, if the price is right, the Arabs will buy them." He laughed under his mustache. "Yes," he said, "there is a little something of Israeli soil in the houses of our friends the Arabs."

Efron was born in Jerusalem and grew up on a kibbutz. Agriculture and politics were mixed up in the life he remembers. "The farmers in the kibbutzim were heroes. They protected the borders. The Israeli people thought they were noble. Now people think farmers are dirty. Stupid." For twenty years Efron was a wheat grower, then he planted potatoes, and for the past few years he has been producing bulbs. Especially lily bulbs. Three years ago he produced the bulbs for our bunch. He froze them, then sold them to Haviv Sela.

Sela's farm is a baked cluster of sheds. There is also a house, a heap of sand shoes in the yard, a broken pot on the window, a goldfinch outspoken on the clothesline. The palm trees have hot leaves; a patch of sand encircles the bottom of each tree. Thirty years ago all of this was desert. Now they grow white lilies from the soil. The farm is just outside the village of Amioz. "We are making our history by single years, not centuries," said Sela, out in the field with his blue cap. He rolled three bulbs in a brown hand. They can be used three, maybe four times, he said. Every June, he will pluck all the bulbs out of the fields, scrub them clean, leave them to dry for a while and then place them in a giant freezer for sixty days. "This makes the bulb think it has been through winter." Once this is done, he will start planting them again. Each bulb to be planted four inches down in the soil. Sela's soil—the soil he calls "my land"—is a difficult shade of red.

The bulbs for our bunch were put into the soil on December 9, 1997. This was the bulbs' third time pregnant: they produced two sets of flowers last year, and had since spent most of October and November in a pretend Siberian winter. Here again in the soil, they began to sprout. They were sprinkled with water for two minutes, eight times a day. They had artificial light at night. The light came down in two-minute bursts. As the flowers grew, the men and women on the farm, who are all from Thailand, would weed the field by hand.

By January, young, green shoots had broken through the soil. Waxy leaves were showing. By February, the flower heads were formed. The cells were turgid with water, bloated with radiant energy. The heads were deep green; they tapered to white at the ends. By March, the stems were twelve inches high. Stout. And two weeks on, they had grown to their height: twenty-two inches. Sun-fed, water-made, chemically charged, carbon dioxide–breathing lilies. White lilies. They swayed easily in Sela's field. Full of life. The blue sky above, the red earth below.

Soon it was time to cut them. Sela took out a small knife. He clipped each of our stems a half inch above the dirt. Thousands of stems were harvested this day: Wednesday, March 11.

Each of our stems had several flowers. Long heads, tight shut. They were carried from the field and placed in buckets of water. For five hours they stand outside in the sun. (This is important: if they aren't allowed to take in water and sun for this period of time, and just breathe, the flowers may never open.) Sela harvested our bunch at ten in the morning. They sat out in buckets until three o'clock. The buckets were then put into the big fridge. They are meant to stay there for not less than sixteen hours. Our bunch went in for the cold night. Meantime, Sela's family came to the yard. A cock crowed. Mrs. Sela drank Diet Coke from a big plastic bottle. "I don't like to feed my body rubbish," she said. The uncut lilies moved in the long field. Acres of them. The lilies of the field.

> I am the rose of Sharon and the lily of the valleys. As a lily among thorns, so is my love among the daughters. (Song of Solomon 2:1-2)

> And why take thought for raiment? Consider the lilies of the field, how they grow: they toil not, neither do they spin: And yet I say unto you, That even Solomon in all his glory was not arrayed like one of these. (Matthew 6:28-29)

Fable says the white lily sprang from the milk of Juno. But Christian fable makes the larger claim upon them: they are everywhere in the Bible. They represent virtue, celestial beauty and purity. To the Greeks and Romans the lily was a medicinal flower. The bulbs were sometimes crushed and made into ointment. The fragrant petals were used as a balm. In the Middle Ages, the white lily was associated with the Virgin Mary (the flower is included in many paintings of her), and also connected with Saints Dominick and Louis. Naturalists are certain that lilies grew plentifully in the Israel of the Bible. Yet they disappeared somehow. No one reported seeing a colony of lilies in Palestine until 1925. On a fine September morning M. N. Naftolsky, a well-known plant hunter who was that day leading a party of students from the Hebrew University in Jerusalem, found a flock of white lilies growing wild in the mountains of upper Galilee. This, he knew, was the lily of the field, the lily of the valley, the lily among the thorns. It had found a way to survive the various ravages of the land.

Sela's cultivated lilies spent the night at 2 degrees Celsius. He took them out of the fridge at 8 a.m. on March 12. It was an especially warm Thursday. Our lilies looked all lushly green. They smelled of trees and soil. The flowers were still clamped shut.

Sela's seven Thai workers were in the packing shed. Chen Singsai is separating the good from the bad. He does this all day. "You must be careful not to give too much water," he said. "Too much water, the leaves go yellow." Singsai comes from a village six hundred miles from Bangkok. "We have to work many more hours for the Mother's Day." He hopes to learn things about farming, things he can take back to his own village one day. He has been in Israel for seven years. His wife, like him, is working at the bench and, just like him, is sitting on a column of up-turned plastic tubs. "We have been working the sixteen hours," says Mr. Singsai. The pay is reasonable. He is able to send something home to his mother. "Not bad life," he said. All the Thai women who work in these sheds have covered their faces. Even in the heat they are covered. "They want to be white," says Singsai. "Like lilias."

Our stems were put onto a machine. It was a kind of sorting machine. At the end, the stems were cut to size by a rotary blade. Many of the leaves were stripped. The man working that end of the machine stood in a pile of mashed plants. A patch of greenery tattooed on the floor. "Many flowers," he said, "and looking the same."

Someone else took bunches of five stems each and placed them in plastic bags. At 9 a.m. our bunch was packed, with some other bunches, into a pink and yellow box, a carton with the word "Carmel" printed on it. At 11 a.m. a truck came to the farm. The cartons were loaded up. A lazy dog lay at the farm's gate. It was panting. It closed its eyes to the dust clouds. The too hot morning; the rumble of trucks. The flowers were on their way to the packinghouse at Mabuim. This place is run by Agrexco—the company behind Carmel—and is one of fifteen packinghouses in Israel. Agrexco is the main exporter of Israeli fruit and flowers.

Liav Leshem, one of the company's young product managers, responsible for flowers, was driving on one of the Negev's new dual carriageways. He had one of those hands-free mobile phones. The phone rang every other minute. He spoke Hebrew to the office, English to customers calling from Holland and Germany. He wore a watch that was lodged in a sweatband. He drove past a spray painting of Princess Diana. Someone had put a mustache on her. The graffito shimmers in the heat.

"It is hard," said Leshem. "We are dealing here with a very perishable thing. Flowers die too early if you don't look after them, give them the right conditions. At every stage of the flowers' journey, we keep the right temperature. It is very hard. There are three ways in the world to lose money—women, gambling and agriculture. Women is the most enjoyable, gambling is the quickest, and agriculture, well, agriculture is the surest."

Agrexco was founded in 1957. Forty years later its turnover was $600 million. Year upon year the company grows: it is one of the biggest suppliers of roses and lilies and gerbera daisies to the English market, and it feeds vegetables into all the main supermarkets. "England wants more of the flowers now," says Leshem. "The supermarkets are taking over. They've increased their orders for next year. They like the quality, and we move fast."

He was moving fast as he said this. Field after field fell away. "Why are the white lilies so expensive?" he said. "I'll tell you: because you have to freeze the bulbs after each planting. They demand a lot of irrigation in the ground. You cannot pack too many in a box, so the transportation costs are high. Very high. We send them all by air. But people love the lilies. Mysterious . . . lilies in England. They use them in the marriages and in the deaths, no? England is our biggest market. What is the difference between a wedding and a funeral? In a wedding, two people are buried."

The packinghouse at Mabuim is across from a cluster of new dwellings. They are middle-income houses; nice terracotta roofs. Three hundred growers—one as far as the Gaza Strip, 120 kilometers away—send their produce to this warehouse. More than 250 million flower stems a year pass through here. Millions of white lilies.

Our bunch arrived at Mabuim at midday on Thursday morning, March 12. They were left in the fridge there for an hour. Then they were stamped. The label has the grower's bar code on it, the plant's name, and the serial number of the country and the customer. The cartons were loaded onto a pallet.

Our bunch went into a truck—bound for the Agrexco terminal at Ben Gurion Airport—at one o'clock. Each carton was passed through a bomb detector machine before being loaded. A young Israeli driver stood by the machine. He was trying to blow a smoke ring through a smoke ring.

There are no accents in Israel. There is no dialect. There are many different kinds of voice, but only one steady inflection.

Unlike other small countries — Denmark or Ireland, say — where the accent can change from street to street. "The heart of the people is more ready for peace now," says Leshem. "More time, more blood on the soil, but eventually peace will come."

Leshem's boss is called Gidon Mazor, a handsome, easy-smiling man in a cotton shirt. "My father," said Mazor, "was a vegetable man. My father pushed me towards the flowers. It was a way of keeping me at home. And my own son is now in the business too." He speaks as if companies such as Agrexco add to the big idea of Israel. Their idea. They show the country working. Another of Leshem's young colleagues said it is all just great: "Britain, which left our country in such a mess in 1948, is now dying for our flowers. They can't get enough of them. Our lilies are the best in the world. We breed them to last long, and to stand up."

Mazor is just as pleased that the company is doing well. But he is more cautious; in his eyes, he looks like he knows more of what success means, and more of what failure means, too. He can guess at the price of things. He has an older businessman's impatience with the trumpets of certainty. "Things are better than ten years ago. Not good enough yet, but improving all the time."

In the Agrexco terminal at Ben Gurion, the loading bay is like the set of a ballet production. Box after box is lifted onto cargo pallets. The forklifts' pas de deux. A symphony of horns and shouts and rubber doors flying open; bells ringing, engines revving up. The sound of tires gripping the chilled tarmac. Everything is cold for the flowers and the cherry tomatoes. Our bunch came in. The carton was placed on a pallet with the other things bound for London. Hundreds of boxes for London that day. Our pallet truck is dragged away by a yellow tractor. Checked for bombs. And soon it is beyond the coolness of the loading bay. Out on the tarmac. Being lifted into the plane, a Boeing 747 with all the seats ripped out. Like a giant garage. Hot, but just the right temperature above the clouds. Five planes leave every day; each carries 110 tons of Israeli produce. The fruits of the soil. The lilies of the field. The plane flew overhead at 7 p.m.

Beeri Lavi spent two years working in Kenya. He helped to set up an irrigation system. He then managed the farms of the president of the Ivory Coast — growing mangoes, pineapples, avocados — and he took what he had learned back to Israel. He now runs Agrexco's operation in London. "The English mentality about flowers is all change," he said. "They want variety. New kinds of flower. The lilies are in the supermarkets now, and not only for death. The narcissus was our first flower. That is the one we brought here first. England loves it. Now it wants everything. They want all the flowers."

Lavi knows that the English used to buy fewer flowers. "There was no money, and it is not a religious country, like Italy. There is less of Easter, less of Christmas. You were spending less on the graves. I was giving advice to the growers. I said, 'Give them more pinks, more light blues, orange, and plenty of white. The English wants soft colors.' And you want them cheap; for children to buy."

The warehouse in Middlesex was Britishly messy. The men at their forklifts were hurried and cursing. Robbie Williams was revving them up on the radio. Our pallet came from Heathrow just after midnight on Friday, March 13. Our carton was loaded into a cage. It was bound for London's New Covent Garden Market.

Roy Stevens was two hours away from waking up. He would soon wash and shave and drive to Vauxhall. He would come in the middle of the night, set out his wholesale stall and try against the clock to sell those flowers. Those flowers that are dying all the time. Our bunch of lilies was going to Mr. Stevens, the first of the English buyers.

The English are funny about flowers. (Not the British: Scots get into trouble for not being flowery enough, although they are catching the bug; and the Welsh prefer vegetables.) But the funniness has changed. It has become postmodern. The old way of thinking about flowers in England was to do with homeliness, domestic security, heritage, national pride. That was the cultural atmosphere then.

But the new oddness about flowers is often to do with estrangement. That's how it seems. Flowers in England, more and more, can seem to give voice to an alien feeling; something of urban disconnectedness. They might speak of a distance from the old steadiness: your parents' easy belief in home and garden, and the English rose. Some people think the new uses of flowers announce a revival of that same English community, but those grotesque piles of wrapped flowers glinting by the roadside might say the very opposite. Their cellophane might say it. They are condomized symbols of how it used to be. People don't touch the flowers; they don't know them. Their softened colors speak boldly of a lack. And the more they are piled, the more certain you become: the England they conjure is dead on the air.

You often see those flowers now. They don't mark soldiers; they mark the fall of people in ordinary life. People who are heroic only in the matter of their having met a surprising death: a car out of nowhere, a gang of crazy youths. Those flower shrines started to appear these last few years: at the sites of football stadium disasters, at the spot where a child was killed. And now they are everywhere in England. They are anonymous expressions of sympathy from one passerby to another. People come with those flowers as if it were an old-fashioned thing to do: laying flowers at the spot where some piece of random violence took place. As if to say, "We didn't used to live like this." As if to say, "Let these flowers remind you of what is best in us."

The people bending there, they act as if they know the flowers on the road could just as easily be piled for them. It is an odd—and oddly compulsive—piece of stage business in the televised culture. Many people use flowers much as they always did. But everything is touched by the new floriation. England suffers bouts of false-memory syndrome. It thinks it remembers flowers, and an age of innocence; it recalls an open-air festival of clean living, and no murders. It knows of a world that was never here, a time when everybody was one, and it marks that time's passing with cellophaned flowers. The pinning of flowers on the palace gates looked like a quiet revolution. It looked like people saying something large in one voice. But it was all in the mind, and all in the mind of television. The flowers were just flowers, and the people bored.

New Covent Garden Market is a gigantic cave of flowers; it lights up while London sleeps. The perfume near knocks you over. Forty or more large wholesalers, their flowers and plants spilling over, lying out in boxes, stacked in high bins. Lilac orchids, red amaryllis, yellow narcissus, pink ranunculus, frosted eucalyptus, a world of roses, a globe of tulips. Lilies.

"A bit wet outside," said Helen Evans, one of the market's employees. All the stand-holders know her. She moves in a cloud of winks and jokes and early-morning hellos. She has noticed the strangeness and importance of the English drama about flowers. It may be to do with memory, or the culture. "But the weird thing," she said, "is that they don't buy a lot of flowers. They spend less on flowers than almost every country in

Europe. The overall retail market is worth £1,240 million per year; about £22 per person a year. But that is not high. The English love flowers — they may think a lot about them — but they don't buy them in a big way." The Swiss spend £102 per person, the Germans £57, the Dutch £47, the French £40. But the English market is growing bit by bit. The market has doubled since 1986.

As for our bunch of white lilies, the lid was off the carton, which sat on the wet concrete. Each stem of the bunch looked pert. They seemed a darker green in the English light. They lay in the stand of S. Robert Allen Ltd., one of the market's big wholesale firms, and were surrounded by blooms from everywhere. The traffic is conducted by Roy Stevens. "We live by the weather," he said. "Too hot, and the flowers are dead on the street; too rainy, and the people won't bother stopping for flowers. It's like that in Britain. I mean, who's going to allow themselves to be dragged out looking for flowers on Cup Final day?"

"That lovely lady Princess Di going so suddenly — it was flowers everywhere. We noticed the rise in demand right away. Bang! All the white flowers were gone. You could just feel it. People needed flowers. And we sold everything we had."

Betsy Kelly is seventy-nine years old. She has been selling flowers since 1930. A small, ambling bundle of cardigans and hats, Betsy is usually too busy to smile; she is famous at the market, as her father was before her, in the old Covent Garden of horses and carts. In all the fluorescence of the new place, Betsy is a star. A curmudgeonly one, for sure, with her waving hands, her rolling eyes, her air of being bothered by this or that nonsense. But Betsy knows her own game. She walked around our box of lilies like someone inspecting a gangrenous leg. Her lips were thinned: one could almost hear her good clock ticking, and see her thoughts, her cold ruminations on pounds, shillings and pence. For all these years, she has got up early, at four or five, and gone down the market to see what's what. Her husband died five years ago. She looked at the lilies, lifted our bunch, scratched her hat and bought them. She looked around when asked a question. "I've forgotten much more than you'll ever know," she said.

Kelly's Flowers is quite far along the Commercial Road. The middle East End. A shop in the heart of Stepney. The road is filled with garment wholesalers and Indian takeaways. People trudge to the hospital. Rows of old houses sit neatly by the road. Layers of flowery wallpaper lying deep in the walls, deep in the modern emulsion. Some of the houses are being taken down. Mrs. Carrington is another old lady from here. She told a story of playing as a child in some of those houses. Some of them lay less than half demolished more than half a century ago. "Most of them had their roofs open to the sky," said Mrs. Carrington. "We fashioned tables and chairs from bricks and boards that lay around in plenty. We would unearth broken pieces of crockery that served as plates, and once, to my joy, I found the bottom half of a blue glass vase. I stood it up in the middle of my table. I filled it with the weeds that grew through the floorboards. Those houses were dark and smelly. But here we lived our pretend lives."

Betsy Kelly was in the back of her shop. She beetled away at her flower arrangements. One of them had a glittery message embedded in red carnations. It just said "Mum." Betsy had taken our lilies back to the shop. They were soaking in buckets in her large fridge. They had spent the weekend in there. It was now five days since the lilies were picked on Sela's farm. They were still very fresh. The heads had whitened some more, and they had softened, too. The flesh of the lily was tender now. There was the beginning of a sweet perfume.

"My mum and dad had the shop," said Betsy, "and they had stalls as well. One up Petticoat Lane and one by the London Hospital. All their lives. You didn't have staff in them days. You just came in as a girl and worked. That was the times. The stuff was different. It was nearly all English-grown. The only bit of stuff that we ever got really was from France or Holland, but not much. It's all the foreign stuff now."

Betsy has been in the present shop for thirty-two years. She and her husband took it over when old Mrs. Kelly became ill. "We kept her," said Betsy. "She had whatsit — Alzheimer's — and in them days the family kept them. Different kettle of fish. We never got much support. Families did it all. When I was at school, I thought I would be a gym instructor. But my mother wanted me in the shop. People were more flower-conscious then. Visiting the hospitals and that; nowadays they'd make you laugh. It's a wonder they go in at all. In them days, they visited the graves more. But this is us now. Do I still like flowers? Well, I suppose really, it's a way of life, know what I mean? I don't suppose for one minute I would like any other trade. I don't think I would like to pack up work 'cause I think to myself, after the hectic life I've led, if I was to pack up work I'd just go senile, and that wouldn't be me."

Most nights of the week Betsy gets home after 8 p.m. She lives in Brentwood, out in Essex. Her two sons come in and out. "Everything's a cost," said one of them. "It's a wonder anybody can make a shilling out of flowers now."

"It was special, once upon a time," said Betsy, "the old Covent Garden Market. You had the personalities. You had the people. They were florists, flower sellers. Today it's all big business. Ask the old ones there now. Ask Tom. Ask Roy. Ask Ken. Any of the old ones will tell you: it was a pleasure to go to the old market. But it's all going multinational. They're killing the small trader. My mother stood in Whitechapel Road. My aunt beside her. Selling flowers. They worked bloody hard. You know St. Clement Danes, the church in Fleet Street? The vicar's wife when I was a girl was Mrs. Pickford. And she used to have teas for the flower girls. Just young women. Between the two wars. And once a year Mrs. Pickford took all the girls to Brighton. Everything was colorful in them days. Not just the flowers, the people."

On Tuesday, March 17, Betsy put the lilies out in the shop. Our bunch was beginning to open: some of the ends were pouting, some were puckered up. One of the ten stems was showing a white tongue. Two tongues. The leaves beneath were very green. Our bunch sat out for two days. The shop was packed on Thursday. Mother's Day was coming up. There were men looking out of place, children shaking their little fists of pound coins. Queues all day. Betsy's assistant, Sue, was plucking and wrapping, counting and cutting, laughing and teasing, and answering the phone.

At 2:30 p.m. a gentleman came in. His brother Amos had died. He had been ill for a long time. "More merciful than tragic." Mr. Copping wanted to leave flowers at the rest home. Sue took our bunch of lilies from the bucket. She laid them on paper, added some daisies, a few white carnations, a bit of spray. She rolled them together and charged him £20. Mr. Copping walked out into the afternoon; the shop bell rang at his back.

Amos Copping died at age sixty-nine. He had never been to Israel. The only time he was ever abroad was during his national service. He'd spent part of a year in Hong Kong. His wife was dead too. Mr. Copping's body lay in Tadman's Funeral Parlour on Jubilee Street and Stepney Way. It was to this address that his brother went with the bunch of flowers. He sat awhile in the chapel with Amos. The flowers were placed in a white vase. Mr. Copping noticed there was a picture of the pope in the chapel. The coffin, the pope, white lilies and the brother. The remains of Amos Copping were buried the following Tuesday. His daughters and his brother were there. "More merciful than tragic," they said.

After that, our flowers stayed on at Tadman's. They were placed on a small table in the hall. The carpets there are ever so blue. Everything is scrubbed. The thing you notice is how clean it all is. Spick-and-span. The air smells of anything but death. "Everybody notices the smell," says Maureen Tadman. "It's the flowers and the scented candles." The carpets look like they are hoovered on the hour. "No," she said. "We don't use air fresheners or what-you-call-it, Shake 'n' Vac. No. It's the natural smell. It's the same with the boys' appearance. They have to look smart. Appearance is so important." The Tadman family has been doing funerals since 1849. The office wall is lined with old pictures of the Tadmans. Men with dark eyes and dark clothes. "Wag" Tadman, the founder, in a portrait taken around the time of the Boer War; Alfred William Tadman, his son, 1882–1935, a man in a tall hat, his mustache so carefully clipped. The two boys he had: Cornelius and Alfred, 1914–1996 and 1902–1980, a couple of characters, upright in their portraits. All dead now, and down in the city cemetery at Manor Park.

Maureen Tadman was dressed in black. She wore owlish glasses. Her demeanor was somewhat melancholy, but now and then she let go of her natural reserve and a smile lit up her face. "With a death," she said, "you really want to do things correctly." She employs only tall men. And she's serious about their smartness. "How would you feel if someone was burying you covered in earrings and ponytails?"

She is conscious of the role she has in other people's stories. She is there at the end of many a life, neatly dressed, efficient, doing things correctly. And she sometimes wonders about those lives too: what they did, how they did it. "Here in the East End, marriage, birth and death mean everything to the people. They live their life a certain way. They are caring, traditional, and the tradition says that neighbors and friends will show support at the time of a death. And the number of floral tributes is evidence of that. It wouldn't be a true East End funeral without them."

One of the funeral directors at Tadman's, Jason Saddington, said you see some funny things when you're driving a hearse. "You don't see people taking off their hats anymore. They just stare. And somebody might cross themselves. The younger folk just stare, and sometimes they rub their chest, like they're embarrassed or something."

Mrs. Tadman twisted her wedding ring around its finger. "I always ask the boys to treat the bodies the same as if they were their own family. We all have our dignity." Jason went up a ladder and washed the windows. "It's a man's world, this," said Mrs. Tadman, "and you need to work that extra bit hard if you're a woman. My own mother was buried by the firm. Aunt Ethel too. And when it comes my turn, yes. I wouldn't want anybody else doing mine. Every person that comes in that door is not a number; they're people, and you must always remember that."

A week later, our lilies were amazing. The white petals were wide to the world. An unopened stem had softened and drooped. It looked like a green silk purse. With their yellow stamens, their moist leaves, the flowers had a powerful scent, something of old earth and the Dead Sea. Life and other business went on around them, and the lilies slowly began to wilt.

The whiteness turned to brown; the petals dried and shriveled up. The fragrance vaporized overnight. Our flowers died about three weeks after Mr. Copping.

They were placed in a bin out the back. On a windowsill there, back against the light, was a tin of air freshener and a tub of Shake 'n' Vac. Each container was covered with pictures of flowers. Live flowers under the sun. The freshness of some other day.

*May 1998*

# Saint Marilyn

NEW YORK — contrary to popular opinion and Frank Sinatra — is never a city that doesn't sleep. It sleeps soundly, in fact. You walk the streets on certain nights and suddenly you can feel quite alone under the buildings. It's not that the place is deserted, there are things going on — taxis, homeless people, late-night walkers, the police — but they can seem to proceed at that hour like things out of step, like odd yearnings of the imagination, or unexpected items in a gasoline-smelling dream of urban ruin.

I stopped one night in front of the Ferragamo shoe shop on Fifth Avenue. The light from the shop was so strong it seemed like daylight spilling over the pavement. I felt drenched in the uncanny whiteness. And there in the window, draped on transparent mannequins or laid on silver boxes, were some of the dazzling relics of the late Marilyn Monroe. "A pair of stilettos by Salvatore Ferragamo, scarlet satin, encrusted with matching rhinestones."

There's no place like home, I thought.

"Estimate: $4,000–6,000." And further along, a hand-knitted cardigan "with a brown geometric pattern and matching knitted belt. Worn by Marilyn Monroe in 1962 and featured in a series of photographs by George Barris taken on the beach in Santa Monica, California. Estimate: $30,000–50,000." In the corner of the window there stood a halter-neck dress from the movie *Let's Make Love*. I thought of Marilyn and Yves Montand posing for the cameras with their unhappy smiles. "Estimate: $15,000–20,000." The Monroe things had been to London, Paris and Buenos Aires, and were now back in New York for auction at Christie's. Ferragamo took the opportunity for a cute bit of public-relations flimflam. The cold air from the ice rink at Rockefeller Plaza—underneath Christie's salesrooms—seemed to be blowing in one great frosty whoop down the avenue.

The people who stopped to look put both hands on the Ferragamo window and the white light made each one a little blonder. One woman said "beautiful"; the glass misted up in front of her mouth. I walked on a few blocks. There was a midnight service going on at St. Patrick's Cathedral. A long line stretched all the way down to the altar, where a glass case stood by itself, with a casket inside containing the relics of Saint Theresa of Lisieux. A hundred years ago, the Carmelite nun Thérèse Martin died, and she died, according to a woman I spoke to at the end of the line, "with a heart as big as the world itself." The last words of Saint Theresa are not open to doubt. "I am not dying," she said. "I am entering into Life." She was canonized in 1925.

I joined the line at St. Patrick's and followed it down, and when it was my turn I touched the glass and walked away. Men to my side were crying and whispering. The relics of Saint Theresa were traveling the world too: last year Russia and Europe, this year America, from New York to Tucson, with a spell over Christmas at the Church of St. Jane Frances de Chantal in North Hollywood.

The Christie's sale of Marilyn's relics raised $13,405,785. The Ferragamo ruby shoes were bought for $48,300 by the son of the man who made them, while lots 51 and 40, the Santa Monica cardigan and the dress from *Let's Make Love,* sold for $167,500 and $52,900 respectively. The big wow of the auction, as expected, was the Jean Louis sheath dress covered in tiny stones, worn by Marilyn at John Kennedy's birthday tribute in 1962, when she sang "Happy Birthday." This went for over a million dollars. The man who bought it (owner of a memorabilia shop called Ripley's Believe It or Not) thought he'd got a great bargain. The Kennedy dress smashed the previous world record for the sale of a female costume: a blue velvet Victor Edelstein dress belonging to Princess Diana that sold for $222,500 in June 1997. The actor and peroxophile Tony Curtis, who must have forgotten that he once said kissing Marilyn was like kissing Hitler, got out of his seat at the auction to tell reporters that Marilyn would have been thrilled. "She'd have enjoyed the fact that people still love her so much," he said.

The sale of Marilyn Monroe's personal property—a plastic cup, a group of blankets, a Plexiglas tissue-box cover, a piece of paper with the words "he does not love me" written in pencil, to name just a few of the 576 lots that were auctioned—may represent the most interesting event to occur in contemporary art since the death of Andy Warhol. Indeed, it takes Warhol's deification of celebrity past its absurdly logical conclusion: why pay more for a representation of Marilyn Monroe, even an Abstract Expressionist one like De Kooning's, or a mass-produced one like Warhol's, when, for a not dissimilar price, you can own a little something of Marilyn herself? The Christie's sale goes so far ahead of Warhol's thinking that we ironically end up back where we started, with the basic principle of authenticity. The threat—the joy—was always that Pop would eat itself in the end, and it has done. The old superstition about High Art — "Rembrandt actually touched this canvas" — can now be applied to the personal belongings of the century's most famous woman — this object actually touched Marilyn — and thus our era's tangled worries over the meaning of fine art are for a moment resolved. Pop culture became its opposite number: the ordinary minutiae of the extraordinary life came to seem as formally expressive as *Guernica*. The designer Tommy Hilfiger pays a fortune for two pairs of jeans Marilyn wore in *The Misfits*. He frames them and hangs them in his apartment. He gets the pleasure of Charles I pacing a banquet hall replete with Van Dycks. Hilfiger gets to feel he has captured the thing that is truly seen to capture his time. The spirit of the age is a bundle of famous rags.

But what of poor Marilyn herself? What is she? And who was she before all this came to pass in her adopted name? What was it about her that allowed it to happen? And who are we that love her so much? These questions rise and fall like the sound of distant applause as you read the Christie's catalogue. And occasional answers can seem to spring from the pictures and descriptions of the objects themselves. The book is a slick and a morbid affair: the clothes are really nothing without Marilyn in them; many of the photographs show her coming out of a film premiere, or sitting hopefully in another tiny apartment. Her possessions, you feel, are there to soften and furnish, to ease and to deepen, the life of a woman who is barely in possession of herself. But without her they seem like tokens of the purest emptiness.

Marilyn's books and stockings and strings of pearls come to ground you in a vivid life that is gone; her existence was so much about projection and luminous performance that you can hardly bear to imagine the macabre earthiness of her leavings. It's a bit like contemplating Ophelia's soaking garments and weedy trophies pulled from the weeping brook; they are cold, modern remnants of desire and the misfortunes of fortune, tokens of the twentieth century's obsession with the nuances of fame and public death.

*Madame Bovary. The Sun Also Rises. The Unnameable. The Fall.* Marilyn's auctioned books are like scripts primed for her long afterlife. And one of the others, *Dubliners,* contains the story that captures something of the eerie and magical grip that personal effects can hold for the living. Her gloves and candlesticks resemble those in Joyce's "The Dead": rows of framed photographs before a pier glass; we might imagine these objects that once belonged to a beautiful, sad young woman can tell us something strange and true about our own lives. The people who queued to see her things around the world were apt to say such a thing. The eternal-seeming fabulousness of a great movie star — like that of a princess — might serve for a while to transform even the dowdiest of realities. That is the myth, anyway. And Marilyn Monroe was nothing if not a sacrifice to the potency of her own mythology. Even her pet dog's tag and license (estimate, $800–1,200; final bid, $63,000) become items of great interest, symbolic pieces of the life of someone who has entered into Life. Frank Sinatra gave her the dog. She called it Mafia. Right now a person is looking at the license and thinking he grasps the meaning of the twentieth century. And who is to say that person is wrong?

Norma Jeane Mortenson was born on June 1, 1926, in the charity ward of Los Angeles General Hospital. Her mother, Gladys Baker, was now and again mad, leaving her daughter troubled but free to dream up an alternative life, and to develop her vital allure reading movie magazines. Norma Jeane had a keen sense of how to conquer people's affections — especially those of men. She wore lipstick. She wore short skirts. She told a sad story of her upbringing. And after a spell modeling and flirting and screwing and practicing her walk, waiting in line with the other girls at Schwab's drugstore on Sunset Boulevard, Marilyn emerged with a brazen sense of how to enliven the fifties.

Marilyn invented a persona — The Girl — that would at first seem to release her from the bad things of her childhood, but which later became like one of her childhood ghouls, leaning over her, making her all sex and suffocating her. The Girl was a fiction and a mask — "Mae West, Theda Bara, and Bo Peep all rolled into one," said Groucho Marx — which served to turn a case of ordinary, everyday wishing into a triumph of calculated stardom. There is hardly a single area of Norma Jeane's life that wasn't fluffed up to enhance Marilyn's exotic stature. The Girl, the resulting character, would seem to carry vulnerability and sexual freedom to a new place in the movies, but in real life, in the decompression chamber of overblown ambitions, the person who called herself Marilyn Monroe could only unravel in a miasma of loneliness and uncertainty and pain. And worst of all, even this, her bad times, her suffering, came in the end to add to the myth of her specialness. In her own lifetime she became the patron saint of sex; and afterwards, in her very modern martyrdom, she made us feel that an engulfing sadness does not in any way preclude a giant success. Marilyn's fans find the combination fatal. And so unfortunately did she.

Encyclopedias exist to bring a constant proliferation of knowledge to rest for a time in one place. *The Marilyn Encyclopedia,* Adam Victor's attempt on the universe of Marilyn Monroe — life, Life, Afterlife, scholarship, clothes, gossip, filmography, addresses, hospitals, drama coaches, superstitions, favorite toys — is truly mind-boggling. It may represent the triumph of detail over proportion, but still, all in all, it serves as a complete concordance to the many Marilyn narratives yet published. Here is a part of the entry on Marilyn's honeymoon with Joe DiMaggio:

> After a night at the budget CLIFTON INN motel in Paso Robles (and a meal in the restaurant of the Hot Springs Hotel, or at the Clifton Inn according to some versions), Joe and Marilyn drove in his dark blue Cadillac to a mountain lodge outside Idyllwild, near PALM SPRINGS, loaned to them for the occasion by Marilyn's attorney, Lloyd Wright. Here they had the uncommon luxury of two weeks alone together.

The uppercase names have entries to themselves. Just as the Christie's sale of Marilyn's knickknacks did better than adjacent sales of German Art and of the Ancient Jewels of Persia, so Victor's encyclopedia, a mini-bible of our times, will do better than many a Complete Guide to This and That, or Encyclopedia of the Other.

There are more biographies of Marilyn Monroe than of any other person in the history of show business. Around seven hundred have been published in English alone, with a dozen or so new ones every year. It is even possible to suggest a typology of writings about Marilyn. It starts off with studio biographies written by publicists, and a kind of memoir by the screenwriter Ben Hecht (later published as *My Story* by Marilyn Monroe), featuring the well-spun tale of Norma Jeane's abused childhood, and the white piano she saved from her mother's house — a piano that sold for three-quarters of a million dollars at the Christie's sale. There were also early biographies by Marilyn's friends (the columnist Sidney Skolsky, the poet Norman Rosten) and her enemies — *Marilyn, the Tragic Venus,* based on the incriminating fibs of Hollywood scribe Nunnally Johnson. There have been plenty of biographies by people who worked for Marilyn, by her housekeeper Eunice Murray, her cleaner Lena Pepitone, by a fan called James Haspiel who used to stand outside her apartment, by one or two guys who slept with her, by any number of guys who wanted to sleep with her, and by a tittle-tattle lifeguard at the Ambassador Hotel in Los Angeles. Her half sister Bernice Miracle wrote a fairly tender little book called *My Sister Marilyn.* Then, to top it all, there was *The Secret Happiness of Marilyn Monroe* by her first husband, James Dougherty.

In fact, you can easily top that too. There has been tome after spurious tome on the subject of her untimely death. Come on down, the Murder Cover-up Theorists. Anthony Summers wrote *Goddess,* an exhaustive, exhausting and paranoid account of how *everyone in the known world* wanted Marilyn dead. He also did the actress the supreme disservice of publishing a picture of her on the slab. There have been many of these sensational books, which mainly show how both Kennedys bugged her, buggered her, drugged her, killed her, collaborated with the Mafia, were set up by the Mafia, were punished by (or in league with) the Teamsters, or the Cubans, or the Rat Pack, and that every intelligence agency in the United States was busy tailing Marilyn or burning her phone records or laying plans to snuff her out.

Monroe's mother blamed her daughter for being born, and the child grew up with a dark memory of people screaming in the hall, of departures and uncertainties, and of men taking advantage of her loneliness and dependence. Even Marilyn seemed to realize that dressing up—going on show—was a way of providing an answer to the gaunt face of her mad mother in the Rockhaven Sanitarium. It might even be possible that Marilyn's efforts to dispel America's fears about sex were somehow related to her attempts to dispel her own fear of madness. At any rate, her grandmother Della Mae Hogan died in a straitjacket. Gladys lived until the 1980s in a Florida loony bin. And Marilyn presented herself to the world as a beacon of confidence, an angel of sex, while all her life she was troubled with the idea that her mind wasn't right.

It was Marilyn's misfortune to think that serious acting could save her from self-doubt. In 1955, after showing America and the world how to relax about sex by allowing her skirt to blow over her head in *The Seven Year Itch,* Monroe ran away to New York to become somebody else. But The Girl would always follow her. She threw a press conference to reveal "the new Monroe":

> Cocktails were served for about an hour as guests awaited a "new and different" Marilyn. Shortly after six, the front door opened and Marilyn blew in like a snowdrift. She was dressed from head to toe in white. A fluttery white mink coat covered a white satin sheath with flimsy, loose spaghetti straps. She wore satin high heels and white stockings. Her long, sparkling diamond earrings were on loan from Van Cleef & Arpels.
>
> Marilyn seemed disappointed when people asked what was new about her. "But I have changed my hair!" she protested. Her hair did seem a shade or two lighter. Asked to describe the new color, Marilyn replied in a child's voice, "Subdued platinum." The crowd received Marilyn with good-natured amusement. They responded as though she were one of her comical, ditzy blond film characters . . . "I have formed my own corporation so I can play the kinds of roles I want," Marilyn announced . . . She declared herself tired of sex roles and vowed to do no more. "People have scope, you know," said Marilyn. "They really do" (*Marilyn Monroe* by Barbara Leaming).

This sad tableau is one of a pair. She went to England the following year to star in *The Prince and the Showgirl* with Laurence Olivier. At the initial press conference one of the straps on her dress broke with suspiciously good timing, whereupon she announced that she would very much like to appear in a film adaptation of *The Brothers Karamazov*. "Which one would you play?" shouted one of the reporters. "Grushenka," said Marilyn, "that's a girl." "Spell it," said another hack.

Marilyn was cursed — or blessed — with an instinctive ability to intellectualize sex and at the same time to sexualize intellectuals. But in time this would constitute a schism in her everyday life: on the way up she tried to please men who wanted her only for sex, and at her height, at the pinnacle of her New York period, from 1955 until her death in 1962, she tried to please men who thought she was better than that. Fundamentally she swithered between giving and wanting: in time she would surround herself with intellectuals who thought they might harness her vulnerability and somehow turn her into a great actress or a happy person. Yet there was something in the material of her early life that made such achievements very difficult: fulfillment remained but a flickering, costly, benighted dream. In some chiefly unhelpful way, she didn't know who she was.

A dozen years ago, I went to look at Marilyn Monroe's grave. She is buried just beyond Hollywood, at a place called Westwood Memorial Park. It was a very quiet place on a hot summer's day. As I walked over the grass, the only real sound was coming from a bell that hung from a branch of a tree over the grave of Natalie Wood. A water sprinkler in the corner of the park made a placid arc over gravestones and shrubs. Not a bad place to live out one's afterlife, I thought. Down a lane called the Walk of Memory you pass Darryl F. Zanuck and Dean Martin, Peter Lawford and Fanny Brice. What I remember most is the atmosphere of the cemetery: the place was more than just a repository of famous bones; a giant investment of common wishes lay deep in the polished stonework. American wishes. The world's wishes. Yet the only scent that moved through the air was the scent of everyday boredom. It could have been any car park in America: a place where children might play on a vapid afternoon, the sun coming down, the future unknown. Yet in that same atmosphere there was something of America's allure to the impressionable world — it was a mood that traveled invisibly over the surface of the manicured grass, a liturgy of success, the psalm of America, with Marilyn as its tragic muse. How could we fail to follow that compelling sound to the ends of the earth?

*July 2004*

# 7/7

**P**EOPLE BEGAN LAYING flowers on the steps of St. Pancras Church the morning after the July 7 bombings, and within a day or two the steps had been transformed into a slope of glinting paper, the flowers strangely urban behind the police cordon. It was also a slope of words: handwritten messages, e-mails, shop-bought cards and pavement script. The church's columns were chalked with words too, and the Word of God—a King James Bible, "User's Guide on Back"—appeared to float unabashed on a sea of London scrawls.

For a few days after the explosions, the atmosphere was bad on the buses. Passengers were looking into every face as they sat on a Number 30 from King's Cross, and if the face happened to be brown, they looked to their bag or backpack. That is how fear and paranoia work: they create turbulence in your everyday passivity; everyone was affected after the bombings, and the botched follow-up on July 21, in ways that won't quickly go away. In the realm of paranoia, the second bombings were more powerful than the first, for they made it clear how very gettable we are, even in a culture of high alert. To anyone with imagination (or who knows anyone who's ever had a second stroke), the most recent attack brings a dimension of constant threat. No one needed to die for this to take effect: July 7 showed us what death on the bus or the tube looks like; the second attack showed that these images wouldn't be allowed to remain just a bad memory. Sitting upstairs on the Number 30 a few days after July 7, I found myself thinking: In this seat, would it be a leg I'd lose, or an arm? Would I die instantly? Or would I be one of those walking around afterwards in a daze? The London bombings are an ontological disaster for anyone who commutes in a big city. The blasts have taken the steadiness out of people's expectations and replaced it with a more or less hysterical dependence on the size of their luck. That sort of thing is OK from a distance, but it can punish your spirit on the down escalator at nine o'clock in the morning.

When the Number 30 passed a statue of John F. Kennedy in Marylebone Road, a teenager looked up at his mother. "It all started with him," he said.

"I know what you mean," his mother said. "He was the first to get this amount of coverage."

In Hyde Park rows of old ladies were sitting in the rose garden. In their white skirts and sandals, they had an air of seen-it-all about them, pointing to beds of flowers and thinking nothing of cellophane. And maybe they *had* seen it all: by the boating pond, fixed to the bandstand, was a plaque engraved with yet more London words. "To the memory of those bandsmen of the 1st Battalion of the Blues & Royals who died as a result of the terrorist attack here on 20 July 1982."

The remains of the Number 30 bus were covered in blue tarpaulin and removed from Tavistock Square a week later. In the days when the street was blocked off, when Upper Woburn Place became a forensic scene and a no man's land, I found myself quietly hankering after the openness of Tavistock Square, and several times that week I went down to look at the barricade and puzzle over the idea that the square had gone. I wondered if the street had not lost its life too, as often happened in the Second World War when people would arrive to mourn both the dead and the place where they used to go. Among many things, the bombings gave those of us who are attached to the city a sense of what it might be like to be very old, to see a graveyard at the corner of every street, a bar where some dead friend used to drink, a bench where you once got a kiss.

There's an essay by Cyril Connolly, "One of My Londons," in which he writes of London as a city of prose. At the point of writing the essay, Connolly found it hard to be in London for more than a few days at a time, so freighted with former lives were the streets around Fitzrovia, so haunted by memory and well-honed sentences. The square that is formed by King's Cross, Lamb's Conduit Street, Tottenham Court Road and Warren Street is one of my Londons, and the very center of that London is Tavistock Square. If London is a city of prose, then this is the capital's capital, a square of reason and memory and imagination. My home's home.

The *London Review of Books* had its offices in Tavistock Square for almost ten years. We were housed in a couple of rooms on the third floor of the British Medical Association building, entrance C, where the great blue door is now shattered and the windows pierced. The paper bears no deeper connection than that to this terrible event, and the pictures of entrance C spattered with gore will alter every Londoner's sense of London, not just those who knew the doors and the square they open onto. Yet proximity is the currency in a culture of bomb fear: those of us who used to go to that place every morning might be allowed to pause for a second in our own way. The *London Review* sent out prose, and poems, from that building every fortnight, and one day a young man came to the door with a bomb strapped to his back.

Standing in the square the other day, trying to ignore the statue of Mahatma Gandhi — it's not hard to ignore, because of its ugliness and the minatory nature of his peaceableness — I reached for the answer. But the answer, of course, was there all along: more thought. More argument. For Tony Blair to deny that the invasion of Iraq influenced the bombers is an insult to both language and morality. For Islamic extremists to pretend that their cause will not be set back in Britain by targeting buses and tube trains is a murderous delusion. Blair's war has been a drafting exercise for young jihadis, and the efforts of the young jihadis will be a drafting exercise for the British National Party. Welcome to Endgame England.

Several of the victims of the bus bombs were taken into the forecourt of the British Medical Association, where they were attended to by as many doctors, and where two passengers died. I was always amazed by the length and circuitousness of the corridors in the BMA building, which made one feel like a lost blood cell traveling through the arteries of some giant corporate body. Our office seemed so small and tight compared to all that expanse, but it was to those rooms, with their windows looking down on Tavistock Square, that Salman Rushdie once delivered his review of Calvino's *Invisible Cities,* and where it was edited, cared for, "washed and ironed," as the editors would say. "Why," he wrote, "should we bother with Calvino, a word-juggler, a fantasist, in an age in which our cities burn and our leaders blame our parents? What does it mean to write about non-existent knights, or the formation of the Moon, or how a reader reads, while the neutron bomb gets the go-ahead in Washington, and plans are made to station germ-warfare weaponry in Europe?" He went on: "The reason Calvino is such an indispensable writer is precisely that he tells us, joyfully, wickedly, that there are things in the world worth loving as well as hating; and that such things exist in people, too."

Those were the same rooms where Tony Blair arrived breathlessly one day before catching the train at Euston. The piece he delivered may have required more ironing than Rushdie's, but it, too, in October 1987, found its place in the paper's pages. He wrote that Mrs. Thatcher "will wield her power over the next few years dictatorially and without compunction" and further predicted that "the 1990s will not see the continuing triumph of the market, but its failure." And it was into those same rooms that Ronan Bennett came with one of the longest pieces ever published in a single issue of the *LRB,* a report on the civil and legal injustices perpetrated by the state in its desperate pursuit of those guilty of the Guildford bombings. Argument in the long run is louder than bombs, even if, as often happened in my day at the *London Review,* people would ring up to cancel their subscriptions when they violently disagreed. It was mostly after we'd run a piece by Edward Said. "I refuse to read pieces written by murderers," one of them said.

"And we're happy not to publish them," I said.

"Said is happy to see Israelis bombed," she said.

"No," I said. "Professor Said is happy to make arguments, and we are happy to publish them."

But it was Tavistock Square itself that was on my mind. It is understandable that condemnation, in such a case as this, will precede contemplation, but perhaps less bearable that we live at a time when it will overthrow honest thinking altogether. The square is a living testament to the opposite view. More than a hundred years before people were phoning to complain about Edward Said's right to write, Charles Dickens was furnishing his new house on the same site, and furnishing his new novel,

*Bleak House,* with characters who struggled to agree about how to live in the world and what to believe. Peter Ackroyd provides a nice picture of the novelist in the agonies of trying to complete his new house, sitting disconsolately on a stepladder while "Irish laborers stare in through the very slates." A later visitor, Hans Christian Andersen, saw a magnificent eighteen-room house, filled with pictures and engravings. But nothing is simply one thing, not even the reputation of a great house, and Dickens's pile on Tavistock Square drew ire from George Eliot. "Splendid library, of course," she wrote, "with soft carpet, couches etc., such as become a sympathizer with the suffering classes. How can we sufficiently pity the needy unless we know fully the blessings of plenty?"

The commentators spoke almost by rote about how the bus explosion in Tavistock Square was "unimaginable," and it was pretty unimaginable, all the more so in a place where so much had been imagined and where people had lived, indeed, fully in accordance with their empathetic capacities. We used sometimes to have a drink after work at the County Hotel, which looks out to Upper Woburn Place with a rather doleful quiver about its nicotine-stained jowls. Everybody who came into that bar — railwaymen from Euston, dancers from the London School of Contemporary Dance — carried a very large sense of particularity about them. Maybe it was the lighting. In among the half pints of bitter and the curly sandwiches, something in the atmosphere of that bar, with its giant 1940s radio, made everyone seem discrete and minutely alive, not like the hordes of Southampton Row. Everybody smoked cigarettes in those days. There was no television and nobody had a mobile phone. They served lemonade out of bottles. It was heaven to me.

Dorothy Richardson lived at 2 Woburn Walk, the narrow passage next to the County Hotel. It was a "flagged alley" in 1905, a "terrible place to live," she wrote. Nearly under the shadow of St. Pancras Church, Richardson's flat stood above a row of shops (as it still does), a stonemason's, in her case, while across the alley, at Number 18, W. B. Yeats had one of his London addresses. Richardson recalled seeing him standing at the window on hot summer evenings, breathing the "parched air." In his biography of the poet, Roy Foster reports that "the flat at Woburn Buildings was scraped and repapered in an effort to remove insect life, though WBY still returned there for his Monday evening entertainments." It appears that Dorothy Richardson was never invited; she and Yeats never actually spoke, though years later she remembered them almost bumping into each other in Tavistock Square. "For memory," she wrote, "we stand permanently confronted either side of that lake of moonlight in the square."

Like Hasib Hussain, the Number 30 bus was a stranger to Tavistock Square. But the eighteen-year-old who wasted his own life and twelve other people's on that bus knew something about the poetry of Yeats. The bomber had seven GCSEs, including one in English, and Yeats was one of his topics. Heaven knows what was on his mind when he set off his terrible backpack that morning, and one can only be sad that it wasn't Yeats, a one-time neighbor to his terrible, beautyless act, or his poem "Easter 1916," a distillation for me of the saving power of two-mindedness, the great theme of old Bloomsbury.

*August 2005*

## Introduction to
# Go Tell It on the Mountain

THE BALLOON OF experience is tied to the earth," wrote Henry James in *The American,* "and under that necessity we swing, thanks to a rope of remarkable length, in the more or less commodious car of the imagination." In 1949, James Baldwin was living in Paris—a measure of rope having been unfurled—yet his ties to Harlem grew stronger by the day. There was little of Hemingway or Gertrude Stein in Baldwin's sojourn; though he enjoyed a little more freedom there, and adventure too, he wasn't there for friendship or freedom or adventure either, but for writing. Baldwin went to Europe in search of his own voice. He went for a clear view of the past. And this exile suited him, sentences at once beginning to bleed out of memory and imagination, old wounds opening into new language.

Baldwin's father was a lay preacher; to his eldest son he was "handsome, proud, and ingrown." The son was born into a religious community, a world where duty joined with pride, where sin battled with high hopes of redemption, where the Saved sang over the Damned, where love and hate could smell similar, and where fathers and sons could be strangers forever. "I had declined to believe," Baldwin wrote in his famous *Notes of a Native Son,* "in that apocalypse which had been central to my father's vision."

> . . . I had not known my father well. We had got on badly, partly because we shared, in different fashions, the vice of stubborn pride. When he was dead I realized I had hardly ever spoken to him . . . He was of the first generation of free men. He, along with thousands of other Negroes, came North after 1919 and I was part of that generation which had never seen the landscape of what Negroes sometimes called the Old Country.

Baldwin was the kind of writer who couldn't forget. He remembered everything, and the pulse of remembering, and the ache of old news, makes for the beat of his early writing. At the age of fourteen he underwent what he later called "a prolonged religious crisis," a confusion too deep for tears, but not for prose. "I then discovered God, His saints and angels, and His blazing Hell," he wrote. "I supposed Him to exist only within the wall of a church—in fact, of our church—and I also supposed that God and safety were synonymous." At this point Baldwin became a preacher too. He knew that something important happened when he stood up and entered deeply into the language of a sermon. People listened, they clapped. "Amen, Amen," they said. And all of it remained with him: the smell of church wood and the crying out, the shimmer of tambourines, the heat of damnation, the songs of the Saved, his father's face and the New York world outside, with its white people downtown who'd say, "Why don't you niggers stay uptown where you belong?" But more than anything it was his father's face.

"In my mind's eye," he writes in *Notes,* "I could see him, sitting at the window, locked up in his terrors; hating and fearing every living soul including his children who had betrayed him, too, by reaching towards the world which had despised him."

Some novelists, in their early work especially, set out to defeat the comforts of invention: they refuse to make anything up. *Go Tell It on the Mountain* is James Baldwin's first novel, a shadow album of lived experience, the lines here being no less real than those on his mother's face. For Baldwin, as for Proust, there is something grave and beautiful and religious about the love of truth itself, and something of sensual joy in bringing it to the page. Baldwin's career as a novelist was spent walking over old territory with ghosts. Things became new to him in this way. "*Mountain* is the book I had to write if I was ever going to write anything else," he said years later. "I had to deal with what hurt me most. I had to deal with my father."

The novel is centered around a "tarry service" at the Temple of the Fire Baptized, in Harlem in 1935. Fourteen-year-old John Grimes, dubious, fearful and already bitter, is about to walk the path to salvation. There are high expectations of John, "to be a good example" and to "come through" to the Lord. The service will last the whole night, and John is there in the company of the elder "saints" of the church, and with his father and mother and aunt Florence. There is a strong sense of John being one of the anointed, but we absorb his slow, terrible doubts about himself. Altogether he is not a happy child on this special night:

> Something happened to their faces and their voices, the rhythm of their bodies, and to the air they breathed; it was as though wherever they might be became the upper room, and the Holy Ghost were riding in the air. His father's face, always awful, became more awful now; his father's daily anger was transformed into prophetic wrath. His mother, her eyes

raised to heaven, hands arked before her, moving, made real for John that patience, that endurance, that long suffering, which he had read of in the Bible and found hard to imagine.

Between the novel's opening and closing – the beginning of the service, with "the Lord high on the wind tonight," and the closing, the morning, with John writhing for mercy on the threshing floor in front of the altar – we read the stories of his relatives: Florence, his aunt; Gabriel, his father; and his mother, Elizabeth. In three long chapters we come to know how the beliefs, the leave-takings, the loves, the honor and dishonor, that have made up the lives of these three people, lives which have animated a host of other lives and which, by and by, have come to animate the life of John Grimes too. There are secrets in the novel, and they emerge in a beautiful, disturbing pattern, uncovered words speaking clearly, soulfully, of this one family's legacy of pain and silence.

In *Go Tell It on the Mountain,* John has a certain dread of the life that awaits him; he feels doomed and he dreams of escape. He has made decisions. "He will not be like his father, or his father's fathers. He would have another life." It might be said that this has been a vain dream of artists – and teenagers – since the beginning of time, but in Baldwin it is neither vain nor merely a dream, for John Grimes represents, in all the eloquence of his wishes, a new kind of American. His father's fathers were slaves. John's father, Gabriel, is free, but he is expected to swear allegiance to a flag that has not sworn allegiance to him, and he lives in a racist land. On this front, Baldwin's America was to become a battleground, but John, given the date of events in the novel, can never be a civil rights cipher. He feels guilty for failing to share Gabriel's unambivalent hatred of white people, but John has additional freedoms in mind – freedom from the local oppressions of Gabriel being first among them. *Go Tell It on the*

*Mountain* is not a protest novel; it is a political novel of the human heart. White men may be evil, but they are neither the beginning nor the end of evil. Baldwin was interested at this point in corruption at the first level of legislative power — the family.

Baldwin wrote about black people. He did not write novels which understood the lives of black people only in terms of white subjugation. At the same time he recognized every terror of segregation, and *Go Tell It on the Mountain* is a shocking, and shockingly quiet, dramatization of what segregation meant in the years when the novel is set. Early on, we see John contemplating the forbidden world inside the New York Public Library, a world of corridors and marble steps and no place for a boy from Harlem. "And then everyone," Baldwin writes, "all the white people inside, would know that he was not used to great buildings, or to many books, and they would look at him with pity." This is a strong thing for a writer to remember, or to imagine, and Baldwin brings it to the page with a sense of anger, and regret. The novel is marked by the dark presence of "down home," the Old South, where all of John's family came from in search of a new life. This was Baldwin's primary milieu: the Harlem of migrant black Americans, bringing with them the stories of their fathers and mothers, one generation away from slavery.

This Northernness was important to Baldwin. It was the world he knew from childhood and the world he cared most about. He had a feeling for the hopes that were invested in the journey north — "North," where, as Gabriel's mother says, "wickedness dwelt and Death rode mighty through the streets." In one of his essays, "A Fly in the Buttermilk," Baldwin wrote of another Southerner's contempt for the North, a man he tried to interview for a piece on the progress of civil rights: "He forced me to admit, at once, that I had never been to college; that

Northern Negroes lived herded together, like pigs in a pen; that the campus on which we met was a tribute to the industry and determination of Southern Negroes. 'Negroes in the South form a community.'"

Baldwin's sensibility, his talent for moral ambivalence, his taste for the terrifying patterns of life, the elegant force of his disputatious spirit, as much Henry James as Bessie Smith, was not always to find favor with his black contemporaries. Langston Hughes called *Go Tell It on the Mountain* "a low-down story in a velvet bag." "A Joan of Arc of the cocktail party" was Amiri Baraka's comment on Baldwin. Some of this could be construed as standard resentment—reminiscent of the kind expressed by Gabriel towards John for not hating whites enough—and some was a reaction against Baldwin's popularity with the white literary establishment. But that wasn't all. By the time he was writing novels, and writing these essays—works of magical power and directness—Baldwin had come to feel that the black "protest" novel was breathlessly redundant. In a recent essay about Baldwin's writing, the novelist Darryl Pickney comments on Baldwin's rejection of Richard Wright, the author of *Native Son:* "In retrospect Baldwin praises Wright's work for its dry, savage, folkloric humor and for how deeply it conveys what life was like on Chicago's South Side. The climate that had once made Wright's work read like a racial manifesto had gone. Baldwin found when reading Wright again that he did not think of the 1930s or even of Negroes, because Wright's characters and situations had universal meanings."

In "Alas, Poor Richard," an essay in the collection *Nobody Knows My Name,* Baldwin concludes that Wright was not the polemical firebrand he took himself to be. Many of Baldwin's black contemporaries hated this view.

Baldwin's first novel, in respect of all this, demonstrates a remarkable unity of form and content; the style of the novel makes clear the extent to which he was turning away from his literary forefathers. It may be sensible to see the novel as a farewell not only to the Harlem of his father, but to the literary influence of Richard Wright and *Uncle Tom's Cabin*. Baldwin was unremitting on this point, and several goodbyes, offered from his Paris exile, became the creed of his early writing. "In most of the novels written by Negroes until today," he wrote, "there is a great space where sex ought to be; and what usually fills this space is violence."

*Go Tell It on the Mountain* is a very sensual novel, a book soaked in the Bible and the blues. Spiritual song is there in the sentences, at the heads of chapters, and it animates the voices on every side during the "coming through" of John Grimes. As he steps up to the altar, John is suddenly aware of the sound of his own prayers — "trying not to hear the words that he forced outwards from his throat." Baldwin's language has the verbal simplicity of the Old Testament, as well as its metaphorical boldness. The rhythms of the blues, a shade of regret, a note of pain rising out of experience, are deeply inscribed in the novel, and they travel freely along the lines of dialogue. There is a kind of metaphorical, liturgical energy in some novels — in Faulkner's *The Sound and the Fury*, in Joyce's *Portrait of the Artist as a Young Man*, in Elizabeth Smart's *By Grand Central Station I Sat Down and Wept*, in Toni Morrison's *Beloved* — which is utterly essential to the art. It may seem at first overpowering, to waft in the air like perfume, or to have the texture of Langston Hughes's velvet bag, but it is, in each of these cases, and especially in the case of Baldwin's first novel, a matter of straightforward literary integrity. Every word is necessary. Every image runs clear in the blood of the novel.

Take John's mother, Elizabeth. Look at the shape of her thoughts on the page, as brought out in Baldwin's third-person narrative:

"I sure don't care what God don't like, or you, either," Elizabeth's heart replied. "I'm going away from here. He's going to come and get me, and I'm going away from here." "He" was her father, who never came. As the years passed she replied only: "I'm going away from here." And it hung, this determination, like a heavy jewel between her breasts; it was written in fire on the dark sky of her mind. But, yes—there was something she had overlooked. Pride goeth before destruction; and a haughty spirit before a fall. She had not known this: she had not imagined that she could fall.

When reading this novel I am always aware of the charge that sex gives to religion, a bond the novel explores and confirms. We think of Baldwin as a figure of the 1960s, a literary embodiment of outrage in the face of American segregation, but actually Baldwin, in his novels, writes more of sex and sin than he does of civil rights. Gabriel, a preacher speaking fiery words from the pulpit, is really a secret sinner, fallen in ways that are known to his sister Florence, and known to his wife Elizabeth too. When younger, "he drank until hammers rang in his distant skull; he cursed his friends and his enemies, and fought until blood ran down; in the morning he found himself in mud, in clay, in strange beds, and once or twice in jail; his mouth sour, his clothes in rags, from all of him rising the stink of his corruption."

This novel tells the story of how John comes to know this. Gabriel uses the church not to raise but to conceal his true character: his hypocrisy is everywhere around him, and nowhere more than in the minds of the women who have suffered him, and increasingly, too, in the mind of John, his "bastard" son. Florence's lover, Frank, was similarly corrupt, yet he, at least, in "the brutality of his penitence," tried to make it up to Florence. It is John's terrible fate — and everyone else's — that Gabriel can neither inspire forgiveness nor redeem himself. He goes on with his lying. He inspires fear. He is hated.

Novels about the sins of men often turn out to be novels about the courage of women. Florence, Elizabeth, Deborah and the tragic Esther, who is made pregnant by Gabriel and sent away to die, are the novel's moral retainers, keeping faith with humanity while all around them Faith rides on his dark horse, cutting down hope and charity. Florence says something for all the women in the novel, and for James Baldwin, one suspects, contemplating the fate of the women in his early life, when she looks at the face of Frank. "It sometimes came to her," Baldwin writes, "that all women had been cursed from the cradle; all, in one fashion or another, being given the same cruel destiny, born to suffer the weight of men." Florence remembers the beginning of her own cruel destiny. It began with the birth of Gabriel. After this her future was "swallowed up" and her life was over: "There was only one future in that house, and it was Gabriel's — to which, since Gabriel was a man-child, all else must be sacrificed."

Baldwin is unusual — and controversial, for more traditional black writers, as well as for the countercultural ones ahead of him — in making the African-American bid for freedom complicated. For Florence, and for her nephew John Grimes, "free at last" would have to mean several things, not only free from the Old South, or free from the evils of segregation, but the freedom to enter the world outside, and freedom from the hatreds of the family kitchen. "And this became Florence's deep ambition: to walk out one morning through the cabin door, never to return." But the novel knows there is a price to be paid for this too. Elizabeth, a long time away from the South, enjoyed walking in Central Park, because "it re-created something of the landscape she had known."

Baldwin never got over his religious crisis at the age of fourteen. He didn't forget. "That summer," he writes in *The Fire Next Time*, "all the fears with which I had grown up, and which were now a part of me and controlled by my vision of the world, rose up like a wall between the world and me, and drove me into the church." He surrendered to a spiritual seduction, falling down before the altar and thereafter preaching for three years. Baldwin recalls his father one day slapping his face, "and in that moment everything flooded back — all the hatred and the fear, and the depth of a merciless resolve to kill my father rather than allow my father to kill me — and I knew that all those sermons and tears and all that repentance and rejoicing had changed nothing."

Baldwin put the essence of all of this into *Go Tell It on the Mountain*. Gabriel has the preacher's traditional love of helplessness, and traditional anger in the face of self-sufficiency. Yet the central issues of Gabriel's life are his hypocrisy and the sexual desire that accompanies the rejoicings of religious life. His treatment of Esther combines the two ("I guess it takes a holy man to make a girl a real whore," she says), but only Florence seems aware of the truth after Esther is dead. At the close of the novel she seeks to name the tree by its fruit. And John, who is no strange fruit of that tree, might live to curse all lies and go free into the world.

Baldwin, all his writing life, insisted he wrote only from experience. That was the kind of writer he was: he meant every word. There would always be something of the pulpit in Baldwin's writing, and something too of the threshing floor. *Go Tell It on the Mountain* is a beautiful, enduring, spiritual song of a novel, a gush of life from a haunted American church. Like many writers with a religious past, the young man who wrote this novel was stranded in the space between his own body and the body of Christ, and strung between the father he hated and the Father who might offer him salvation. John Grimes finds the beginning of his redemption in the very place where his father lived out his hypocrisy, the church, where Gabriel spawned so much of the trouble in their lives. Here, at last, after all is said and done, John Grimes can go in search of the Everlasting, "over his father's head to Heaven—to the Father who loved him."

*2001*

# On the End of British Farming

**T**HIS LAST WHILE I have carried my heart in my boots. For a minute or two I actually imagined I could be responsible for the spread of foot-and-mouth disease across Britain. On my first acquaintance with the hill farmers of the Lake District, on a plot high above Keswick, I had a view of the countryside for tens of miles. I thought of the fields that had passed underfoot, all the way back to Essex, through Dumfriesshire, Northumberland or Sussex. Later I would continue on my way to Devon, passing through other places waking up in the middle of the worst agricultural nightmare in seventy years. My boots are without guilt, but in all the walking here and there, in the asking and listening, I came to feel that British farming was already dying, that the new epidemic was but an unexpected acceleration of a certain decline.

In the last few weeks nearly 100,000 head of livestock have been condemned. The industry has lost £300 million. A freeze still holds on the export of livestock. Country footpaths are zones of reproach, and supermarkets are running out of Argentinian beef. The agriculture minister is accused of doing too much and doing too little. The questions surrounding the foot-and-mouth epidemic – Where will it all end? How did it all start? – might be understood to accord with anxiety about every aspect of British agriculture today. The worst has not been and gone; it is yet to come. Still, one thing may already be clear: British farming hanged itself on the expectation of plenty.

One day not long ago I was in the Sainsbury's superstore on the Cromwell Road. Three of the company's top brass ushered me down the aisles, pointing here, gasping there, each of them in something of a swoon at the heavenliness on offer. "People want to be interested," said Alison Austin, a technical adviser. "You've just got to capture their imagination." We were standing by the sandwiches and the takeaway hot foods lined up in front of the whooshing doors. Alison swept her hand over the colorful bazaar of sandwich choices. "This is a range called Be Good to Yourself," she said, "with fresh, healthy fillings, and here we have the more gourmet range, Taste the Difference. We have a policy of using British produce where we can. With carrots, for example, we want to provide economic profitability to the farmer, using the short carrots for one line of produce and the bigger ones for another."

The Cromwell Road branch of Sainsbury's is what they call a flagship store. It's not only a giant emporium, it is also grander than any other store in the chain, selling more champagne, fresh fish, organic meat and Special Selection food. Six varieties of caviar are available all year round.

"People are gaining more confidence in sushi," said Peter Morrison, Manager, Trading Division. "We have joined forces with very credible traders such as Yo! Sushi and we aim to educate customers by bringing them here." Alison handed me a cup of liquid grass from the fresh-juice bar, Crussh. There was something unusually potent about that afternoon – the thoughts in my head as I tilted the cup – and for a moment the whole supermarket seemed to spin around me. People wandered by. The place was a madhouse of bleeping bar codes. "How do you like it?" one of them asked. I gulped it down and focused my eyes. "It tastes like an English field," I said.

The store manager guided me to the cut flowers. "We are the UK's largest flower sellers," he told me. "The biggest year-on-year increase of any product in the store is in flowers." The bunches before me were a far cry from the sad carnations and petrol-station bouquets that now lie about the country as tributes to the suddenly dead. The ones he showed me had a very smart, sculptural appearance, and they sold for £25 a pop. "We have forty kinds of apple," Alison said, "and again, we take the crop, the smaller ones being more for the economy bags."

"Someone came in on Christmas Eve and asked for banana leaves," the keen young product manager over in fruit and vegetables told me, "and you know something? We had them."

You would have to say that Sainsbury's is amazing. It has everything—fifty kinds of tea, four hundred kinds of bread, kosher chicken schnitzels, Cornish pilchards—and everywhere I turned that day there was some bamboozling elixir of the notion of plenty. Their own-brand products are made to high standards: the fresh meat, for example, is subject to much higher vigilance over date and provenance than any meat in Europe. "Some things take a while," Peter Morrison said. "You can put something out and it won't work. Then you have to think again, about how to market it, how to package it, where to place it, and six months later you'll try again and it might work." We stopped beside the yogurts. "Now this," he said, picking up a tub of Devon yogurt, "is made at a place called Stapleton Farm. We got wind of how good it was: a tiny operation, we went down there, we got some technical advisers involved, and now look, it's brilliant!" I tasted some of the Stapleton yogurt; it was much better than the liquid grass. "It's about the rural business grow-ing," Peter said. "Real food is what people want. This couple in Devon"—he gestured to the yogurt pots—"started from virtu-ally nowhere. Of course they were nervous at first about work-ing with such a major retailer. But these people are the new kind of producer."

Passing the condiments aisle, I saw an old man standing in front of the Oxo cubes. He looked a bit shaky. His lips were mov-ing and he had one of the foil-wrapped Oxo cubes in the palm of his hand. "People go to Tuscany," Alison was saying, "and they eat Parma ham and they come back here and they want it all the time. So we go out and find the best." You are always alone with the oddness of modern consumption. Walking under the white lights of Sainsbury's, you find out just who you are. The reams of cartons, the pyramids of tins: there they stand on the miles of shelves, the story of how we live now. Cereal boxes look out at you with their breakfast-ready smiles, containing flakes of bran, handfuls of oats, which come from fields mentioned in the Domesday Book. We went over to the aisle with the cook-ing oils and Alison did one of her long arm-flourishes: "When I was a child," she said, "my mother used a bottle of prescription olive oil to clean the salad bowl. Now look!" A line of tank-green bottles stretched into the distance. "Choice!" she said.

Supermarket people like to use certain words. When you are with them in the fruit department they all say "fresh" and "juicy" and "variety" and "good farming practices." (Or, as the head office puts it, "In 1992 Sainsbury developed a protocol for growing crops under Integrated Crop Management System principles. Following these principles can result in reduced us-age of pesticides by combining more traditional aspects of agri-culture and new technologies.") In the meat department there is much talk of "friendly," "animal well-being," "humane," "safe," "high standards" and "provenance." The executives spent their time with me highlighting what they see as the strength of the partnerships with British farming which keep everyone happy. "The consumer is what matters," said Alison, "and we believe in strong, creative, ethical retailing."

Down at the front of the store again, I put one of the gourmet sandwiches on a table and opened it up. The bread was grainy. The lettuce was pale green and fresh. Pieces of chicken and strips of pepper were neatly set out on a thin layer of butter. The open sandwich was a tableau of unwritten biographies: grains and vegetables and meat were glistening there, uncontroversially, their stories of economic life and farming history and current disaster safely behind them.

When I was a boy we had a painting above the phone table. It was the only real painting in the house, and it showed a wide field in the evening with a farm at the far end. The farmhouse had a light in one of the windows. The painting had been a wedding present, and my mother thought it was a bit dour and dirty-looking, so she did the frame up with some white gloss, which flaked over the years. I used to lie on the hall carpet and look at the picture of the farm for ages; the field was golden enough to run through and get lost in, and the brown daubs of farmhouse were enough to send me into a swoon of God-knows-what. I suppose it was all part of a general childhood spaced-outness, and it meant nothing, but it seemed very heightening at the time. The painting raised my feelings up on stilts, and made me imagine myself to be part of an older world where people lived and worked in a state of sentimental peace. All rot of course. But lovely rot. Sometimes I would go downstairs in the night and shine my torch on the painting.

At one time it seemed as if all the farms around our way had been abandoned or pulled down to make room for housing. Past railway lines and beyond the diminishing fields we would find old, dilapidated Ayrshire farmhouses with rusted tractors and ancient wooden drinking troughs lying about in the yard, and we'd play in them for half the summer. Cranberry Moss Farm, McLaughlin's Farm on Byrehill, Ashgrove Farm, the Old Mains—nowadays they are all buried under concrete, except for the farm at Toddhill, which became a home for the mentally handicapped. In my youth they had been like haunted houses. There were echoes in the barns.

Those farms seemed as remote from the daily reality of our lives as the one in the wedding picture. We would never live there: computer factories and industrial cleaners would soon replace them as providers of jobs, and it was these new places, in our Ayrshire, that spoke of the lives we were supposed one day to live. We took it for granted—much too early, as it turned out—that farming was a thing of the past, a thing people did before they were sophisticated like us. We never considered the stuff on our plates; we thought the school milk came on a lorry from London. Never for a second did my friends and I think of ourselves as coming from a rural community; like all British suburban kids, we lived as dark, twinkling fallout from a big city, in our case Glasgow, and we thought carports and cinder blocks were part of the natural order.

But of course there was plenty of agriculture. It surrounded us. The farms had just been pushed out a wee bit—and wee could seem larger than it was, at least for us, shocked by the whiteness of our new buildings into thinking a thatched roof was the height of exotic. Everything changed for me with the discovery of Robert Burns: those torn-up fields out there were his fields, those bulldozed farms as old as his words, both old and new to me then. Burns was ever a slave to the farming business: he is the patron saint of struggling farmers and poor soil. But now, as I write, the situation of farming in this country is perhaps worse than it has ever been, and the countryside itself is dying. We are at a stage where it is difficult to imagine British farming surviving in any of its traditional forms; and for millions living on these islands, a long-term crisis has been turning into a terminal disaster.

The total area of agricultural land is 18.6 million hectares, 76 percent of the entire land surface. According to an agricultural census in June 1999, there has been a decrease of 5.3 percent in the area given over to crops, as a result of a decrease in cereals and an increase in set-asides. According to a recent report from the Ministry of Agriculture, Fisheries and Food (Maff), the 1999 figures show a drop in the labor force of 3.6 percent, the largest decrease in a dozen years. "These results," the report continues, "are not unexpected given the financial pressures experienced by most sectors of the industry over the last few years."

Farmers' income fell by over 60 percent between 1995 and 1999. Despite increases in production, earnings were lower in 1999 by £518 million. The value of wheat fell by 6.5 percent and barley by 5.4 percent. Pigs were £99 million down in 1998, and lambs £126 million down; the value of poultry meat fell by £100 million or 7.4 percent; the value of milk fell by £45 million; and the value of eggs by 10 percent or £40 million. A giant profit gap has opened up throughout the industry: rapeseed, for example, which costs £200 a ton to produce, is selling for £170 per ton (including the government subsidy); a Savoy cabbage, costing 13p to produce, is sold by the farmer for 11p, and by the supermarkets for 47p.

Hill farmers earned less than £8,000 a year on average in 1998–99 (and 60 percent of that came to them in subsidies), but late last year, when I first started talking to farmers, many were making nothing at all, and most were heavily in debt to the bank. A suicide help line was set up, and the Royal College of Psychiatrists expressed concern at the increased number of suicides among hill farmers in particular. A spokesman for Maff said that agriculture was costing every British taxpayer £4 a week. After Germany and France, the UK makes the largest annual contribution to the Common Agricultural Policy, and yet, even before the great rise in the strength of the pound, British farmers' production costs were higher than anywhere else in the European Union, to a large extent because of the troubles of recent years.

"Everything is a nightmare," one farmer told me. "There are costs everywhere, and even the subsidy is spent long before you receive it. We are all in hock to the banks — and they say we are overmanned, but we don't have anybody here, just us, and children maybe, and an absolute fucking nightmare from top to bottom." The strong pound, the payment of subsidy checks in euros, the BSE (mad cow disease) crisis, swine fever and now foot-and-mouth disease, together with overproduction in the rest of the world's markets — these are the reasons for the worsened situation. But they are not the cause of the longer-term crisis in British farming: local overproduction is behind that, and it is behind the destruction of the countryside too. For all the savage reductions of recent times, farming still employs too many and produces too much: even before the end of February, when diseased livestock burned on funeral pyres 130 feet high, some farmers were killing their own livestock for want of a profit, or to save the fuel costs incurred in taking them to market.

In Britain nowadays most farmers are given aid — a great deal of aid, but too little to save them — in order to produce food nobody wants to buy. The way livestock subsidies work — per animal — means that there is an incentive for farmers to increase flocks and herds rather than improve the marketing of what they've got. As things are, subsidies save some farmers, but they are a useless way to shore up an ailing industry, except perhaps in wartime.

The evidence of what is wrong is out in the British land itself. It is to be found in the particularities of farming experience now, but also in a historical understanding of what farming has meant in this country. Farming—more even than coal, more than ships, steel or Posh and Becks—is at the center of who British people think they are. It has a heady, long-standing, romantic and sworn place in the cultural imagination: the death of farming will not be an easy one in the green and pleasant land. Even shiny new millennial economic crises have to call the past into question. How did we come to this?

In the eighteenth century, farmers were still struggling out of the old ways depicted in *Piers Plowman,* or the Bayeux Tapestry, where English farm horses are seen for the first time, bringing vegetables from the fields to the kitchen table. Jethro Tull, one of the fathers of modern agriculture, devoted himself to finding ways to increase yields—he invented the seed drill, a machine that could sow three rows of seed simultaneously—and collected his ideas in *The New Horse-Houghing Husbandry; or, An Essay on the Principles of Tillage and Vegetation* (1731). His ideas were widely accepted by the time he died, at Prosperous Farm near Hungerford in Berkshire, ten years later. Arthur Young, an agricultural educator and zealot of Improvement, set out in 1767 on a series of journeys through the country. *A Six Months' Tour Through the North of England* gives a spirited first-person account of changing agricultural conditions. "Agriculture is the grand product that supports the people," he wrote. "Both public and private wealth can only arise from three sources, agriculture, manufactures and commerce . . . Agriculture much exceeds the others; it is even the foundation of the principal branches." But the new improvements came at a price, and they changed forever the relationship between the land and the people who tried to live by it. British peasant life was effectively over. "The agrarian revolution was economically justifiable," Pauline Gregg writes in *A Social and Economic History of Britain, 1760–1965,* but "its social effects were disastrous. Scores of thousands of peasants suffered complete ruin. The small farmer, the cottager, the squatter, were driven off the soil, and their cottages were often pulled down." The British countryside, in the face of all improvements, and with every prospect of sharing in the coming wealth of nations, became as Oliver Goldsmith described it in "The Deserted Village":

> *Ill fares the land, to hastening ills a prey,*
> *Where wealth accumulates, and men decay.*
> *Princes and lords may flourish, or may fade;*
> *A breath can make them, as a breath has made:*
> *But a bold peasantry, their country's pride,*
> *When once destroyed, can never be supplied.*

In the spring of 1770 British cows were so disabled by starvation that they had to be carried out to the pastures. This business was known as "the lifting." *The General View of Ayrshire,* published in 1840, records that as late as 1800 one-third of the cows and horses in the county were killed for want of fodder. By the end of winter in this period, according to John Higgs's *The Land* (1964), every blade of grass had been eaten and the animals were forced to follow the plow looking for upturned roots.

The social structure of the country had changed, the population had grown, the plow had been improved, the threshing machine had been invented, and crop rotation had taken hold. William Cobbett, in his *Rural Rides* — originally a column that appeared in the *Political Register* between 1822 and 1826 — captured the movements which created the basis of the farming world we know. Cobbett rode out on horseback to look at farms to the south and east of a line between Norwich and Hereford; he made an inspection of the land and spoke to the people working on it. He addressed groups of farmers on the Corn Laws, taxes, placemen, money for agricultural paupers and the general need for reform.

In one of his columns he describes meeting a man coming home from the fields. "I asked him how he got on," he writes. "He said, very badly. I asked him what was the cause of it. He said the *hard times.* 'What times?' said I; was there ever a finer summer, a finer harvest, and is there not an old wheat-rick in every farmyard? 'Ah!' said he, '*they* make it hard for poor people, for all that.' '*They*,' said I, 'who is *they?*' " Cobbett yearned for a preindustrial England of fine summer days and wheat-ricks, and yet his conservatism did not prevent him from becoming an evangelist of Improvement. As for "they" — Cobbett knew what was meant; he later called it "the Thing," and sometimes "the system." He railed against everything that was wrong with English agriculture: low wages, absentee landlords, greedy clergymen, corruption; and he was prosecuted for supporting a riot by these same agricultural workers the year after he published *Rural Rides.* Cobbett saw how self-inflated governments could sit by and watch lives crumble. His discriminating rage has the tang of today. "The system of managing the affairs of the nation," he wrote in *Cottage Economy,* "has made all flashy and false, and has put all things out of their place. Pomposity, bombast, hyperbole, redundancy and obscurity, both in speaking and writing; mock-delicacy in manners, mock-liberality, mock-humanity . . . all have arisen, grown, branched out, bloomed and borne together; and we are now beginning to taste of their fruit."

Rain was running down Nelson's Column and Trafalgar Square was awash with visitors inspecting the lions. An American woman stepping into the National Gallery was worried about her camera lens. "This British weather will be the end of us," she said as her husband shook out the umbrellas. In the Sackler Room — room 34 — children with identical haircuts sat down on the wooden floor; they stared at the British weather of long ago, spread in oils with palette knives, and they, too, asked why it was always so fuzzy and so cloudy. One group sat around Turner's *Rain, Steam and Speed — The Great Western Railway.* The instructor encouraged them to express something about the atmosphere of the picture. "Does it make you shiver?" she asked. "It's like outside," one of the children replied. But most of them were interested in the hare running ahead of the train. "Will it die?" one of them asked. "Where is it running to?"

The future. You feel the force of change in some of these weathery British pictures. Over the last few months I kept coming back to this room, and sitting here, further up from the Turners, looking at Constable's *The Cornfield.* We see an English country lane at harvest time where nothing is unusual but everything is spectacular. Corn spills down an embankment, going to grass and ferns, going to pepper saxifrage or hog's fennel, dandelion and corn poppy, down to a stream. Giant trees reach up to the dark, gathering clouds. At their foot, a small boy lies flat on his front, drinking from the stream. He wears a red waistcoat and has a tear in the left leg of his trousers. A dog with a marked shadow looks up and past him with its pink tongue out. The sheep in front of the dog are making for a broken gate that opens onto the cornfield. A plow is stowed in a ditch; the farmer advances from the field; and in the distance, which stretches for miles, you see people already at work.

The picture has philosophical currency: people will still say it is an important part of what is meant by the term "British"—or at any rate "English." This is the country delegates sing about at party conferences, the one depicted in heritage brochures and on biscuit tins, the corner that lives in the sentiments of war poetry, an image at the heart of Britain's view of itself. But here's the shock: it no longer exists. Everything in Constable's picture is a small ghost still haunting the national consciousness. The corn poppy has pretty much gone, and so have the workers. The days of children drinking from streams are over too. And the livestock? We will come to that. Let me just say that a number of the farmers I spoke to in the winter of 2000 were poisoning their own fields. The Constable picture fades into a new world of intensive industrial farming and environmental blight.

*The Cornfield* is said to show the path along which Constable walked from East Bergholt across the river Stour and the fields to his school at Dedham. Last October I made my way to Dedham. It was another wet day, and many of the trucks and lorries splashing up water on the M25 were heading to the coast to join a fuel blockade. On the radio a newscaster described what was happening: "The situation for the modern British farmer has probably never been so dire, and a further rise in the price of fuel could kill many of them off."

Before leaving, I had rung a pig farmer, David Barker, whose farm is north of Stowmarket in Suffolk. Barker is fifty years old. His family have been farming pigs in Suffolk for four generations; they have lived and worked on the present farm since 1957. He owns 1,250 acres and 110 sows, which he breeds and sells at a finishing weight of 95 kilos. Among his crops are winter wheat, winter-sown barley, grass for seed production, some peas for canning, 120 acres of field beans, 30 acres of spring oats and 100 acres of set-aside.

"Five years ago I was selling wheat for £125 a ton and now it's £58.50," David Barker said. "I was selling pigs for £90 and now they're down to £65. And meanwhile all our costs have doubled: fuel, stock, fertilizer. There's hardly a farmer in East Anglia who's making a profit. The direct payments from Europe have declined also, because they're paid out in euros."

"What about swine fever?" I asked, innocent of the epidemics to come.

"There are over five hundred farms that haven't been able to move pigs since August," he said. "Immediately, this becomes an agricultural nightmare. The pigs are breeding, the feed is extortionate, and you end up relying on things like the Welfare Disposal Scheme, where pigs are removed for next to nothing. Gordon Brown's bright idea: they give you £50 for a pig that costs £80 to produce."

"What can be done?" The stormy weather was making his phone crackly.

"Well, this government has no interest in farming," he said. "People in the countryside in England feel they are ignored and derided, and frankly, it appears that the government would be much happier just to import food. This is the worst agricultural crisis in dozens of years. We're not making any money anywhere. Take milk: the dairy farmer receives 7p in subsidy for every pint; it takes between 10p and 12p to produce, and it costs 39p when it arrives at your door. A lot of farmers are giving up, and many of those who stay are turning to contract farming — increasing their land, making prairies, to make it pay."

"Is that the only way to reduce costs?"

"Yes. That, or by going to France."

David Barker used the word "nightmare" at least a dozen times during my conversation with him. He told me about a friend of his, another Suffolk farmer, who, earlier in the swine fever debacle, had sold his 250 pigs into the disposal scheme, losing £30 on each one. Barker himself was waiting for the results of blood tests to see if his pigs had the fever. "If it goes on much longer it will ruin me," he said.

When I arrived at Nigel Rowe's farm near Dedham, only the weather was Constable-like. Out his window the fields were bare and flat. "European pig meat is cheaper to produce," he said, "because we have higher standards and higher production costs. As soon as foreign bacon gets cheaper by more than 10p per kilo, the housewife swaps. That is the rule."

I asked him if he felt British supermarkets had been good at supporting bacon produced in Essex or Suffolk. "The supermarkets have been very clever at playing the different farming sectors off against each other," he said. "The Danish model is very centralized—they are allowed to produce and market something called Danish Bacon. We are very regional over here, very dominated by the tradition of the local butcher. Supermarkets want the same produce to be available in Scotland as you get in Sussex. Only the Dutch and the Danish can do that, and some of these foreign producers are so powerful—the Danish producers of bacon are much bigger than Tesco."

Nigel has 2,000 pigs. But he's not making money. As well as working the farm, he has a part-time job as caretaker at the local community center. "In the 1970s we were all earning a comfortable living," he said, "and when I was at primary school in the 1960s at least thirty of my schoolmates were connected with farming. Now, in my children's classes, there are three. I had 120 acres and I had to sell it recently to survive. I also had to sell the farm cottage my mother lived in, in order to stay here. That's what I was working on when you came—a little house for my mother."

He looked out the window at the flatness beyond. "The arithmetic is simple," he said. "When I started in this game it took five tons of grain to buy the year's supply of fuel for the tractor. Now it takes five *hundred* tons. What do you think that means if your acreage is the same? The government seem hellbent on the old green and pleasant land, but they won't get behind the people who keep it that way." Nigel sat in his living room wearing a rugby shirt and jeans speckled with paint from his mother's new house. "They're not thinking straight," he said. "Our product needs to be marketed—branded, with a flag, which is presently not allowed. It's all wrong. We have to import soya as a protein source for our pigs now because we can't use other animal meat or bone fat. But this country imports tons of Dutch and Danish meat fed on bone fat."

As we walked out of the living room I noticed there were no pictures on any of the walls. We went outside to the pigsties. The rain was pouring down, the mud thick and sloppy on the ground, and one of Nigel's pigs was burning in an incinerator. As we looked out I asked him what had happened to the land. "The subsidies from the Common Agricultural Policy have got out of hand," he said, "because they are linked to production rather than the environment. Did you know the rivers around here are polluted with fertilizer and crap? We're seeing a massive degradation of rural life in this country. Bakers and dairies have already gone, onions have gone, sugar beet is gone, beef is pretty much gone, lambs are going."

Before we went into the sty, he asked me if I was "pig-clean." "I'm clean," I said, "unless the fever can come through the phone." Hundreds of healthy-looking pink pigs scuttled around in the hay and the mud. He picked one up. "Farming is passed down," he said, "or it should be. A farm is built up for generation after generation, and when it starts to slip and go — you feel an absolute failure. That's what you feel."

We went around the farm and Nigel explained how things work. The notebook was getting very wet, so I put it away. "You feel a failure," he said again, looking into the wind. "The other night I was at a meeting: a hundred and forty farmers at a union meeting paying tribute to four hill farmers under forty-five who'd committed suicide." He leaned against the side of the barn. "We are no longer an island," he said. "Everything's a commodity."

Charles Grey, the leader of the Whig Party, won a snap election in 1831 with a single slogan: "The Bill, the whole Bill and nothing but the Bill." The Reform Act, which was passed the following year after several reversals and much trouble from the Lords, increased the British electorate by 57 percent and paved the way for the Poor Law and the Municipal Corporations Act; this in turn killed off the oligarchies which had traditionally dominated local government. The misery and squalor that Cobbett had described in the late 1820s worsened during the Hungry Forties; it was not until after the repeal of the Corn Laws and the subsequent opening up of trade that British farmers found a brief golden moment. By the end of 1850 Burns and Wordsworth and Constable were dead, and the countryside they adored was subject to four-crop rotation and drainage. Something had ended. And the census of 1851 shows you what: for the first time in British history, the urban population was greater than the rural. Yet the cult of the landscape continues even now as if nothing had changed. Today some parts of East Sussex look like Kansas.

In 1867 it became illegal to employ women and children in

gangs providing cheap labor in the fields. This was a small social improvement at a time when things were starting to get difficult again: corn prices fell; there was an outbreak of cattle plague; cheaper produce arrived from America; refrigeration was invented in 1880 and suddenly ships were coming from Australia loaded with mutton and beef. At a meeting in Aylesbury in September 1879, Benjamin Disraeli, by then Earl of Beaconsfield, spoke on "The Agricultural Situation" and expressed concern about British farming's ability to compete with foreign territories. "The strain on the farmers of England has become excessive," he said. The year before, he claimed, the opposition had set "the agricultural laborers against the farmers. Now they are attempting to set the farmers against the landlords. It will never do . . . We will not consent to be devoured singly. Alone we have stood together under many trials, and England has recognised that in the influence of the agricultural interest there is the best security for liberty and law." British farming struggled to compete in the open market until 1910, when the Boards of Agriculture and Fisheries and Food were established and the state became fully involved in supporting it. No one was prepared for what was coming next: squadrons of enemy airplanes would darken the fields, and out there, beyond the coast, submarines were about to reintroduce the threat of starvation.

The year 1914 was yet another beginning in British farming. John Higgs argues that the war found agriculture singularly unprepared:

The area under crops other than grass had fallen by nearly 4.4 million acres since the 1870s . . . and the total agricultural area had fallen by half a million acres. When the war began the possible effects of submarine attacks were unknown and there seemed no reason why food should not continue to be imported as before. As a result only the last two of the five harvests were affected by the Food Production Campaign. This came into being early in 1917 with the immediate and urgent task of saving the country from starvation.

This was the start of a British production frenzy, a beginning that would one day propagate an ending. Free trade was cast aside in the interest of survival, and agricultural executive committees were set up in each county to cultivate great swaths of new land, to superintend an increase in production, with guaranteed prices. The Corn Production Act of 1917 promised high prices for wheat and oats for the postwar years and instituted an Agricultural Wages Board to ensure that workers were properly rewarded for gains in productivity. Some farmers objected to having their produce commandeered for the war effort. One of them, C. F. Ryder, wrote a pamphlet entitled *The Decay of Farming*. A Suffolk farmer of his acquaintance, "without being an enthusiast for the war," was quite willing to make any sacrifice for England which might be essential, but as a dealer in all kinds of livestock, he knows the shocking waste and incompetence with which government business has been conducted, and thinks it grossly unjust that, while hundreds of millions have been wasted, on the one hand, there should be, on the other, an attempt to save a few thousand by depriving the agriculturalist of his legitimate profit.

Despite the words of the non-enthusiast, the war had made things temporarily good for farmers. But the high prices of wartime couldn't be maintained, and in 1920 the market collapsed. This was to be the worst slump in British agriculture until the present one. With diminished world markets and too much grain being produced for domestic use, the Corn Production Act was repealed in 1921. British farmers were destitute.

In *A Policy for British Agriculture* (1939), a treatise for the Left Book Club, Lord Addison, a former minister for agriculture, tried to explain the devastation that took place during those years.

> Millions of acres of land have passed out of active cultiva-
> tion and the process is continuing. An increasing extent of
> good land is reverting to tufts of inferior grass, to brambles
> and weeds, and often to the reedy growth that betrays wa-
> ter-logging; multitudes of farms are beset with dilapidated
> buildings, and a great and rapid diminution is taking place
> in the number of those who find employment upon them . . .
> Since the beginning of the present century nearly a quarter of
> a million workers have quietly drifted from the country to the
> town. There are, however, some people who do not seem to
> regard this decay of Agriculture with much dismay. They are
> so obsessed with the worship of cheapness at any cost that
> they overlook its obvious concomitants in keeping down the
> standard of wages and purchasing power, and the spread of
> desolation over their own countryside. Their eyes only seem
> to be fixed on overseas trade.

There are those who argue that it was this depression—and the sense of betrayal it engendered in farmers between the wars—that led the government to make such ambitious prom-ises at the start of the Second World War. Addison's policy, like many agricultural ideas of the time, was based on a notion of vastly increased production as the ultimate goal. "Nothing but good," he wrote, "would follow from the perfectly attain-able result of increasing our home food production by at least half as much again . . . A restored countryside is of first-rate importance."

It was too early in the twentieth century—and it is perhaps too early still, at the beginning of the twenty-first—to see clearly and unequivocally that the two goals stated by Addison are contradictory. The vast increases in production at the start of the Second World War, and the guarantees put in place at that time, set the trend for overproduction and food surpluses — and began the process of destruction that continues to threaten the British countryside. The pursuit of abundance has contributed to the creation of a great, rolling emptiness. But in the era of the ration book, production was the only answer: no one could have been expected to see the mountains on the other side.

Two years before Addison took office, Thomas Hardy died, and voices were raised in Westminster Abbey invoking his own invocation of the Wessex countryside:

> Precisely at this transitional point of its nightly roll into darkness the great and particular glory of the Egdon waste began, and nobody could be said to understand the heath who had not been there at such a time. It could best be felt when it could not clearly be seen, its complete effect lying in this and the succeeding hours before the next dawn.

It was in Addison's time that glinting combine harvesters began to appear in the fields.

You hear the Borderway Mart before you see it. Driving out of Carlisle, beyond the roundabouts and small industrial units, you can hear cattle lowing and dragging their chains, and in the car park there are trucks full of bleating sheep arriving at a market that doesn't especially want them. Inside, you can't breathe for the smell of dung: farmers move around shuffling papers, eating rolls and sausages, drinking coffee from Styrofoam cups. Some of them check advertising boards covered with details of machinery for sale, farm buildings for rent — the day-to-day evidence of farmers selling out. "It could be any of us selling our tractor up there," an old man in a tweed cap muttered at me.

The PA system crackled to life. "The sale of five cattle is

starting right now in ring number one," the voice said. A black heifer was padding around the ring, its hoofs slipping in sawdust and shit, and the man in charge of the gate, whose overalls were similarly caked, regularly patted it on the rump to keep it moving. Farmers in Wellington boots and green waxed jackets hung their arms over the bars taking notes. One or two looked more like City businessmen. The heifer was nineteen months old and weighed 430 kilos. The bidding was quick and decisive: the heifer went for 79p a kilo.

"If you were here in the prime-beef ring six or seven years ago," the auctioneer said later, "you would have seen the farmers getting about 120p per kilo. That is why so many of the farmers are going out of business. Four years ago, young female sheep would be going for eighty-odd pounds, and today they are averaging thirty."

Climbing to Rakefoot Farm outside Keswick, you see nothing but hills and, in the distance, the lakes like patches of silver; tea shops and heritage centers and Wordsworth's Walks serve as punctuation on the hills going brown in the afternoon. Will Cockbain was sitting in front of a black range in a cottage built in 1504. "There are ghosts here," he said, "but they're mostly quite friendly."

Will's father bought Rakefoot Farm in 1958, but his family have been working the land around Keswick for hundreds of years. "There are more Cockbains in the local cemetery than anything else," he said, "and they have always been sheep farmers. Sitting here with you now, I can remember the smell of bread coming from that range, years ago, when my grandmother was here." Will has 1,100 Swaledale sheep and 35 suckler cows on the farm. "Seven thousand pounds is a figure you often hear as an annual earning for full-time farmers round here," he said.

"Quite a few are on Family Credit—though not many will admit it. We farm 2,500 acres, of which we now own just 170, the rest being rented from five different landlords, including the National Trust. The bigger part of our income comes from subsidies we get for environmental work—keeping the stone walls and fences in order, maintaining stock-proof dykes, burning heather, off-wintering trees."

"Can't you make anything from the sheep?" I asked.

"No," he said. "We are selling livestock way below the cost of production. Subsidies were introduced in 1947 when there was rationing and food shortages, and the subsidies continued, along with guaranteed prices, and now even the subsidies aren't enough. We've got the lowest ewe premium price we've had for years. In hill farming the income is stuck and the environmental grants are stuck too. Fuel prices are crippling us. We are in a job that doesn't pay well and we depend on our vehicles. We are responsible for keeping the landscape the way people say they are proud to have it—but who pays for it? The people down the road selling postcards of the Lake District are making much more than the farmers who keep the land so photogenic."

Will Cockbain was the same size as the chair he was sitting in. Staring into the fire, he waggled his stocking-soled feet and blew out his lips. "I think Margaret Thatcher saw those guaranteed prices farmers were getting and just hated it," he said. "And now, though it kills me, we may have to face something: there are too many sheep in the economy. Farmers go down to the market every other week and sell one sheep, and then they give thirty or forty away. They're not worth anything. There are mass sheep graves everywhere now in the United Kingdom." Will laughed and drank his tea. "It's only those with an inbuilt capacity for pain that can stand the farming life nowadays," he said. "I like the life, but you can't keep liking it when you're running against the bank, when things are getting out of control in ways you never dreamed of, relationships falling apart, everything."

On the walls of Will Cockbain's farm there are dozens of rosettes for prize-winning sheep. A picture of Will's son holding a prize ram hangs beside a grandfather clock, made by Simpson of Cockermouth, and an old barometer pointing to Rain. "This is a farming community from way back," Will said, "but they're all getting too old now. Young men with trained dogs are a rarity, and hill farming, of all kinds, needs young legs. We've lost a whole generation to farming. My boys are hanging in there for now, but with, what, £27,000 last year between four men, who could blame them for disappearing?"

"It's going to be a nightmare if they let farming go the same way as mining," said another farmer, "but still, we all vote Conservative up here. The Tories were much better to us."

As early as 1935 there was panic in the Ministry of Agriculture about the possibility of another war. The First World War had caught British agriculturalists on the hop; this time preparations had to be made. And it was this panic and this mindfulness that set in train the subsidy-driven production that many feel has ruined (and saved) the traditional farming economy in this country, creating an "unreal market" and a falsely sustained industry, the root of today's troubles. Before the outbreak of war, policies were introduced which favored the stockpiling of tractors and fertilizers; there were subsidies for anyone who plowed up permanent grasslands; agricultural workers were released from war duty; and the Women's Land Army was established. Farming became the second front, and the "Dig for Victory" campaign extended from public parks to private allotments.

With the war at sea, British food imports dropped by half

while the total area of domestic crops increased by 63 percent: production of some vegetables, such as potatoes, doubled. Farmers in the 1920s had complained that their efforts to increase production in wartime had not been rewarded by an undertaking of long-term government support. The mistake would not be repeated. Promises were made at the start of the second war, and in 1947, with food shortages still in evidence and rationing in place, an Agriculture Act was passed which offered stability and annual price reviews to be monitored by the National Farmers' Union. Parliament instituted a massive program of capital investment in farm fabric and equipment, and free advice on the use of new technologies and fertilizer was made available. Water supplies and telephone lines were introduced in many previously remote areas. Farmers working the land in the 1950s and 1960s, though there were fewer and fewer of them, had, it's true, never had it so good. At the same time, increased use of artificial fertilizers and chemical pesticides meant greater yields and what is now thought of as severe environmental damage: motorway bypasses, electricity pylons, larger fields attended by larger machines, with meadows plowed up, marshes filled in, woods and grasslands usurped by acreage-hungry crops—what the writer Graham Harvey refers to as "this once 'living tapestry'" was being turned into "a shroud . . . a landscape of the dead."

Government subsidies and grants in wartime, cemented in postwar policy, prepared British farmers for the lavish benefits they were to enjoy after Britain joined the Common Market in 1973. Today, the Common Agricultural Policy (CAP) gets a lashing whatever your view of the EU. One side sees quotas and subsidies and guaranteed prices as responsible for overproduction and the creation of a false economy. The other accuses it of being kinder to other European states and not giving enough back to British farmers, a view generally shared by the farmers themselves, but secretly abhorred by the government, which is handing out subsidies. The two sides agree, however, that the CAP doesn't work, and as I write, a new round of reforms is being introduced.

In 1957, when the Common Market came into being, there was a deficit in most agricultural products and considerable variance in priorities from state to state—some to do with climate and dietary needs, some to do with protectionist tendencies. (British farmers who feel ill served by the CAP often say it was formed too early to suit British needs.) When the CAP went into effect in 1964, it was intended to rationalize the chains of supply and demand across member states. This was to be achieved by improving agricultural productivity and promoting technical progress; by maintaining a stable supply of food at regular and sensible prices to consumers; by setting up a common pricing system that would allow farmers in all countries to receive the same returns, fixed above the world market level, for their output. Agricultural commissioners were given the right to intervene in the market where necessary, and a system of variable levies was established to prevent imported goods from undercutting EC production. The vexed issue was the common financing system, which still operates today, and which means that all countries contribute to a central market-support fund called the European Agricultural Guidance and Guarantee Fund. All market support is paid for centrally out of this fund, with budgetary allocations for each commodity sector. Cash is paid to producers in member states regardless of the level of a country's contribution to the fund.

One consequence of this protectionist jamboree has been an increase, across the board and in all member states, in the variety and quality of available products, from plum tomatoes and cereals to hams and wines and cheeses, with supermarkets now carrying a vastly increased range of produce at comparable prices. (This may have pleased British consumers, but it hasn't pleased British farmers, who argue that supermarkets have exploited this abundance, breaking traditional commitments to local producers and "shopping around Europe" for supplies which could be got in Britain.) A second consequence has been the familiar overstimulated production and the creation of surpluses. It may even be that by continuing to offer not only guaranteed prices but production subsidies to boot, the CAP can be considered one of the chief instigators of the current crisis.

In the early 1990s European agriculturalists, seeing the need for the CAP to give direct support to an ailing industry—"to protect the family farm," as they often put it—and to protect the environment, began to speak a different language. The European Commission, in its own words,

> recognised that radical reforms were necessary in order to redress the problems of ever-increasing expenditure and declining farm incomes, the build-up and cost of storing surplus food stocks and damage to the environment caused by intensive farming methods. A further factor was the tensions which the Community's farm support policy caused in terms of the EC's external trade relations. Various measures have been adopted since the mid-1980s to address these problems, e.g. set-aside, production and expenditure quotas on certain products and co-responsibility levies on others. However, these proved inadequate to control the expansion of support expenditure.

A constant refrain during the Thatcher period was that measures like these would serve only to impede market forces. The bucking of market forces, however, was one of the founding principles of the CAP, and even today, when we finally see the bottom falling out of the system of rewards and grants for over-production, the tendency is towards "relief" packages, which New Labor supports through gritted teeth. It would appear that for a long time now British farming has been faced with two choices: a slow death or a quick one. And not even Thatcher could tolerate a quick one.

Consumers stand to save more than a billion pounds from the cuts in support prices; and the Blair government is largely in agreement with these proposals, although there are elements which, according to documents available from the Scottish Executive, it finds less than satisfactory:

> While the general proposals for addressing rural policy lack detail, they look innovative and offer possibilities for directing support to rural areas. The downside of the proposals is that the compensation payments look to be too generous, there is no proposal to make farm payments degressive or decoupled from production . . . The Government has also declared its opposition to an EU-wide ceiling on the amount of direct payments which an individual producer can receive. Because of the UK's large average farm size, this proposal would hit the UK disproportionately. Elsewhere, there is uncertainty about how the proposals would work in practice. This includes the proposal to create "national envelopes" in the beef and dairy regimes within which Member States would have a certain discretion on targeting subsidies.

A modern journey across rural Britain doesn't begin and end with the Common Agricultural Policy. Since the end of the Second World War, and escalating through the period since the formation of the EEC, what we understand as the traditional British landscape has been vanishing before our eyes. Something like 150,000 miles of hedgerow have been lost since subsidies began. Since the underwriting of food production regardless of demand, 97 percent of English meadowlands have disappeared. There has been a loss of ponds, wetlands, bogs, scrub, flora and fauna — never a dragonfly to be seen, the number of tree sparrows reduced by 89 percent, of song thrushes by 73 percent and of skylarks by 58 percent. "Only 20 acres of limestone meadow remain in the whole of Northamptonshire," Graham Harvey reports. "In Ayrshire only 0.001 percent remains in meadowland . . . None of this would have happened without subsidies. Without taxpayers, farm prices would have slipped as production exceeded market demand . . . Despite years of overproduction, farmers continue to be paid as if their products were in short supply."

I set out on my own rural ride feeling sorry for the farmers. I thought they were getting a raw deal: economic forces were against them; they were victims of historical realities beyond their control and of some horrendous bad luck. They seemed to me, as the miners had once seemed, to be trying to hold on to something worth having, a decent working life, an earning, a rich British culture, and I went into their kitchens with a sense of sorrow. And that is still the case: there is no pleasure to be had from watching farmers work from six until six in all weathers for nothing more rewarding than Income Support. You couldn't not feel for them. But as the months passed I could also see the sense in the opposing argument: many of the bigger farmers had exploited the subsidy system, they had done well with bumper checks from Brussels in the 1980s, they had destroyed the land to get the checks, and they had done nothing to fend off ruin. When I told people I was spending time with farmers, they'd say, "How can you stand it? They just complain all day, and they've always got their hand out." I didn't want to believe that, and after talking to the farmers I've written about here, I still don't believe it. But there would be no point in opting for an easy lament on the farmers' behalf, despite all the anguish they have recently suffered: it would be like singing a sad song for the 1980s men-in-red-braces, who had a similar love of Thatcher, and who did well then, but who are now reaping the rewards of bad management. As a piece of human business, British farming is a heady mixture of the terrible and the inevitable, the hopeless and the culpable, and no less grave for all that.

Britain is not a peasant culture. It has not been that for over two hundred years. Though we have a cultural resistance to the fact, we are an industrial nation – or, better, a postindustrial one – and part of the agricultural horror we now face has its origins in the readiness with which we industrialized the farming process. We did the thing that peasant nations such as France did not do: we turned the landscape into American-style prairie, trounced our own ecosystem, and with public money too, and turned some of the biggest farms in Europe into giant, fertilizer-gobbling, pesticide-spraying, manufactured-seed-using monocultures geared only for massive profits and the accrual of EU subsidies. A civil service source reminded me that even the BSE crisis has a connection to intensive agribusiness: "Feeding animals with the crushed fat and spinal cord of other animals is a form of cheap, industrial, cost-effective management," he said, "and it would never have happened on a traditional British farm. It is part of the newer, EU-driven, ultra-profiteering way of farming. And look at the results." Farms in other parts of Europe, the smaller ones dotted across the Continent, have been much less inclined to debase farming practices in order to reap the rewards of intensification.

The way ahead is ominous. In a very straightforward sense, in the world at large, genetically modified crops are corrupting the relation of people to the land they live on. Farmers were once concerned with the protection of the broad biodiversity of their fields, but the new methods, especially GM crops, put land use and food production in the hands of corporations, which are absent from the scene and environmentally careless. By claiming exclusive intellectual property rights to plant breeding, the giant seed companies are gutting entire ecosystems for straight profit. It is happening in India, Algeria and increasingly in places like Zimbabwe, and it is among the factors threatening to make life hell for the traditional farmers of Yorkshire and Wiltshire.

In 1998, in a leaked document, a Monsanto researcher expressed great concern about the unpopularity of GM foods with the British public, but was pleased to report that some headway had been made in convincing MPs of their potential benefits. MPs and civil servants, the document says, have little doubt that over the long term things will work out, with a typical comment being: "I'm sure in five years' time everybody will be happily eating genetically modified apples, plums, peaches and peas."

In 1999 the Blair government spent £52 million on developing GM crops and £13 million on improving the profile of the biotech industry. In the same year it spent only £1.7 million on promoting organic farming. Blair himself has careered from one end of the debate to the other, swithering between his love of big business and his fear of the *Daily Mail*. Initially, he was in favor of GM research in all its forms. "The human genome is now freely available on the internet," he said to the European Bioscience Conference in 2000, "but the entrepreneurial incentive provided by the patenting system has been preserved." Other voices — grand ones — disagreed. "We should not be meddling with the building blocks of life in this way," Prince Charles was quoted on his website as saying. The government asked for the remarks to be removed. "Once the GM genie is out of the bottle," Sir William Asscher, the chairman of the BMA's Board of Science and Education, remarked, "the impact on the environment is likely to be irreversible." The Church of England's Ethical Investment Advisory Group turned down a request from the Ministry of Agriculture to lease some of the church's land—it owns 125,000 acres—for GM testing. More recently, Blair has proclaimed in the *Independent on Sunday* that the potential benefits of GM technology are considerable, but he has also introduced the idea that his government is not a blind and unquestioning supporter. "We are neither for nor against," said the Labour MP Mo Mowlam.

Poorly paid, unsung, depressed husbanders of the British landscape, keeping a few animals for auld lang syne and killing the ones they can't afford to sell, small farmers like Brian Carruthers, the man who lives outside Keswick with his Galloway cows and keeps his children on Family Credit, or the pig farmers in Suffolk, told me they felt as if they were under sentence of death from the big agricultural businesses. I asked one of them what he planned to do. His response was one I had heard before. "Move to France," he said with a shrug. Graham Harvey is in no doubt about where the fault lies: "In the early 1950s," he writes, "there were about 454,000 farms in the UK. Now there are half that number, and of these just 23,000 produce half of all the food we grow. In a period of unprecedented public support for agriculture almost a quarter of a million farms have gone out of business . . . It is the manufacturers and City investors who now dictate the UK diet."

The government has been stuck in farming crisis after farming crisis, but it recognizes—though until now somewhat mutedly—the accumulating evils of the subsidy-driven culture. Its public position is to undertake large-scale, environmentally friendly tinkering with European funding, attended by vague worries about changes in the world market. An unofficial spokeswoman for Maff told me there were much deeper worries than the policy wonks would be heard admitting to. "It is like the end of the British coal industry," she said,

> but no one wants to be Ian McGregor. In the time since BSE 110,000 head of cattle have disappeared: it seems that farmers were burning them on their own land. It's a cultural thing, too: no one wants to admit that a certain kind of farming, a certain way of English life, has now run to the end of the road. People will supposedly always need bread. But there is no reason to believe it will have to be made with British ingredients. The disasters in farming aren't so temporary. And they aren't mainly the result of bad luck. No. Something is finished for traditional farming in this country. Not everything, by any means, but something — something in the business of British agriculture is over for good, and no one can quite face it.

The day before I set off for Devon there was a not entirely encouraging headline on the front page of the *London Evening Standard:* "Stay Out of the Countryside." Just when it seemed there was little room for disimprovement in the predicament of British farmers, news came of the biggest outbreak of foot-and-mouth disease in more than thirty years. Twenty-seven infected pigs were found at Cheale Meats, an abattoir in Essex, a place not far from Nigel Rowe's pig farm in Constable country. Infected animals were quickly discovered on several other farms. Suspect livestock began to be slaughtered in their hundreds. Such was the smoke from the incineration site in Northumberland that the A69 had to be closed for a time. British exports of meat and livestock (annual export value £600 million) as well as milk (of which 400,000 tons are exported a year) were banned by the British government and the EU. "It is like staring into the abyss," Ben Gill, the president of the National Farmers' Union, said. "On top of the problems we have had to face in the last few years, the impact is unthinkable."

The National Pig Association estimates that the relatively small outbreak of swine fever last year cost the industry £100 million. The last epidemic of foot-and-mouth disease, which took hold in October 1967, led to the slaughter of 442,000 animals—a loss of hundreds of millions of pounds in today's terms, only a fraction of which made it back to the farmer in compensation. Last month's ban affected more than half of Britain's farmers, and no one doubts that many of them will be ruined.

The county of Devon seemed dark green and paranoid when I traveled there the day after the ban was introduced. It seemed to sit in fear of the disinfecting gloom to come, and as the fields rolled by, I considered the ongoing assault on Hardy's Wessex, the trouble on all sides, and the sense of an ending. Yet I'd originally planned my visit there as an opportunity to gaze at a vision of farming success. Stapleton Farm, my destination, was the one named by the Sainsbury's executives, on the day I walked with them around the flagship store on the Cromwell Road, as an example of the new kind of partnership that can exist between supermarkets and farmers. Stapleton produces the quality brands of yogurt and ice cream admired by the people at Sainsbury's: their optimism seemed hard to recapture on the way to Devon that morning.

Stapleton Farm is not far from Bideford, near Great Torrington, and there isn't a cow to be seen there. The farm uses brought-in milk to make the yogurt and ice cream that is so highly regarded by Sainsbury's. No livestock, no fields, no manure, no tractors, just a small manufacturing unit that couldn't be doing better. This is the enterprise Sainsbury's put me on to when I asked about the partnerships with farming that mattered to them. This is the new thing.

I found Carol Duncan in a Portakabin she uses as an office. She was surrounded by Sainsbury's invoices and office stationery. Like her husband, Peter, who soon arrived with a marked absence of flat cap or Wellington boots, Carol considers herself a modern rural producer. "I was absolutely delighted when we managed to get rid of the very last cow off this farm," she said. "That's the thing about cows, you know, they just poo all the time." Peter's father and his grandfather had run Stapleton Farm in the traditional West Country way: they had livestock and they worked the fields through thick and thin. "But from an early age I wasn't interested in that kind of farming," Peter admitted. "I wanted to be inside reading books. And then, when my time came, I was interested in the different things you can do with milk. In the 1960s we farmers needed to diversify and head ourselves to somewhere better. The traditional way had been to stand around waiting for the government price review. I wanted to make yogurt and change things around here. My father would say, 'Who's going to milk the cows?'"

"He just wouldn't stop being a farmer, his father," Carol said.

Peter laughed. "Yes. But we started with three churns. Carol was an art teacher, and that kept us going through the difficult years. We made yogurt and started selling it to independent schools."

"That's right," Carol said. "If you're paying between £13,000 and £16,000 a year for a school, you want to make sure your children aren't going to be eating rubbish. We had to fight for our markets. In 1994 the price of milk in Devon went up by 29 percent. We had to increase the price of the yogurt by 5 percent, and we lost some of our German contracts. I went out and fought to get them back. It was horrible: two-hundred-year-old cheese makers were shut down, and hardly a Devon clotted-cream maker was left standing. But there's too much milk. It's in oversupply. Six years ago we thought we were going out of business."

"We started exporting our stuff," Peter said, "to Belgium especially. We supply an upmarket supermarket chain called Delhaize."

"Until this morning," Carol said. "We've just been banned from exporting."

"We're hoping it will only be a matter of weeks," Peter said, "but this is the sort of thing that can ruin people. We're praying it doesn't spread."

There were a number of people coming and going outside the Portakabin window. They seemed different from most of the farming people I'd met: they were young, for a start, and they seemed like indoor types, a different color from the fieldworkers I'd come across in Essex and Cumbria, Kent and Scotland. The Duncans have more than thirty people working at Stapleton Farm — chopping, grating, mixing, packaging, labeling, loading. The buildings where the yogurt and ice cream are produced are old farm buildings that have been converted. They look typical enough among the high hedges of north Devon, yet inside each shed there are silver machines and refrigerated rooms that are miles away from the world of cows. Peter tells the story of the Sainsbury's development manager coming down to see them in 1998 as if he were relating a great oral ballad about a local battle or a famous love affair. "The woman came down," he said. "I thought she seemed so fierce. They had already taken samples of our yogurt away. They said they liked them. But when the woman came that day, she just said, 'I suppose you'd like to see these,' and it was the artwork for the pots. They'd already decided we were going into business. I nearly fell off my chair."

Carol laughed in recognition. "Yeah," she said, "and they say, 'How many of these can you produce a week?' So we started aiming for 10,000 pots a week in a hundred Sainsbury's stores. They were very pleased with the way it was going, weren't they, Peter?"

"Oh yes," he said, "and we were putting yogurt into the pots by hand and pressing the lids on. It was incredibly hard work."

"Then they wanted to double it," she said.

"Oh yes," he echoed, "they wanted to double it. We had to get better machinery. So it was off to the bank for £80,000. Come February 1999, we were doing 50,000 to 60,000 pots a week."

Carol swiveled in her office chair. "We think Sainsbury's are geniuses," she said. "We just give them yogurt and they sell it."

Stapleton Farm processes all its own fruit by hand. All the milk they use comes from three local farms. Recently, they started giving the milk farmers half a penny more per liter, because of the hard time the farmers are having.

"It's been a music hall joke for years," Peter said, "about farmers complaining. But now that the worst has come true, the whole thing's beyond belief."

In the face of all this seriousness, I remembered some lines of George Crabbe's, from "The Parish Register" (1807):

> *Our farmers round, well pleased with constant gain,*
> *Like other farmers, flourish and complain.*

"The ladies who work for us all come from within three miles of here," Carol said, "and they're working for housekeeping money. The farms they live on are struggling, and they are here to earn money to feed their kids. But it's a struggle for us too. Most of the people who work here take more away from it than we do, but it's our little dream."

The Duncans' dream has been one of survival and self-sufficiency, and of being free of that last cow. But as environmentalists they may have trouble living with the price of their own success: expansion. The week I spoke to them, the Duncans were reeling from having bought a £68,000 machine that wasn't yet working. Sainsbury's wants them to produce more and more, and they are aware of the fact that doing well entails spending more, so that demand can be met. They are now heavily in debt but also rejoicing at their own success. In the autumn of 1999 their contact at Sainsbury's suggested they have a go at making ice cream.

"Oh God," Carol said, blushing at the recollection, "I didn't know how to make ice cream. I just made a liter in my little kitchen Gelati and we sent it off. They said they had eighty samples to try. And they decided they liked ours the best. So that was it."

"Yes," Peter said, "that was a visit to the bank for another hundred grand. We had about ten weeks to get the production into full swing. And in the first twelve months of production we sold £750,000 worth of ice cream."

Carol is more forthright, and I would say more conservative, than her husband. She obviously hates the idea of farming but likes the idea of country-related things. "An art student wouldn't be seen dead near a farm," she said at one point. "Farmers just have the wrong attitude."

"No," Peter said, "not all of them. The problem was the marketing boards, which gave farmers the wrong idea. They thought someone would just take their produce away and turn it into money. This has been the situation since the end of the war. No other country in Europe was like that. That is why we are so far behind."

Carol heaved a huge sigh. "I'm so pissed off about the foot-and-mouth disease. We had a whole lot of ice cream going into Spain next week. Not now. I hope it doesn't spread to here."

"Starting to do business with Sainsbury's feels a bit like being mown down by a bus," Peter said.

"Yes," said Carol, "but I was so relieved when we got rid of that last cow and that old farm. That's the thing with a lot of the farmers around here: they have the potential to get into tourism, get into the farm cottages side, caravans and all that."

Supermarkets want to be able to rely on volume. If Stapleton Farm's yogurt continues to grow in popularity — which it will, as part of Sainsbury's Taste the Difference range for the more discerning shopper, costing 45p, against the Economy brand's 8p — then it will have to get bigger. The charm of Stapleton's smallness cannot last; the supermarket culture requires commitment and tolerance of the highest order from producers. "I remember once thinking," Peter said, "that maybe yogurt would end up being produced by about three factories in Europe. And it may go like that."

"Our girls," Carol said, "have been brought up to believe that Europe is their oyster. And at this moment we are just what Sainsbury's wants."

I asked the Duncans if they were worried about having all their eggs in one basket. What happens if people get fed up with Devon yogurt? What happens if Sainsbury's finds somewhere cheaper, or somewhere better able to meet the volume required? Or if it falls for the new kid on the block? Carol met my gaze evenly. "We'll survive," she said.

Before going into the factory with Peter, I had to put on white boots and a white jumpsuit, sterilize my hands and pull on a hairnet. Peter stopped in the middle of a chilled room, with the sound of clicking going on further along the line, the sound of mass production. "This was a cattle shed when I was little," he said. "I can remember it quite clearly." We stood beside a pallet of strawberry yogurts bound for Sainsbury's. It had the special label already attached. I asked him who paid for the Sainsbury's packaging. "Oh, we do," he said.

That afternoon, Tim Yeo, the shadow agriculture spokesman, said that the government had responded in chaotic fashion to a chain of farming crises. "I wish he would shut up and go away," Nick Brown replied. "He is trying to make political capital out of a terrible situation." And when I was barely out of the West Country, news broke of another farm where livestock was found to have contracted foot-and-mouth disease. The farm was in Devon. And the farmer owned thirteen other farms.

The most comprehensive guide to British farming performance is provided by Deloitte & Touche's *Farming Results*. "Despite cutting costs and tightening their belts," the report for autumn 2000 concludes, "farmers have suffered the lowest average incomes since our survey began 11 years ago." Several facts stand out, so unreasonable do they seem, and so shocking. "In the last five years the net farm income of a 200-hectare family farm has plunged from around £80,000 to just £8,000 . . . Those farmers who have expanded their operations dramatically in recent times . . . cannot sustain profitability in the face of tumbling commodity prices." "The bad news," says Mark Hill, the firm's partner in charge of the Food and Agriculture Group, "is that we predict small profits becoming losses in the coming year. This is due to a further fall in output prices and yield plus rising costs of £25 per hectare in fuel alone."

An equally gloomy drizzle was making a blur of Otford the

day I visited. Hedges were loaded like wet sponges, the short grass squeaked underfoot, there was mud in the road and mud at the farm gate, with a cold whiteness in the Kent sky that darkened quickly in the afternoon. Ian and Anne Carter were sitting in the drawing room of their farmhouse. She is a justice of the peace, groomed to a fine point of civic order, wearing a blue suit with a poppy pinned to its lapel. She is well spoken, opening up her world in good clear Southern English, the language of the prep school and the shipping forecast, and her generosity seems to go perfectly with the rationale of the teacups. Ian stretched out his long legs like a teenager: he is likably comfortable with everything he knows and everything he doesn't know; he is right as rain and habitually nice. They both shook their heads.

"You need to have 2,500 acres to make farming work nowadays," he said. "Not so long ago you could have 600 acres and secondhand equipment and send your kids to a good school and holiday in the south of France. That's all gone now."

"Absolutely," said Anne, "there has been pressure from the fertilizer companies to use certain fertilizers. There are too many sheep owing to these awful subsidies. The whole countryside out there has changed almost beyond recognition." Over the fireplace hangs a Constable painting, a portrait of one of Anne's ancestors. There is something darkly lively about the picture. For a while we all sat and stared into it. "It's not at all famous," Anne said. "All the famous ones are out there being admired."

A British Legion–type couple came to lunch. "It's funny the way things go," the man said, "when you think of all those British companies that went to the wall. British manufacturing took such a hammering, and now you see that a whole way of living and working has disappeared."

"Do you think the land will eventually be nationalized and given to the National Trust?" his wife asked.

"You mean heritaged?" someone else asked.

"Very interesting what's happened to *The Archers,*" Anne said. "This year Nigel, who has the big house, Lower Loxley, is involved in some sort of shooting gallery. They didn't have that before. *The Archers* has become less and less farming and more sex."

We braved the weather and walked several miles over the fields. Anne spoke about a spiritual connection she felt with the countryside and a hope she retained in the balance of nature. There were milky pools beside the trees, and when I walked with Ian he tried to give an account of why things had gone the way they had, a story of overproduction and subsidy distortion and diseased animals and the threat of bad seeds. It seemed less imposing that the land belonged to the Carters, and much more interesting, in an easy, uncomplicated way, that they belonged to the land thereabouts. They seemed to walk it knowingly. We stopped at the family chapel, dedicated to Saint Jude, in a building which dates from 1650. A book inside the chapel tells the story of the ownership of this piece of land—the lay ownership from 1066 to 1521, the removal of the house and the farm from a nobleman to one of the wives of Henry VIII. Across from the chapel is a disused cowshed that Anne's father built in 1946. Water dripped from the lintel, and an inscription is carved above. "To the glory of agriculture," it says, "and the working man."

*March 2001*

# England and the Beatles

THERE IS SOMETHING very English in the marriage of boredom and catastrophe, and the England that existed immediately after the Second World War appears to have carried that manner rather well, as if looking over its shoulder to notice that lightning had just struck a teacup. Reading the work of V. S. Pritchett or the absconded Auden, you pick up the notion that Europe had just come through a spell of bad weather, as though the only important question emerging from the war was about how it might have affected the course of English normality. The great horror was that things would remain the same, second only to a fear that things would never be the same again. The mood is captured nicely in "1948" by Roy Fuller, a poet who happened to spend his life working for the Woolwich Equitable Building Society:

> Reading among the crumbs of leaves upon
> The lawn, beneath the thin October sun,
> I hear behind the words
> And noise of birds
> The drumming aircraft; and am blind till they have gone.

*The feeling that they give is now no more*
*That of the time when we had not reached war:*
*It is as though the lease*
*Of crumbling peace*
*Had run already and that life was as before.*
*For this is not the cancer or the scream,*
*A grotesque interlude, but what will seem*
*On waking to us all*
*Most natural —*
*The gnawed incredible existence of a dream.*

England appeared then to be a country of old men, a place in which dreams were routinely gnawed down by broken teeth, while America in 1948 appeared to the English like a stately pleasure dome, housing this great new phenomenon, the teenager, and busy with every kind of plan for the future, from abbreviated hemlines to the hydrogen bomb. The compulsions of teenagers have come to so dominate the world that we might sometimes forget they used not to exist. In 1900, for instance, 20 percent of American kids between ten and fifteen were in fulltime employment and, even as late as D-Day itself, Andy Hardy represented a world where young people did useful things and had fun before going to bed alone at ten o'clock. What was the teenage market in 1945 but comic books, bobby pins and the Toni home perm? But in 1948 the transistor radio was invented (kids could suddenly listen to music in their own rooms), and the 1948 Cadillac came with tail fins and a radio console, a vehicle customized for teenagers and featured in a blazing new magazine called *Hot Rod.*[1] It was also the year of the Kinsey Report. Ed Sullivan's *Toast of the Town* was first aired in that summer of

---

1. For some of this information I am indebted to Lucy Rollin, *Twentieth-Century Teen Culture by the Decades: A Reference Guide* (1999).

1948, and it would eventually promise a world in which the likes and dislikes of young people in blue jeans could appear to run the culture.

In a bombed-out Liverpool, a dozen years later, new shining buildings were being erected, and English normality was erupting into something of a classless, American-accented meritocracy: four cheeky lads with scuffed shoes, the Beatles, came bursting with new harmonies and even newer energies, and they appeared to be telling young people they had choices. John Lennon, quoted in *The Beatles Anthology:*

> America used to be a big youth place in everybody's imagination. We all knew America, all of us. All those movies: every movie we ever saw as children, whether it was Disneyland or Doris Day, Rock Hudson, James Dean or Marilyn. Everything was American: Coca-Cola, Heinz ketchup . . . The big artists were American. It was the Americans coming to the London Palladium. They wouldn't even make an English movie without an American in it, even a B movie . . . They'd have a Canadian if they couldn't get an American . . . Liverpool is cosmopolitan. It's where the sailors would come home on the ships with the blues records from America.

Devin McKinney's intelligent study of the Beatles, *Magic Circles: The Beatles in Dream and History,* finds the four in a Liverpool coated in the grime of empire; among the cellars, bunkers and back streets of postwar Britain, they "listened to America and lived on fantasies of everything their culture lacked." McKinney listens to a tape of the sixteen-year-old John Lennon singing with the Quarry Men, the ramshackle group that preceded the Beatles, at a church garden fete. It is the day Lennon met Paul McCartney. "The music," writes McKinney, "though it *resembles* rock and roll, sounds as if it owes nothing to any form, because it is so completely itself. It feels like ugly British kids make it, and sounds as if it comes from under the ground."

Like most British pop groups of the time, the Beatles sang with American accents, which shows you what Britain was becoming in those years. Yet the group was the first to echo the sound of America back on itself, only louder, newer, with more screams, and their story, rightly divined in McKinney's book, is about how they came to represent the thrill of rock music as a high form of dreaming in the present tense of history. It is exactly forty years since the Beatles landed at JFK. What did they bring with them apart from an instant legend of old Europe transmogrified by America? Greeted by "a squall of unmediated adolescent emotion," the Beatles never questioned the meaning of the sobbing girls who crowded around them, or of the outraged adults who would later oversee the burning of their records. America was ready for something new in 1964, and the Beatles surprised even themselves at their agility when it came to meeting that readiness. Paul McCartney in the *Anthology:*

> There were millions of kids at the airport. We heard about it in mid-air . . . The pilot had rang ahead and said, "Tell the boys there's a big crowd waiting for them." We thought, "Wow! God, we have really made it." I remember, for instance, the great moment of getting into the limo and putting on the radio and hearing a running commentary on *us:* "They have just left the airport and are coming towards New York City . . ." It was like a dream. The greatest fantasy ever.

Ringo Starr, the drummer, showed all the excitement of a wallflower suddenly plucked onto the dance floor by the college jock. "On the plane," he said, "flying into the airport, I felt as though there was a big octopus with tentacles that were grabbing the plane and dragging us down into New York."

That madness was a fulfillment of the promise of 1948: Elvis came first, then came the Beatles, but the Liverpudlians failed to lose themselves in Hollywood as Elvis did, and instead they began, after that first innocent bout in America, to travel into the nature of their own psyches and the character of their own time and place, journeys that still offer the most articulate definition of the decade. Looked at properly, the Beatles really were the sixties: they started out as one thing and ended as another, and that is the core of their story, how they changed from ultramelodic laughing boys to revolutionary art-heroes, making an entire generation imagine itself differently. Another story emerges too when you look at the Beatles' music and its reception, a story about the cultural relationship between Britain and the United States, an odd friendship in which loyalties, enmities and anxieties of influence have been animated in a climate of increasing American power.

The Beatles appeared on *The Ed Sullivan Show* on February 9, 1964,[2] and the direct influence of that event is still being felt in new ways. In 1961, a teenage John Kerry played bass guitar in a band called the Electras. The boys rehearsed in the halls of St. Paul's School in Concord, New Hampshire; they cut a record

_____

2. The anniversary is marked by several publications and republications about the Beatles, including Martin Goldsmith, *The Beatles Come to America* (2004), a rather sweet beat-by-beat account of the band's appearance on *The Ed Sullivan Show*. "Such was the nationwide fascination with the Beatles that, so the story goes, crime decreased to almost nothing while the music played . . . And evangelist Billy Graham broke his own rule of not watching television on the Sabbath, tuning in to the Beatles to try to understand his three teenage daughters. After turning off the set, he proclaimed the Beatles symptomatic 'of the uncertainty of the times and the confusion about us. They are part of the trend towards escapism. I hope when they are older they will get a haircut.' "

and described their music as "early surf." Tony Blair's band was called Ugly Rumours; he played guitar and sang. Only the other day, on a tour of China, a group of students asked the British prime minister to sing a Beatles song. He blushed and looked at his wife, Cherie, who picked up the microphone and gave a rather croaky rendition of "When I'm Sixty-four." John Edwards plays the saxophone and "admires" the Beatles. Former governor Howard Dean plays the harmonica and the guitar and his favorite Beatle is George Harrison. Wesley Clark's favorite album of all time is *Yellow Submarine* (Kerry's is *Abbey Road;* Dennis Kucinich's is *The White Album*). Who can forget Bill Clinton's saxophone solo on *Arsenio Hall?* "There was not only a new sound," said Al Gore, speaking about the Beatles to the editor of *Rolling Stone.* "There was something else that was new with the Beatles. A new sensibility . . . that incredible gestalt they had." The great exception to all this is George W. Bush. He was at Yale from 1964 to 1968, and liked some of the Beatles' first records. "Then they got a bit weird," he has said. "I didn't like all that later stuff when they got strange." Bush also told Oprah Winfrey his favorite song is the Everly Brothers' "Wake Up Little Susie" (1957), but overall, he said, he prefers country music.

The Beatles are the super-boomers' house band. Even people who don't care about popular music—especially those, one might argue—are conscious of how these English songwriters may have harnessed the properties of their own time, or were harnessed by them, down to every teenage sob and every kink of modern marketing. McKinney crunches the facts and pulps the possibilities before tossing everything into a great metaphysical soup, and his book carries sentences not unlike those Norman Mailer used to write forty years ago in the *Village Voice:*

Despite feeling paralyzed at the center of the mania, the Beatles would draw their audience in by pushing it to new places. They would speak contentious, unprecedented words; offer upsetting, incomprehensible images of themselves; make disorienting musical noises. Just as their music would be the best and most challenging they had yet made, their collective persona would be more provocative, richer in dimensions than ambition or circumstance had previously allowed—or required. They would answer and interpret their suddenly hostile world in the language of symbol, the logic of dreaming; and they would, by accident and intent, seduction and aggression, tumult and meditation, sound early shots in the ferocious battle over consciousness which consumed the latter half of their decade.

If this seems a tad overheated, it's only because the writer is very close to the heat: there has never been another group so perpetually *involved* as the Beatles were, and to seek the source of their power is to interrogate the culture of then and now to a degree only just below melting point. You'll forgive the prose for being a bit drugged when you get used to its modes of perception: McKinney is writing about a time, perhaps the first time, that history and society were apt to be understood through the movements of its youth, and McKinney is right for the job so long as one agrees that the occasion calls for something more infiltrating than the objective rigors of Hugh Trevor-Roper.

If you ask anyone what the Beatles sang about, they will say "love" if they're thinking of "Love Me Do" and "She Loves You," or they'll say "loneliness" if they're thinking of "Eleanor Rigby" or "She's Leaving Home." Some people will mention drugs if they're remembering "Strawberry Fields Forever" or "Lucy in the Sky with Diamonds." Those who care about, as it were, crotchets and quavers are known to compare Paul McCartney to Schumann, as Ned Rorem did when he wrote in the *New York Review of Books* in 1968,[3] or liken John Lennon to Chopin. But the true, workaday beauty of the Beatles' words and the music is related to the matter of mutation — the foursome's great theme. They were a wonderful group because they truly inhabited their own ambivalence, making music that grew as it changed, songs that were loaded with an experience of contradiction and exploration. As with many of their contemporaries, they could have remained a charmingly harmonic pop band forever; they could have scattered their perky songs like coins before the crowd and never been resented for it; they could have been Gerry and the Pacemakers. But the individual members of the Beatles spent a decade growing in and out of themselves, moving towards and apart from each other and their fame, until they finally spun into legend.

We take their innovations for granted now, as if those young men had not been real people living in a world of small, actual discoveries, but supersonic characters in a comic strip. Yet when people first bought the album *Revolver* and heard the guitars going backwards, it seemed that some sublime disjunction was taking place and that the Beatles knew something that other people did not. They knew something about their current moment and something about the fantasies of their audience, and that is perhaps the largest single thing to know in show business. While the *Revolver* LP created the impression, *Sgt. Pep-*

---

3. "The Music of the Beatles," January 18, 1968. This was the essay in which Rorem also called the Beatles "cockneys," a designation which thrilled the denizens of East London but caused chaos in the affections of Liverpudlians everywhere. Rorem, by the way, is still unburdening himself on such topics. See the latest volume of his diaries, *Lies* (2000): "All art dates, from the moment it is made," he writes. "Some dates well, some badly. Giotto, *Le Sacre,* the Beatles date well. Beethoven's Ninth, Lautrec, the Rolling Stones date badly. (Pick your own examples: personal taste is risky, even when the argument's solid.)"

*per's Lonely Hearts Club Band* made people feel that the group could offer not just hidden truths but a whole new way of life, and *The White Album* of 1968 seemed to millions like a rather grand echo chamber of moral concerns, from My Lai and civil rights to sexual liberation.

I was born the year that album was released, so it was nothing to do with me at the time, but the album has since come to seem to me the most that can be done with rock music. If Bob Dylan and Lou Reed were more genuinely literary, the Beatles produced more puzzling and penetrating art. "The people gave their money and they gave their screams," said George Harrison, "but the Beatles gave their nervous systems, which is a much more difficult thing to give." In their talk and in their jibes to the press, the Beatles always seemed sweetly at home in themselves, just lads from Liverpool underneath all the mania. But in fact they carried some heady enigmas into the public sphere, not least of them the bringing of English dirt and chaos into the homes of clean-living America. Their career shows a trailblazing democratization of cultural authority. Seventy years before them, what did it take to tinker with the old consciousness? The single-mindedness of Nietzsche? The martyrdom of Oscar Wilde? The almost private experiments of Gustav Mahler? A group of Impressionists? The Beatles had no training, no permission and no great tradition either, but they had their own hungers and the instinct of a popular mandate. The real surprise was how they turned a mirror on that populism, song by song, album by album, in some measure showing their fans the new society that they had begun to constitute.

Four quite ordinary boys from Liverpool. In 1966, in the Philippines, the year after the Marcoses came to power, who do you think was on the flamboyant leader's wish list of artists who could come and appear to confirm his "democratic" revolution? Only one name: the Beatles. The band played a concert but, failing to turn up at a palace function, they were more or less deported, and Brian Epstein, the Beatles' manager, had to pay back their earnings before the plane was allowed to take off. It was perhaps the dangers of excessive populism that Lennon was commenting on when he observed that the Beatles were more popular than Jesus; he was pilloried in America for the statement, but actually he was saying something very straightforward and real. He wasn't calling for the overthrow of religion by rock and roll but, more simply, expressing surprise at the way religion's ancient fantasia had given way to cries for the newer, more prosaic messiahs, a bunch of Merseyside vandals. Nowadays it is no big deal to notice that more young people watch *The Simpsons* than attend church, but in 1966 the insult burrowed into the heart of an American paranoia—American specifically: the comment was actually made to an *Evening Standard* journalist in London, where nobody cared—and the result was that Beatlemania found its dark opposite in people who couldn't burn their images fast enough.

In four years the Beatles had become as complicated as their decade, and by the 1966 American tour things had turned nasty. The America that had both nourished them as English kids and received them as heroes in 1964 was now beginning to buckle under the shock of the new, under the demands and freedoms that forces such as the Beatles had brought into play. Beatlemania ended at that point and something else took its place—the Beatles as soft revolutionaries and agitators, the Beatles as harbingers of strangeness and great changes to come. The songs were showing the Indian influence—also the influence of hallucinogenic drugs—and musical transformation had been the hallmark of that *Revolver* LP of 1966, with its squealing amplifier feedback and lyrical accounts of fear and death and tension.[4]

America behaved that year as if its innocence was being corrupted. "One night on a show in the South somewhere [Memphis] somebody let off a firecracker while we were on stage," said Lennon later. "There had been threats to shoot us, the Klan were burning Beatle records outside and a lot of the crew-cut kids were joining in with them. Someone let off a firecracker and every one of us — I think it's on film — look at each other, because each thought it was the other that had been shot. It was that bad."

Here's McKinney:

The demonstrations were, by one set of symbols, an assertion of white Christian supremacy. By another, they were the most extreme Beatle fantasy yet devised. They showed how far the Beatles had gone in engaging with the world, how deeply they had penetrated even its sickest and most ancient passions, and how complex were the burdens their ambitions had forced them to assume. The burnings were deplorable and stupid, but as a social and mass-psychological reaction to a certain provocation they were not without their logic. Fear of the Beatles and fear of social tolerance were not only compatible; each was implied by the other. At certain points in the '60s, the feelings people had for the Beatles and for the world around them came together and formed a circle — a magic circle, a sphere of fantasy within which mutations of

---

4. Take one song, "She Said She Said," a menacing and regretful track on that album, heralding a very different group from the one that sang "I Wanna Hold Your Hand." "The antithesis of McCartney's impeccable neatness," writes Ian MacDonald in the best account of the Beatles' music, *Revolution in the Head* (1994), "Lennon's anguished 'She Said She Said' is a song of tormented self-doubt struggling in a lopsided web of harmony and metre . . . It draws its inspiration from the day in August 1965 when Lennon took LSD with Roger McGuinn and David Crosby in Los Angeles."

thought were formed, the unimaginable was imagined, and action was taken.

This was clearly not the sixties that everyone experienced – not the sixties of J. Edgar Hoover, for instance, or George W. Bush – but the modern personality the Beatles promulgated is the one that broke the old culture's back. As much as John F. Kennedy, the Beatles brought a new attitude front and center, creating at once a ferocity of love and hatred, the kind of appeal, we now understand, that sometimes finds its resolution at the tip of an assassin's bullet. The Beatles' songs got so complicated they couldn't be played by the band live, and the lyrics, from one album to another, grew very keen to recognize the delirium that lives somewhere inside democracy.

Paul McCartney was the more optimistic and melodic of the pair – and the more shallow, according to conventional wisdom. Lennon could be shallow enough when he wasn't trying – but generally Lennon was the more visionary, seeing terror, and some kind of resignation to terror, as one of the potential out-growths of freedom in our time. Lennon's powerful ambivalence was four-fifths of his genius: "Half of what I say is mean-ingless," he wrote in a song to his dead mother, "but I say it just to reach you." Lennon and McCartney found beauty in chaos, and that is rock and roll's oldest and most natural secret. But in uglier minds, such as Charles Manson's, songs such as "Happi-ness Is a Warm Gun" and "Helter Skelter" became manifestoes for some of the purest and least ambiguous badness known.

America's counterculture was a dark fairy tale, and it was Joan Didion's *The White Album,* a beautiful portrait of the dec-ade's voids and erasures, which brought out, in Flemish detail one might say, the very proximity of that fairy tale to nightmare;

it is a book in which the Beatles' long dance of innocence and experience is fixed and pinned like a butterfly in a glass case. Those boys who met at the church garden fete in Liverpool could hardly have imagined their lyrics would one day end up painted in blood on the walls of Sharon Tate's house on Cielo Drive. "Many people I know in Los Angeles," wrote Didion, "believe that the sixties ended abruptly on August 9, 1969, ended at the exact moment when word of the murders on Cielo Drive traveled like brushfire through the community, and in a sense this is true. The tension broke that day. The paranoia was fulfilled."

McKinney's book maps that development rather brilliantly, and one begins to see exactly how the harmless, tuneful, teeny-bop band of 1962 came, quite alarmingly, over time, to conduct those discordant investigations into death and chaos and crisis in the second half of its career. Where the *Sgt. Pepper* album had been a rather fey acid trip, an escape from social reality into some color-saturated hippie nothingness, the Beatles' *White Album* is the most perfect rock album ever made, one with a social and psychological resonance that people are still conjuring with today. Can an album of rock music do that? Well, nobody really thought so before then, but nobody would doubt it now, especially not those legions who believe so completely in their own buying power as the truest expression of the will to choose life and alter the world. Charles Manson may have been, as McKinney says, jealous of the Beatles' screams, and the band may have awakened in him, as in so many, "a latent sense of entitlement," the certainty "that he had something to say that was worthy of being attended to by those awed millions." For others, the song "Revolution" was a denunciation of student revolt in 1968, a hymn to appeasement in the face of Mayor Daley's storm troopers. In any event, the Beatles had come to seem like moral rabble-rousers whether faced with screaming girls, Jesus freaks, leftist warriors or the FBI. At one time or another, everybody has had at least one good reason to love the Beatles and at least one good reason to hate them. "Radical critics were wrong," writes McKinney,

> in failing to acknowledge that the Beatles had done their bit for the revolution. Had begun doing it when they climbed their first coal wagon as the Quarry Men; had gone on doing it battling the crowd in Hamburg, banging a new sound against the Cavern walls, giving themselves to audience after audience, drawing in one here, alienating another there; and had paid for it in the rain of jelly babies and Manila fists and Jesus hysterics and mad love, in the sacrifice of their safety and the burning of their youth.

A great deal of writing about the 1960s seems to helium-huff its way into intelligibility, but McKinney is right: as journeys for artists go, the Beatles' journey into their time now appears in its own way no less surprising and world-modifying than the developments of Picasso. "I say in speeches that a plausible mission for artists is to make people appreciate being alive at least a little bit," wrote Kurt Vonnegut in *Timequake*. "I am then asked if I know of any artists who pulled that off. I reply, 'The Beatles did.'" The group's story is an inspired dream sequence about self-transformation. Lennon and McCartney were two scruffs with poor school results; they each lost their mothers very young, in those first years in England after the war. Your mother is dead, your world is bombed and dirty. What are you going to do? That's the question. And the simple answer—"we're going to pick up our guitars and change the world"—now acts like an unconscious mantra for generations who take their entitlement for granted, including those people whose busy, sixties-experienced shadows begin to spread over everything, from the carpets in the House of Lords to those lawns just in front of the White House.

*May 2004*

# On Lad Magazines

A SPOKESMAN ADMITS THAT the cancellation of the Saturday-night sleeper from London to Aberdeen "until the end of time" is a bitter blow for those who like to wake up on a Sunday morning to the munching of Highland cattle, but there can be no question of having the train back, say the men at Euston. They can't find a single soul who'll agree to work the shift.

"It was like an alcoholic bullet flying through the night," a former guard says, poetically. "You just couldn't cope with those guys on their stag nights. That's what did it. The buffet car was a cesspool. They were climbing into the berths with Christ knows who. It was madness. They'd pull the emergency cord. They'd fling the bog roll down the aisles. They'd vomit. Break guitars over each other's heads. You can't be having that on a nice train." You'll find the same sentiment echoing around the hostelries of Dublin's Temple Bar, where stag nights have been banned, proprietors believing that the Ryanair generation has made a mockery of the art of running amok. Over on cheap flights from Prestwick and Stansted, these boys were often to be found floating trouserless in the Liffey at dawn, or staggering up Grafton Street, their T-shirts clinging to them with alcopops and spilled sambuca.

Britain's newsstands are heaving with magazines devoted to the rough magic of being a bloke. On first sight you think they are what my friends used to call scud mags; the girls who adorn the covers — legs wide, breasts atumble, nipples fit for pegging a couple of wet duffle coats on — tend to be among the nearly famous, a tribe of models admired by laddish editors for their friendly shagability and the hunger in their eyes. The market for male "general interest" magazines has grown massively in the UK, as if young men suddenly needed to be celebrated and serviced in a new way, as if there were a new demand among them for reassurance about the wonders of male normalcy. They look for all this in the way people like Tony Parsons have taught them, in a spirit of soft-core irony and hard-core sentiment. But apart from reassurance and a sort of avenging pride, what are these magazines selling to their readers? With their grisly combinations of sensitivity and debasement — "How to Bathe Your New Baby" vs. "Win the Chance to Pole-Dance with Pamela!" — it may be time to consider whether these men's magazines aren't just the latest enlargement on the old fantasy of men having everything they want to have and finding a way to call it their destiny.

*Stag & Groom* magazine is edited by a woman who has no end of tolerance for the male love of male company. She has the modern lifestyle writer's addiction to life as it might be lived in a pink paperback, and that means her men are allowed to be very bad and also to know that their badness is quite lovable. But maybe she's just having a monumental laugh. "Stags!" she writes in the editorial of the second issue:

Are you doing all you should? Have you partaken of sufficient extreme sports, fine dining and wild women to ensure that your sense of adventure is fully sated in advance of the big day? Have you, in short, succeeded in scaring yourselves silly enough to be ready for a little marital peace and harmony? No? Well, what the deuce are you waiting for, old boy? Get out there in the mud and allow your dearest friends to shoot seven shades of crap out of you. When you've finished, it's your stagly duty to adjourn to a fine establishment for haute cuisine, Courvoisier and Cuban cigars, perhaps followed by some clinical observations of the gentler sex at play.

The "old boy" thing—as well as the advertisements for honeymoons in the Maldives and for Mayfair jewelers—might suggest *Stag & Groom*'s target readers are a level or two up the social scale from the alcopopoholics, but the thing about new laddishness is that it has something of Tony Blair's classless, open-palmed, universalizing, "we are all feeling this pain together" baloney (an attitude that understands courage to be a strong mixture of earnestness and easily available empathy), so the magazine will speak to every marriageable young fellow who is happy to see himself as just another upholder of simple truths about modern men and how we are. A gentleman's magazine of the old sort could rely on the notion that nobody confused gentlemen and guttersnipes, but it is fashionable now for grandees to drink pints and plebs to drink champagne, allowing *Stag & Groom* to do its thing in an untroubled way, talking about football and chest-waxing in the same quick breath, murmuring piously about the best man's duties and the wisdom of choosing the Lotus Elise as a wedding car, as if the trials of manhood were a holy pilgrimage, as if, indeed, the rites of male vanity were aspects of a religion into which we have all very recently been born again.

After reading a few issues of the newest men's weeklies, *Zoo* and *Nuts,* I began to wonder if the readers of these magazines might want to have sex with their chums. It's like men who want to sleep with their best friend's wife: why don't they just cut out the decoy? *Zoo* presents a world of men joined by the same desire, not for the same women (though they wouldn't say no), but for a community of leering men. All these magazines are, in the end, about providing a sense of belonging, but few are as blatant in their invitation to the fantasy of tribal kinship as *Zoo,* which runs a regular item called "Guilty Wanks: Toss Off and Then Think About What You've Just Done." The list underneath, detailing the people readers are ashamed of thinking about when they're having sex with themselves, includes the child pop group S Club 8, "*National Geographic* bare-breasted tribeswomen," Natalie Portman in the film *Leon* and "your best mate's girlfriend." *Zoo* loves the notion that all men are the same at heart: dirty and funny and fucked-up and violent, slaves to their needs and not ashamed — the articles about football brutality snuggle up quite naturally with "The Ten Sexiest Rears in the World." The editors borrow the notion of male universality from the spirit of Britain under Blair, but the unfunny barbarism of the magazine's content shows there are still differences between men, if only in degree.

You'll find that no pride is greater than the pride that comes with being thick. Britain is filled with people who are really proud of their stupidity. I'm surprised *Nuts* hasn't made this its rubric — "We're Thick. And Everybody Else Is a Tosser" — yet, for all that, it wears its density more or less lightly. It favors stories about gangland hitmen (Brian "The Milkman" Wright, "during his drug-dealing days he always delivered"; John "Goldfinger" Palmer, once "one of Britain's richest men, owning a fleet of private planes, helicopters, boats and cars"), and every few pages there's a soap star in her knickers, usually followed by a report, written with barely contained excitement, about a massive pileup on some notorious bend of a foreign racetrack. A delicately positioned article called "Please Smash Me in the Face!" accompanies photographs of a bloodstained skinhead with a face like a plate of steak tartare:

> Being thrown head first into a barbed-wire fence doesn't sound like much fun — but this senseless gibbon does it as his hobby. During a blood-spattered Backyard Wrestling match between shaven-headed fighter Karnage and his rival Sic, Karnage was repeatedly smashed in the face with a strip light then elbow-dropped onto a bed of barbed wire and cacti.

Alas, poor Karnage. The popularity of *Nuts* is, in some ways, as hard to understand as the success of the *Sun* — unless you take it for granted that a frightening percentage of young British men are sociopaths. In that sense, *Nuts* and *Zoo* are closer to their tabloid newspaper cousins than to other men's magazines. Mostly, though, what they resemble are mad-dog football fanzines and the kinds of websites that carry pictures of suicide victims.

The thirst for a beery men's magazine — not a girly magazine, but something that could both celebrate and make common cause with men's worst habits — was first attended to ten years ago with the inauguration of *Loaded*. The anniversary campaign last month featured billboards across the country showing a large-breasted girl with the words "Loaded: Ten Years Fighting for Feminism" printed across her skimpy top. The cover of the June issue offers free beer and Durex, but my copy just contained a packet of Extra Strong Mints, which I'm trying not to take personally. *Loaded* tries to be bubbly about its degeneracy, but it's mostly a jokeless, pulpless exercise in self-abuse. Of course it tends to like lagers and motors, fighting and hooligans, and imagines the rest of the world is fraudulent and missing out because it has other things on its mind. What's sad about the magazine is that, despite its defensive bluster, it has no convictions to be courageous about, and there's nothing in its contents worth attacking. It shows as many pictures as it can of coy girls concealing their nipples, and sandwiches these between rubbishy little sections flogging after-shave. *Loaded,* too, likes the notion that it's conducting a conversation with real men, a conversation that needs very few words. Yet the British lad magazine is not about men at all, or about the business of being a grown-up person; it's fueled by a childish notion of hedonism — pills, thrills and bellyaches — which sees politics as a mug's game and wives as a curse. They may be right about that, but if so, they are right in a fairly boring way: no man older than twenty-one wants to be told he's a failure unless he lives like George Best. And that's *Loaded*'s central anxiety: it exhibits a very British smallness of style in its understanding of male recklessness, and its world of Saturday nights is really a lament for passions spent or never experienced.

So why are men's magazines in Britain so largely devoted to a tittering schoolboy's understanding of life and laughter? In America, where publications such as *Esquire* and *GQ* originated, men's magazines weren't scuzzy in the way ours are, and quite often they were venues for some of the country's best and most expensive journalism. *Playboy* and *Esquire,* particularly, could produce, and have, anthologies of first-rate political and cultural journalism, and even this month, when the newish British lad mag *Jack* flags on its cover "A Speed Special Starring Fast Planes, Bikes and Women," the much-derided *Playboy* advertises a long piece by Gore Vidal on God and the state. *Jack* runs a piece about British wrestling in which even the writer seems completely bored with the subject:

> I ask Keith to tell me the difference between the British wrestler and the new breed of Americans who seem to have moved wrestling on a notch. Apart, of course, from one being built on steak puddings and the other on steroids. "British wrestling is somewhere the family can go and have a good night out. It represents a typical good night's entertainment," says Keith.
>
> When the ring is up the wrestlers hurry into the dressing rooms to get changed. The audience is already arriving. There will be 100 to 150 people, mainly made up of friends and family and a few obligatory old ladies sucking on boiled sweets. As the audience shuffle in carrying chairs I scan a borrowed running sheet.

Say what you like about the 1960s, and say what you like about America: the original *Esquire* would have sent George Plimpton to write about the wrestling, and would have given him space for twenty thousand words. It's hard to know what *Jack*'s editors are offering readers, or how they look at the world. Perhaps they're just fed up and *Jack* is a magazine for fed-up blokes, or a magazine edited by people who are badly hung-over from reading *Loaded*. In any event, when a men's magazine lacks care and conviction to this extent — when even its pieces on Italian football and foreign bloodbaths are stale — you begin to ask yourself if the British male it's supposed to attract isn't perhaps a little disastrous. Is he tired? Is he upset? Is he depressed?

Nostalgia and small-mindedness are among the most exhausting things to hum a tune about, but so is loneliness, and a lot of what you see when you look into these magazines is men being confused about what to make of themselves. If you look closely at the stuff, you see how many of the men either writing or being written about associate aging with isolation: the smell of fear rises out of the after-shave ads and the free sachets of facial scrub on every other page. Who am I? What am I becoming, and can I stand it? *Esquire,* which tends to be the best written of these publications, and which maintains its connection to its own traditions by running the odd piece you might care to read, has a copy of Jonathan Franzen's essays to give away with the current number. It still has some "Sexy but Deadly" microceleb on the cover, but inside, the anxieties I've been talking about are more humanly displayed. Henry Sutton writes about being a "Broken-up Man." It starts with him crying in front of his seven-year-old daughter:

> A friend of mine keeps ringing me up to say that being a bloke and getting divorced means I'm on a one-way ticket to a bedsit in Balham. "You'll get screwed," he says. Having spoken to a couple of lawyers, having realised how things are stacked against me legally, well, yes, I probably am going to get screwed. I'm screwed already. I'm 40. I'm totally broke and I'm almost homeless. How the fuck did I let this happen?

A few years ago Robert Bly celebrated the notion of men running into the woods to beat their own chests, but many of the newer bibles of male self-realization unwittingly celebrate something else: the notion that men might flee to the big cities and grow their own breasts. At any rate, there is a very strenuous blend of women-envy in some of the magazines for men. Richard Wollheim has just finished telling us, in *Germs,* his frighteningly good memoir, about wanting to be a woman sixty years ago. "I knew that what I wanted," he wrote, "was, not so much to have her, though I also wanted that, as to be her." And later: "The way to a woman's heart, I had come to believe, was along the hard, stony, arduous track of effeminacy."

Another kind of men's magazine has been busy turning that arduous track into the primrose path. *GQ*, like the others, always has a glossy girl on the cover, but the magazine is actually quite gay, at least in the sense that the late Ian Hamilton used the term. Hamilton thought it was gay to look left and right when you crossed the road, and he thought it was gay for men to blow-dry their hair. This went on for a while, until one day he made the point to Martin Amis that it was actually quite gay to sleep with a woman. *GQ* is gay in that way: it appears to envy women more than lust for them, and its pages are full of tips on how men should depilate, breast-enlarge, slicken, tart up and generally make themselves a bit more attractive to members of the non-opposite sex.

On one page, the film director Eli Roth, described as the maker of the "body-horror-in-the-woods" movie *Cabin Fever* (nothing to do with Robert Bly), says: "I'm a closet metrosexual. I try to look like I've just rolled out of bed but the truth of the matter is I have spent thousands of dollars on Kiehl's products. Plus, when girls come over, my stock of Kiehl's is the deal-breaker for them spending the night." Then there's an article about the latest sex thing: from Japan, obviously, and now big in America, called bukkake, where men don't have sex with women but all stand around together in a room and masturbate over the girl. Then there's a piece about the joy of not wearing underpants. The agony uncle makes Quentin Crisp look like Charles Bronson, or is it Charles Bronson like Quentin Crisp? "Quilt covers or eiderdowns?" an anxious letter writer asks. "Blinds or curtains? Carpet or wooden flooring? Wallpaper or paint? Wall lights or free-standing lamps? Mirrored or wooden wardrobes? I've just got my first house and need some advice on how to decorate my bedroom. I don't want to put the ladies off."

"You could use sacks as blankets," comes the reply, "have bin bags as curtains, spray graffiti on the walls, only have a torch for a light—ANYTHING as long as you don't install mirrored wardrobes." Later on, there's a two-page spread of the young actor James Franco's lips. That's *Gentlemen's Quarterly* for you: a magazine for men who want to have what women have—clean nails, hairless chests, fresh armpits and moist lips. A magazine for men clever enough to want to look like the kind of person they're supposed to want to sleep with themselves. And seeing as half the people who read *GQ* probably do sleep with themselves, this might be considered sound editorial policy.

Since good-looking naked men started appearing on the covers of magazines aimed at men, the incidence of bulimia among British males has risen by 100 percent. Women still account for more than 90 percent of bulimia sufferers, and of the men a great proportion are gay, but the numbers are also going up for men in general, as if to confirm what the experts always said about the pressure exerted by images of the perfect on the imperfect. The June issue of *Men's Health* offers Britain's eager blokes the chance to "Be Built Like Brad Pitt." The magazine shows men how to have sex, how to shave, how to book a holiday, but mainly—relentlessly—how to change the shape of their bodies, always accompanied by pictures of men with chests as broad and pert as the plains of Montana. Of course, women have been putting up with this sort of harassment for years, and perhaps the success of *Men's Health*—among those of us who love it, and the figures are rising—is God's way of torturing us with unguents, dumbbells, fancy toothbrushes and canoes, to make up for years of magazines telling women about the need-fulness of dieting if you want to keep your man, with helpful pictures of the smilingly skinny. I've heard men saying the men in *Men's Health* make them sick: they don't mean they disapprove of them, they mean they disapprove of themselves in relation to them, and that's a comeuppance. The threat of the male gaze has been making many women and gay men ill for years, but men's magazines show that the threat has now become general enough to be counted a cultural worry. All men now experience other men's looks, and that is one of the anxieties these magazines sometimes exploit and sometimes suppress.

All the men in *Arena Homme Plus* look like Greta Garbo, like Marlene Dietrich, or like women done up to look like Valentino. The editors declare that they edited the issue — "The Boys of Summer" — with photographs of Hollywood legends pinned to the wall, and the result is perhaps the highest form of camp you'll encounter this season, unless you happen to be a roadie on Cher's next "farewell tour" of Britain. Fashion is answerable to nothing but fashion, and male vanity has a million fresh occasions every day, so the fact that the men in *Homme Plus* dribble over one another and rest their hair-gelled heads on one another's shaved chests should be no great cause for worry. It's just a prettier version of the sort of thing that used to happen on the London-to-Aberdeen sleeper every Saturday night.

*June 2004*

# Four Funerals and a Wedding

WHEN I WAS YOUNG, people didn't die and they didn't pass away. They certainly didn't expire, or perish, though there was a woman in our street called Hazel who dabbled in spiritualism while her philandering husband went out to fix people's Hotpoint twin-tubs, and she quite often spoke of people who had "crossed to the other side." I thought that was sick. Hazel had a lot of anger in her, as people now say, and I felt that must explain her hazardous use of words. She'd met Sandy, her husband, when he drove one of the Alexander buses about the town of Elgin. She happened to be the clippy on the same bus, and she would often tell me about the beauty of those single-decker vehicles ("the Bluebird") and the handsomeness of Sandy behind the wheel. Now she was furious all the time, and took it out on her accordion, playing Strathspey reels until the red varnish flaked off her fingernails.

In our town it was all in the words. Nobody was ever "dearly" anything, certainly not "departed." "Deceased" seemed a bit high and mighty, even allowing for the fact that in Scotland everyone's station is slightly raised by their having enjoyed, if you will, the process of personal death. People in my childhood found the word "death" unsayable, and got round it by saying, of someone whose corpse lay in the next room, that "something had happened."

"If anything ever happens to me," my mother would say, "you'll find the Liverpool Assurance policy book in the cupboard up above the stock cubes."

"If something happens to me," my grandmother said, "don't put me up in that Dalbeth Cemetery. It's a cold place."

And my father too. "If anything ever happens to me, you'll know what life's all about."

"What do you mean 'if'?" I would say. "Why can't you just say 'when I die'?"

"You think you're that smart," my granny would say. "But that's just a morbid thing, to use that word."

"Death!"

"Don't say it! It's a horrible word."

"Death!"

"Stop it," my mother would say. "I hate talking like this, but if something happens to me . . ."

"What do you mean 'if'? And what do you mean 'something'? The thing that will happen to you is called death, and there's no ifs or buts about it."

"He's so pessimistic, him, isn't he?" my granny would say. "Always had a dark side. Probably got it from his uncle John. He was like that as well. Morbid."

"You're just trying to draw attention to yourself," my father would say. "If something ever happens to you, I suppose you'll want one of them statues to yourself up in the Glasgow Necropolis."

"Yes," I said. "The sign could say: 'Up here, something did

happen to Andrew O'Hagan. Like each of us, he wondered if it would happen. And it did.'"

Something happened to my second-ever schoolteacher, Mrs. Wallace. We saw her totally somethinged in her coffin under a huge crucifix of Jesus Christ, to whom, by the look of the nails and the blood running down his arms and toes, there might also have been a question of something happening. Mrs. Wallace was a champion smoker and worrier of rosary beads. She took a liking to me, giving me the not entirely popular task of writing pupils' names on the blackboard if they spoke while she was out having a fag. I was so unremitting and keen with the chalk that Mrs. Wallace figured me to be a potential candidate for the priesthood; she got me my first gig ringing the bell on the altar at St. Winnin's, though a combination of sleepiness and professional jealousy on my part was to harm my chances of advancement in the eyes of Father McLaughlin.

Mrs. Wallace's funeral was my first one, and in some senses no funeral could ever have the same intensity, not even my own, in the event that anything should ever happen to me. I sat through the funeral mass, at age seven, in a state of shock, with all the pasty-faced solemnity of a Pre-Raphaelite mourner confronting the eternal, my intense concentration broken only for a second by the gentle passing of the family, who I knew instantly must be counted the stars of the occasion, each of them, top to toe, in respectful, chalk-free, something-comprehending black. My seniority in the diocese was not marked by an invitation to the graveside, but I did go there two years later, taking the bus to a populous cemetery in the small town of Stevenson. Mrs. Wallace's spot was up against the right-hand wall, deep in the shadow of the Ardeer Explosives Factory. Of course, something has since happened to the factory and its cooling towers too, but I remember their real presence in that Stevenson graveyard. In a tangle of crosses and angels it said on the gravestone "Mary Wallace," the chiseled words seeming to embody in some powerful and menacing way the mysteries of faith.

In the via Monserrato, a few weeks before the death of Pope John Paul II, the light seemed yellow against the rain, and Rome seemed a place not of eternities but of passing trade. Cardinal Cormac Murphy O'Connor entered the restaurant in his civilian uniform of open-necked shirt and windcheater, smiling to the waiters and taking his usual table. I didn't approach him, but took time to notice the high-spiritedness of his friends, happy to be in the company of the head of the English Catholics, a man not given to any obvious show of relaxation but, rather, seeming constantly anxious about being behind with business.

Nearby is the English College, or the Venerable English College, as its fan base likes to call it. Father Clive was waiting on the steps for me. He was in his late twenties, very neat, soft-toned and red-cheeked, and he welcomed me into the building in the manner of someone obeying time and tradition, naming the exact moment on his watch before telling me I was the latest visitor in a tradition of literary visitors stretching back to John Milton. He said it very kindly, but I wanted to laugh. However, something high in his red cheeks warned me neither to laugh nor to make any reference to *Paradise Lost.* I simply smiled and composed my wits and followed him over the black and claret tiles to the Martyrs' Chapel.

"This is a fourteenth-century floor," Father Clive said. "The college is the oldest of all English institutions abroad." He showed me a little pond in the garden where students swam in the hot months. They called it "the tank," and it conveyed to me an image of passengers bathing in the swimming pool of a sinking ship. But the mood of the college did not suggest sinking: there is a form of religious devotion which can, at a certain time in the evening in a place such as Rome, seem to shape the very air itself, though I presume only Catholics could suppose so. In any event, the English College had the kind of peacefulness that ancientness alone can bestow — the young men walked the halls knowing the world they walked in possessed the texture of meditation and martyrdom, of prayers uttered and strong beliefs confirmed. Yet round the corner in the Campo de' Fiori, the statue of Giordano Bruno stands high above a modern center of bar snacks, designer scarves and trendy beers, a statue reminding those who care to be reminded that modernity has its martyrs too.

My paternal grandmother ran a fish shop in Glasgow that had nothing on the walls but a framed print of the dying Christ. She used to tell children that they should mind to behave themselves, because — and she'd point at the picture — "that's what he got for being good." My grandmother took the modern world to be a simple affront to her sense of right and wrong; Protestants were barbarians to her mind, and she refused to attend my cousin's wedding when he married one. I remember the conversation. My father said to her, "Do you hate Pakis as well?"

"No, Gerald," she replied. "I don't hate anybody. I've never stepped inside a Protestant church in my life and I'm not going to start doing it now."

I once wrote some words on a piece of paper and pushed them to her across the sofa. They said: "You like authority more than freedom." She just looked at me. I like to think that inside the moment that contained the look, she told me, without saying anything, that I was trouble. My father had once thrown a lemonade bottle through her window, and that was a kind of trouble she could dislike but understand. Her look told me that my kind of trouble was worse. She looked away and crumpled up the paper and put it on the fire.

I was ten years old when John Paul II came to power. My granny instantly adored him, loving his feudal side without reservation and simply ignoring the freedom-upholding aspect. The only thing she was truly agnostic about was politics: she never mentioned that, and her only concern when it came to sports was whether Celtic was likely to beat Rangers. She had no worries about communism, though; she worried about poor people and she came from poor people, but that was it, except she might say that poor Protestants had brought it on themselves with a well-known aversion to a day's work. She didn't live long enough to see John Paul II's visit to Glasgow and his giant mass in Bellahouston Park. (She missed it by a year.) "There is one Lord," he said on that occasion, "one faith, one baptism, and one God who is father of us all, all over, through all and within all." She would have levitated with pleasure at that line, and the whole business of him saying it in Glasgow would have represented to her a victory far greater than anything achieved at Bannockburn.

The night before the pope died, Rome became a great character in its own fiction, seizing and displaying all parts of itself to the world's television cameras. But two rather complicated images of Rome came back to me. The first was of Dorothea Brooke stuck in the via Sistina while her husband worked all day in the Vatican Library. George Eliot gave us to believe that Dorothea felt bleached and drained of blood by the ruins, basilicas and colossi of Rome, those "long vistas of white forms whose marble eyes seemed to hold the monstrous light of an alien world." For the new Mrs. Casaubon, Rome's spiritual splendor, its role as a historic center, could only suck the color from the present day, and I wondered, looking at those two high, lighted windows in the pope's apartments, whether there wasn't something overblown and cinematic about the event of his death, like the drama of the great operas which can sometimes seem the wrong sort for the small human business at hand. An old man was dying in those rooms; the pomp of history had the will to rob the matter of its most present sadness.

"Dorothea all her life," George Eliot wrote, "continued to see the vastness of St. Peter's, the huge bronze canopy, the excited intention in the attitudes and garments of the prophets and evangelists in the mosaics above, and the red drapery . . . spreading itself everywhere like a disease of the retina." On the day of the funeral the Church showed much of the strength that lies in its hierarchical weave. The coffin had layers too, cypress and zinc inside oak, and was flanked by scarlet cardinals who themselves were flanked by purple bishops and black-clad dignitaries, in the folds of which stood Cherie Blair with her mantilla blowing in the wind, and further in again, the Bushes looking bored and slightly vexed as they always do abroad, him especially, forever scanning the middle distance for un-American mirages. Fold within fold the dignitaries stood, queens, princes, heathen courtiers, and in some dark pocket at the outer edge the future king of England lowered his eyes to shake the hand of Robert Mugabe.

We live in cultish times — not to say occultist ones — in which it seems not unreasonable for people, en masse, to weep in the streets for public figures they previously cared little about. Pope John Paul II was pretty much like that himself, creating more saints than any other pope, and so it appeared natural that thousands of mourners interrupted the funeral with cries of "Santo Subito!" The papers said the mourners were mostly Poles, but in fact they were mainly Italians, giving him back a little bit of what he gave them: an excited neediness for suprahuman entitlement. There was a great deal of clapping as Cardinal Joseph Ratzinger offered his words of appreciation to the dead pontiff. Clapping is the way it is always done nowadays, clapping in church, clapping by roadsides, as if a surge of assent had no outlet bar through the palms. What is a saint these days but a celebrity whose fame is guaranteed forever? And so we have it: applause, the currency of fame.

"Shhh, we are in a church," Anita Ekberg says as she climbs to St. Peter's dome in *La Dolce Vita.* "This is where I want to write my name," she says, and the photographers chase her up the steps with flashbulbs popping. Ekberg at the top of St. Peter's basilica, as much as her dip in the Trevi fountain, looking almost bleached with attention, is an image of public-personhood becoming a sort of religion. Her hat is blown off and she giggles as it falls down to St. Peter's Square, to the place where the princes of the Church and the princes of the world now attend this funeral, watched in their turn by cameras from every corner of the earth.

The very best ironies live their lives inside other ironies. Henry VIII changed his relationship with the Catholic Church so as to enable himself to marry his chosen bride. (Sadly, something happened to her.) Five hundred years later, Prince Charles changes the date of his wedding to his chosen bride so as to attend the funeral of the head of the Catholic Church. We can be sure of only one dissimilarity between these two English royals: Henry wasn't forced into his decision by a fear of the *Daily Mail.* Charles, like Henry, has come to find fame despicable, and also to find himself shadowed by the public image of a dead former wife, but unlike his Tudor forebear, he appears to have no ability to force his will, allowing every potential show of principle to appear like a fluttering of small resentments.

It may be the chief characteristic of the Windsor dynasty, this ability to make grand things small. The British poet laureate Andrew Motion wrote a poem for the wedding which rather effectively takes them out of the great tide of history and into the more local business of the heart,

> *. . . which slips and sidles like a stream*
> *Weighed down by winter-wreckage near its source —*
> *But given time, and come the clearing rain,*
> *Breaks loose to revel in its proper course.*

This was nicely said, more nicely said than the matter was achieved, as Charles and Camilla Parker-Bowles came down Windsor High Street to the Guildhall in the style of two people going to a Saturday-morning jumble sale, their hearts not yet very obviously reveling in their proper course but still detained by the weight of year-round wreckage. As they emerged from their car, a local steel band tried to add lightness, and cover a few boos, with a rendition of "Congratulations," a song once sung by Cliff Richard to remind people that happiness is a feeling constantly under threat from the songs that celebrate it. "Beautiful white dress," the woman from the BBC said.

"Hardly white," the person beside me said. "She's got two huge children."

"It wasn't quite white," said Trinny, one of those women off *What Not to Wear.* "More like oyster."

There's a bit of bunting round the pubs and a few grannies waving Union Jacks and eating buns. No tea trays. No street parties. In almost every respect it was like the suburban wedding of two elderly people who got it wrong the first time around.

Camilla did look happy: she's the sort of person who goes to lunch with her daughter and steals her chips and smokes her cigarettes, so she must be fine. She and Charles signed the register on a little table below a stained-glass window bearing the legend of George VI and the year 1951, when Charles was three years old and his mother was four years married, still a princess in a world before British steel bands and Cliff Richard.

"Here they come," the BBC said.

"Oh, they look a bit awkward," said James Whitaker, Royal Expert. "Oh, well. Never mind. She's finally got him in her grip."

"I don't think I am wallowing in exuberant excitement," said Piers Morgan, former editor of the *Daily Mirror.* "I think there will be a sigh of relief among the public that there is now some legitimacy about this couple." Mr. Morgan managed to be consistently polite about the royal pair, quite forgetting, perhaps, the stuff about Camilla he'd included in his book of diaries, *The Insider.* At one point in the book he describes having lunch with William and his mother. "Oh, Mummy, it was hilarious," he has William say about a television show. "They had a photo of Mrs. Parker-Bowles and a horse's head and asked what the difference was. The answer was that there isn't any." Morgan adds: "Diana absolutely exploded with laughter."

Everybody at the royal wedding was watching everybody else to such an extent that the BBC commentator Sophie Raworth dressed in a dutiful pea-green suit by Caroline Charles, entirely lost her footing when Piers Morgan pointed out that she was wearing exactly the same outfit as Virginia Parker-Bowles, the second wife of Camilla's first husband. Raworth was clearly put out that something so suitable for her own foxy self should be thought appropriate for Granny Frump, and went unprofessionally silent for a while. It used to be that the British public looked on these occasions with a subject's sense of inclusion, seeing clearly their own role and their own station in the whole affair. Now they watch as one might watch a freak show or a procession of soap stars, which is more or less the same thing.

"Eeeeech," the person next to me said as the guests arrived. "He's got super-posh hair! Like sparse candyfloss. Look at these people, they're so well bred they're practically wraiths. Look. No hips at all."

"They don't look especially clean," I said.

"Yes," she said. "That's super-posh. Like the Queen Mother, who didn't do anything about her little brown teeth. In that respect they're like the working-class people who love them."

"They can't help it," I said.

"Yes they can. They're just out of touch. Everybody's got fabulous teeth now. Diana had great teeth. These skinny men are all a terrible throwback."

"With bad teeth."

"Yeah. Toilet teeth. Eeeeech! There's Trudi Styler. She's super-dirty. Look at her loving the camera. Oh, look at her. She just wants to lift up her skirt and do it."

During the blessing in St. George's Chapel, Grieg's "Last Spring" from *Two Elegiac Melodies* bled into Wordsworth's "Immortality" ode, and Camilla stood at the altar wearing a hat which put one in mind of a cross between Julius Caesar and the Statue of Liberty, a combination appropriate, perhaps, to her position in the royal household. Generally, however, the white suburban theme managed very well to survive the austere beauty of the fifteenth-century chapel. The groom cajoled his bride to remember her words, the young guests waved and blew kisses, the mother-in-law sat through the whole thing with a face like fizz, the buses waited outside to take everyone to the reception—"pragmatic, pragmatic, pragmatic," the BBC said—and the people outside looked exactly like people who hadn't waited outside all night for a place at the front (as people did in their thousands when Charles married Diana), but, rather, as if they'd stopped for a peek on their way to Sainsbury's. The royals walked out of the chapel to the theme music from *Antiques Roadshow*, or was it Handel's *Water Music*?

Saul Bellow seemed to me to possess more moral luster than your average pope, but then I only read him, I didn't marry him, as five people did. The pope and Saul Bellow were enemies of nihilism in one form or another, and I would have given anything to hear a conversation between the two, the Pole so miniature in his certainties on the one side, and the novelist so grand with his Russian genes and his American talk, so large in his openness to being absolutely sure about nothing. Great writers are fonts of ambivalence, and the coverage of Bellow's death (a subject he had covered very precisely himself) seemed allied to his greatest efforts as a maker of life on the page. Bellow was better at seeing things—the true good and the true bad in things—than the routines of politics and religions would have allowed him to be. No one said it, but he was always at his least imaginative when he offered his political opinions.

Lying between the West and Connecticut rivers, the town of Brattleboro, Vermont, was built on modest profits from water and music. It was a resort town before the Civil War, famous for the "water cure" at the Brattleboro Hydropathic Establishment, which drew on the pure springs along Whetstone Brook. The town later produced reed organs—"providing music for the whole of America"—but the once flourishing factories of the Estey Organ Company are closed now, the buildings empty in their acres, representing in that windowless way a complete view on another time.

Saul Bellow's funeral took place in the Jewish section of the town's large cemetery. Brattleboro has a complicated relationship with still waters, but the rabbi made reference to them in both Hebrew and English, via Psalm 23. Bellow's imagination was no stranger to the valley of the shadow of death; that same shadow picks out the true lineaments of Herzog or Citrine or Albert Corde — "death," Bellow said, was "the black backing on the mirror that allows us to see anything at all." Still, it is not easy to think of Bellow's grave, the people there putting a soul to rest whose excellence had lain in its modern restlessness.

A friend of mine tells me there were about sixty at the grave. The rabbi explained that Bellow had asked for a traditional Jewish burial — quite spare and simple. He also said that Bellow had wanted them to finish the job, that his funeral should not be merely figurative, that each person at the graveside was to throw a shovel of dirt onto the coffin. The family went first, using the shovel, then came Philip Roth, who threw the soil into the grave with his hands. Almost everyone else went up to pick up the shovel. "What was remarkable," my friend said, "was that one was reminded of the sheer labor it takes to replace all that soil. For half an hour, it must have been, there was silence, as we dug into the mound and threw the earth onto the coffin."

In Rome, as the wind fluttered the pages of Holy Writ laid on top of the pope's coffin, it seemed, for all the hosannas, that the coffin contained someone who had spent many years denouncing the reality of the world in favor of an elevated fiction. Yet, of the two men, of the two imaginations, who could argue that Bellow was not the real pro-lifer? It might be counted a shame, considering the size of his constituency, that the pope never saw the funny side of eternity, a side that even Bellow's minor characters were apt to cozy up to. But still it is hard to think of all that invention and hilarity encoffined.

Prince Rainier of Monaco believed in miracles. "Either prayer works or it doesn't," he once said. "And I believe it works." With these words he made his way to Lourdes in the mid-1950s in the company of his personal priest, an American, Father Francis Tucker, to pray to Mary the Blessed Mother for the safe delivery to him of a good and beautiful Catholic bride. Grace Kelly was the answer to his prayers: "I want to thank you for showing the prince what an American Catholic girl can be," Father Tucker wrote to the Hollywood star, "and for the very deep impression this has left on him."

When Kelly left New York on the SS *Constitution,* on April 4, 1956, she was turning her back, as the newspapers liked to say, on Hollywood dreams in order to live a real-life fairy tale. But there were more than a hundred reporters on board the ship, a fact which begins to tell you how her tale was also a nightmare. Like Anita Ekberg's climb to St. Peter's dome, Grace Kelly's wedding a decade earlier was a dramatic moment — a poetic moment, one might say — in the destruction of private life. In 1981, a year before she died, Kelly attended a gala event in London and stood next to Diana, the new Princess of Wales, who wept on the older princess's arm when they went to the loo. "Don't worry, dear," the former actress said, "it will only get worse."

Flags were tied back with black ribbons, coastal waters were off-limits to all shipping, the casinos were closed, and Monte Carlo's manhole covers were sealed against the possibility of terrorists the day they buried Prince Rainier. The fort above the bay sent cannon fire into the empty waters, and half the principality's six thousand residents lined the road to the cathedral, the building where Rainier Grimaldi married Grace Kelly fifty years earlier and where he was soon to join her remains in the family crypt. Several of the dignitaries were suffering from Eurolag — Rome, London, Windsor, Monaco — but *Monaco-Matin* declared it "an intimate but planetary funeral."

The Grimaldis have brought more libel and invasion-of-privacy lawsuits than any other family in Europe. Where the cardinals in Rome had almost strutted for CNN, Monaco's female royals hid behind black lace headscarves, crying alongside Barber's Adagio for Strings, seemingly exhausted by loss and a lifetime's trial by cameras. Prince Rainier got his sweet Catholic girl and people got their fairy tale, but strangely, under the arc lights and the pageant colors signifying seven hundred years of continuous reign, the Grimaldis looked done-in, as if they had come to realize that love was not the story after all. Prince Albert stared through the mass, and I wondered if that look on his face did not acknowledge the fact that his life was not his own. The funeral was not a celebration of love but another reckoning with cruel fate. "History is the history of cruelty," Herzog said. "Not love, as soft men think."

This has been an odd fortnight for the authorities. New lights have appeared in the Vatican apartments. The tombs are sealed and Cardinal Ratzinger has mounted the throne as Pope Benedict XVI. In Brattleboro, trains trundle past the cemetery and summer visitors begin to stand in line for the Estey Organ Company Museum. The casinos are open in Monte Carlo, and private boats once again take their own chances with romance and death in the clear blue of the Mediterranean. The bunting is down in Windsor High Street, and children continue to rendezvous at the doors of Burger King and up the street and round the corner at the gates of Eton College. It's all nothing in the children's eyes.

*May 2005*

# After Hurricane Katrina

THE SKY OVER North Carolina was showing red the night Sam and Terry decided to leave for the South. The red clouds traveled to Smithfield from the western hills, the high Appalachians and the Blue Ridge Mountains and the Great Smokies. Sam Parham is twenty-seven years old and weighs 260 pounds. For an hour or so, right into the dark, he pulled on the starter rope of an electric generator he'd borrowed from his father until the top of his T-shirt was soaked with sweat. "Goddamn bitch," he said. "This muthafucker is brand new. I want the goddamn thing to work. We're sure gonna need its ass when we get to New Orleans."

Sam's neighbor had chickens outside his trailer, and frogs were hiding in the pine trees along the drive. An American flag hung limply on the porch as Sam inspected the back of his truck with a giant torch, the crickets going *zeep-zeep-zeep* and red ants crowding in the oil at his feet. "I just can't watch those TV pictures of children stranded and not go down there," Sam said, while Yolande, his pregnant girlfriend, sat on the porch and opened a can of Mountain Dew and lit another cigarette.

Yolande was wearing her uniform from the Waffle House,

where she works the night shift. "You can't expect me to agree," she said. "But I respect you for doing it, Sam. I just think it's the government should be doing it."

"I'm just a blue-collar guy or whatever," said Sam. "And I'm gonna do what I can if the country needs me."

Terry Harper is a coworker of Yolande's at the Waffle House. As we drove along Interstate 95 to pick him up, house lights flared in the distance and Yolande started talking about God. "My daddy knows the Bible one hand to the other and when he starts speaking at you it's like preachin'," she said. North Carolina was the birthplace of Billy Graham and three US presidents—Andrew Johnson, James Polk and Andrew Jackson—and also, among the twinkling lights out there, you could find the uncelebrated birthplace of Thomas Wolfe, the North Carolinian who wrote *Look Homeward, Angel*. As the truck got nearer the Waffle House, someone on the radio made the point that North Carolina was itself no stranger to hurricanes—Hazel (1954), Hugo (1989), Fran (1996), Floyd (1999). It's no stranger to racism either. The Neuse River, the Roanoke River and the Yadkin River, named, like so much in the state, by the native Indian population that was cleared to make way for the twinkling lights and Interstate 95, have been known to burst their banks and flood the plains. The radio was silent on the fact that America's first-ever sit-in occurred at Greensboro, North Carolina, to protest against segregation at a lunch counter.

"They're not cookin' more than $200 a night," said Yolande, "and I can do that on coffee and Coca-Cola if I'm tired." She was planning to take over Terry's shifts so that he could make the trip south. Terry was mild-mannered, imperturbable, sucking juice out of a Waffle House cup. He is a fifty-year-old black man with a short mustache and a gap between his teeth. He was born in Pitt County but spent his happiest days in Atlanta.

Terry sat at the counter of the Waffle House waiting for a decision. It turned out he needed more than Yolande to cover his shifts, so we went in search of another worker, Ashley, who has kids on her own and needs the money. She doesn't have a telephone, but Sam found her house in the rundown Wilson area, next to a railway crossing. It was 75 degrees in the dark. Ashley came out from a house that flashed blue with television pictures, and she jumped up and down on the porch at the prospect of having more shifts at the Waffle House. "It's the lowest of the low works for the Waffle House," Sam said. "Would you look at her jumping up and down, the immaturity of her. She's got kids. Look at where we're at." He took a long look into the bleak houses at the edge of the projects. "My sister was murdered," he said. "She was killed by an injection of liquid crack cocaine. They tried to say she had a drug problem, but she had no drug problem. She was killed."

Ashley's two kids were cowering in their pajamas in the back of the truck with the neon of the fast-food marquees shining in their eyes. They were delivered to a babysitter in Lenoir Drive, a place that seemed to be exclusively black, young women sitting on the stoop while boys played basketball on the street in cap-sleeve jerseys. Ashley says she gets $2.85 an hour. Driving back to the Waffle House, Ashley and Yolande were gossiping about other members of the staff. "You know that TV show *As the World Turns*?" Yolande said. "Well, there's more soap in the goddamn restaurant. We call it 'As the Waffle Burns.'"

Sam was using the Internet as he drove at 70 miles per hour. He kept the laptop balanced between the two front seats, and had a wireless connection, so he was able to look up weather and news reports as he drove, clicking on the keypad and sometimes using the shift key. When not on the Internet, and not talking about the shape and meaning of his life, Sam was often on his mobile phone. He has, as he keeps saying, "unlimited," which means that his payment plan allows him to call anywhere in America as often as he likes. He spent great portions of every day on the phone to Yolande, or to his former wife, or his children, usually when he was driving, and the calls often ended in arguments. "You know about the hurricane, right?" Sam said to his son Zak. "I'm going down there to help the people. It's what we have to do. The people need our help."

After speaking to his children, Sam would grow listless for a while, as if love and regret were together taking their toll. He stared into the windscreen as the night came on and his plans fell into alignment. "I seem to get myself into these situations where I just help people all the time," he said. Then he rang his grandmother and put her on speakerphone.

"Don't run into a brawl or anything, Sammy, 'cause a lot of those people are just crazy right now."

By 12:10 a.m., the back of the truck heaped with a chain saw, a power generator, a giant toolbox and assorted jacks, Sam and Terry had left Smithfield and before long were heading down the Purple Heart Memorial Highway. Sam split his attention equally between the road and the laptop. His love of the Internet explained my presence in the back of the truck: like tens of thousands of Americans in the days after the hurricane, Sam had advertised himself on the net as a willing volunteer, and I found him and followed him. "Here," he said, chucking Terry a carton of painkillers. "Don't say I ain't good to you." Terry has a bad case of gout in his right leg, and it makes him hobble. When not on the phone, Sam talked into thin air, addressing himself. "Why did the Good Lord bring Hurricane Katrina?" he asked. "Man, it's life, it's evolution. Shit happens. But the thing that matters is what you do about it as a person. If some guy comes to rape my wife, why, this is America: I'm gonna put a cap in his ass. I'm gonna give him a hot one and let him leak." As if to confirm his point, Sam lifted a small blue medical bag that was hanging on the rear-view mirror. It contained a gun with the clip inserted and the safety catch on. He waved the gun over the steering wheel. "They're gonna get this in the ass," he said.

Terry wanted to sleep a little until the painkillers took hold. And when he woke, somewhere in South Carolina, Sam was saying how much he admired George W. Bush. "I voted for Bush last time," he said. "I liked the way he handled 9/11. He's a strong president. Hell, he's my commander in chief." Terry gave him a long, weary look and rubbed his eyes. Neither Sam nor Terry has ever possessed a passport, and they speak of the world beyond America as if it were a hidden territory of oddness, weakness and unreality. Sam stopped the truck at a gas station.

"I feel better," Terry said. "I'm gonna smoke me some Turkish Jades." And with that he hopped out of the truck and headed for the all-night window.

"He's poor as shit, man," said Sam. "No money at all. And he's going down to Mississippi in this bitch to help with somethin' that's got nothing to do with him." The road south — the flashing grass, the beat of the signs — seemed to direct Sam into a landscape of clear memory. He was born in Palm Beach, Florida, and within six months had been adopted by his grandmother. His mother was an alcoholic, and he was left on a window ledge in Pennsylvania in the dead of winter. That's when his grandmother came and took him to live in Maine.

"We got some of the same issues," said Terry. "My mother dropped me off in North Carolina when I was four years old and I never saw her again."

"We came to North Carolina in 1984," said Sam. "We moved into my uncle's camper and then spent a while living in a tent. We got a house eventually. I remember my biological mother coming to the house in Greensboro and she tried to kidnap me. She took me out in the middle of the night when I was asleep. The cops came and I'd never seen so many blue lights."

"A white baby kidnapped," said Terry.

"Yeh," said Sam. "If a black kid disappeared nobody cared back then, but if a white kid was taken there would be cops crawling outta the grass."

At the gas station, water was leaking from a drainpipe, and it ran down the wall to arrive on top of a newspaper vending machine. Terry paused beside it to light one of his menthol cigarettes. The paper was out of date, but, through the glass, there was a story about the desperate situation in New Orleans. It said the government was under fire for the slowness of the rescue operation. "It now looks like the South will be relying on volunteers. It may turn out to be one of the greatest volunteer operations this country has ever seen. President Bush said it made him proud to witness the response of everyday working Americans." A second story said the ordeal had opened "an old wound" about race in America.

Not far from the Chattahoochee River, Sam parked the truck in a rest area and reclined his seat for a few hours' sleep. As he snored, Terry saw a great blue heron fly over the truck and swoop down towards the interstate. "Heading south in search of water," he said. "Just like us."

Terry believes that racism has followed him all his life. He grew up only twenty minutes from the ocean in North Carolina and helped truck tobacco when he was ten years old. "That was my first job," he said. "My second job was in the grave-yard, burying bodies at fifty dollars a grave. I was sixteen and still at Ayden-Grifton High School. That was how I paid for everything, sports, prom: digging graves." At school, Terry got deeply involved in civil rights actions. He speaks of a white state trooper who was cleared of murdering two young black men, the Murphy brothers. There was a dawn-to-dusk curfew at that time, but Terry and his friends would go out at night and set fire to cornfields. Terry says he tried to shoot the state trooper one night with a borrowed rifle. He waited all night in a ditch, and when he fired he missed the policeman by three inches. Later, Terry and a group of his friends got some dynamite from a demolition company and tried to blow up their high school. Terry was detained by a teacher and so was not present when the bomb was set off. His friends were charged and found guilty. "Yep," said Terry, "those boys went down. Two of them, the Raspberry twins, got twenty years apiece."

In the early 1970s, Terry joined the Black Panthers. A number of things drew him into the movement: his childhood experience of racist murders, an instinct for self-defense, and the charismatic influence of the Panther members from Chicago who visited North Carolina to inspire younger black men to force a change in the fabric of America and, Terry said as the truck sped forward into the Alabama sun, "to kill a few people."

"Cool," said Sam. Though he'd taken a week off from his work as a cable television engineer to help with the relief effort, Sam still had to deliver his work records and invoices from the previous week. He worried about it across several states and eventually pulled into a Days Inn near Birmingham, Alabama. Terry looked up. "This is where Bull Connor, the police chief, turned his damn German shepherds on those little black girls," he said. "Then he turned a fire hose on those poor fuckers who were marching."

"Cool," said Sam, parking the truck with one hand. As the woman at the Days Inn took her time to book us into the room, Sam disconnected the Internet cable from the back of her computer. "Whore," said Sam.

"Let's just get inside and rest awhile," said Terry.

The room was dirty and the sheets didn't fit the bed. Terry decided to call reception to complain. "For seventy-eight dollars a person might expect hot water and fitted sheets," he said.

Meanwhile, Sam marched into the room and put his gun down on the table and held up a bunch of papers. "This represents fifteen hundred fuckin' dollars," he said. "And if I don't get them faxed to fuckin' North Carolina in ten minutes I don't get paid next week. This shit's fucked up. The bastard machine only takes three fucked-up papers at a time." Quietly, Terry removed the clip from the gun.

"George Wallace, the governor, said, Over my dead body would any nigger go to school here."

"It was them blacks that started racism in the first place," Sam said. Sweat was dropping onto the pages he aimed to fax.

Terry wanted to stop in Atlanta on the way back to see his son, who was refusing to go to school. Terry hadn't seen his son in several years and said he just needed ten minutes. "His black ass is on the fifty-yard line," Terry said. "Not going to muthafuckin' school. That's unacceptable to me. I'll kick his black ass when I get him."

The TV was showing a movie about a police SWAT team, and Sam, his pages traveling slowly through his mobile fax machine, stuck out his tongue and made shooting noises at the screen. "You're one dead fucker," Terry said to Colin Farrell, the actor on the screen. "You're gone." As he watched the movie, Terry opened a tin of clam chowder and ate it cold with a stolen spoon, following it with a red drink called Tahitian Fruit Punch.

Terry woke up to find Sam lying on the next bed and the TV saying that New Orleans was depending on the kindness of strangers. "It's a known fact," Terry said, "that the police and emergency services are, minimum, fifteen minutes slower to attend calls in black areas, so it's no surprise that they were slower to help the South when it was in trouble. If this had happened in a white area, they would've been out there the same day plucking them white folks out the water."

It had grown dark outside and we were thinking of setting off again. Sam was surfing the net for porn and talking to his ex-wife at the same time. "I'd hope that if I was stuck up on a roof that someone would come get me offa there," he said. "This is America. People do their best." His ex-wife was niggling him about family duties. "If something terrible happens to me, you're gonna feel bad," he said. "Yes, ma'am. You surely are." After a minute of silence and finger-flicking, Sam's tone changed and he seemed to lean further into the phone. "Do you know what tantric sex is?" he asked. He was still looking at his laptop. "It's mind-fucking!"

Terry was in the bathroom when Sam came rushing into the motel room with a giant grin on his face. "Terry! Hey. Hot blondes outside!" Terry immediately came through and started whistling from the door. Sam laughed. "You ain't gonna get them by whistling like they was dogs, dude." A while later, a handsome young couple, Cory and Aimee Exterstein, arrived at the Days Inn reception desk with their two children. Cory was wearing a baseball cap that said Louisiana State University. They looked exhausted, and the children were half asleep. Their house had been destroyed by floodwater in New Orleans, and they had managed to escape with the children and a few blankets. They told the woman at the desk that FEMA was saying that evacuees could stay at Days Inn motels and FEMA would pay the costs.

"I don't know nothin' about that," the woman said.

The young man was getting frustrated and his wife began to cry. "We're just looking for some help here," he said. "We don't have anything and the boys are tired. We've been driving all day."

The woman behind the desk suddenly grew hostile and self-pitying. "I don't get paid enough to deal with this," she said. "This gentleman"—she pointed to Terry, who was standing in the foyer—"is looking for more towels and I don't have any kind of help here."

Mr. Exterstein used the motel phone to call FEMA, but things were chaotic and the person he spoke to didn't know how to help them. His wife put her elbows on the desk and sobbed behind her hands.

"Listen, man. You can have our room," said Terry.

"What?" said the man.

"Our room," said Terry. "We've only been resting for a coupla hours and we're clearing out soon. Forget them: they're so rude around here. Take our room."

When they arrived at the room, Sam was combing his hair so that it sat round his head like a bowl. Delighted to see the family, he gave them bottles of water and money out of his pocket. "You guys are so kind," Aimee said. "It's just unbelievable, all this. And you guys are so kind."

"That's awesome, man," her husband said. "We only have two hundred dollars between us, and we wish we could do something for you guys."

"All we want to do is help," Sam said.

It turned out the young couple had worked together at a bar

called the Cajun Cabin on Bourbon Street — "the French Quarter's only authentic Cajun bar and restaurant" — a place with red-and-white-checked tablecloths and live music every night. But it was now under six feet of water, as was the Extersteins' house. "It's completely destroyed," Aimee said. "I didn't even have time to get my framed pictures or any of the personal stuff. It's all just gone forever now."

"And when we went back to see if anything was salvageable," Cory said, "the door had been kicked down and it was obvious the looters had been there. My Xbox was gone. Aimee's jewelry. Everything."

"They locked everybody inside the Convention Center," Aimee said. "It was just crazy down there. It was as if gangs had taken over New Orleans." They put the children into one of the beds and then hugged each other in the middle of the room.

"I had to go into the bathroom and do stuff when they hugged," Sam said later. "It choked me up to see them upset, and it made me feel great to know we'd done something."

On the edge of Mississippi, Sam called his girlfriend to tell her what happened back at the motel in Birmingham. "We're finally doing something," he said. Even in company, Sam always seemed a little lonely without his cell phone flipped out on his hand. Terry woke up and stared at the car in front. "Oh, man!" shouted Sam. "I see the whites in the nigger's eyes! I sees the whites!"

"You're stoopid," said Terry. "Some things just ain't worth gettin' upset about."

"I see the whites, muthafucker!"

Snapped branches began to appear by the side of the freeway. Then the road signs started to look ragged and the fields blasted. "Hurricane territory," Terry said.

The truck seemed to be moving faster as Sam was losing patience with his ex-wife. "Listen, young lady. You're being rude! You're cutting me off. Listen, you fat pig. You fat fuckin' pig. I'm losing power here."

She wouldn't accept that Sam was on a mercy mission. She thought he was bragging about what he had done, and she would rather he had gone back home and tended to his own business. "Listen to me and shut the fuck up," he said. "I don't give a damn fuck what you put up with. You fat little piggy-piggy, stinky little pussy-pussy. Fat pig. Fat pig. Stinky pussy. I'm trying to talk, you fuckin' pig. I just want to be an American hero. Yes. That's why I wanted to be in the military. I would love to do something and be a hero." He then hung up.

Terry and Sam talked a lot about the vehicles in front. One of the cars had a bumper sticker that said YEE-HA IS NOT A FOREIGN POLICY, and Sam laughed at this at first, but then, correcting himself, he began to get excited as Mississippi Interstate 55 filled up with military Humvees. With an increasing number of bent or snapped trees lining the road, the military personnel whizzed past in the afternoon sun, wearing claret berets and designer sunglasses and chewing gum like teenagers in an ad for American nonchalance. Sam bashed his fist on the steering wheel and whooped. "I say praise them all," he said. He beeped the truck's horn and shook Terry. "Hey, bitch," he said, "I wanna flag. Reach out the window and grab the flag off the back of that fire truck."

"I wouldn't touch that flag with a two-hundred-foot pole," Terry said.

After giving his partner the finger, Sam logged on to the Internet, then reached out and flipped open his phone. "Damn," he said, "I ain't got a single bar on my phone. I can't call out."

"Great," said Terry.

"Fuck you, you black African-American bitch."

When Hurricane Katrina grazed New Orleans, people thought the city had got off lightly. Trees were uprooted, some verandas collapsed in the city's older districts, shutters were blown into the street, windows were shattered in a number of downtown office blocks, but that first night, people were still drinking hurricane cocktails in Pat O'Brien's bar in the French Quarter: four ounces of good dark rum added to four ounces of hurricane mix, garnished with an orange slice, a maraschino cherry and tons of laughter into the night. It was only during the following days that the disaster put a stop to the music: the levees broke, and slowly at first, then very quickly, the bowl-shaped city began to fill up with water and then to drown in its own toxic effluent.

The worst inundations happened in poor areas. Almost a third of New Orleanians live below the poverty line — 67 percent of the population is black — and in the most densely populated areas the water, after several days, had flooded the houses past the second floor. Relations between the New Orleans Police Department and the city's poorest citizens are notoriously bad: the previous year, according to the columnist Jack Shafer, when seven hundred blank rounds were fired in one of those neighborhoods, nobody called the police. New Orleans's homicide rate is ten times the national average. "Unless the government works mightily to reverse migration," Shafer wrote, "a positive side-effect of the uprooting of thousands of lives will be to de-concentrate one of the worst pockets of ghetto poverty in the United States."

As the days passed, the federal and local authorities that had ignored long-standing and much-publicized warnings about deficiencies in New Orleans's system of levees took up a position that people quickly recognized as having about it the putrid odor of an old wound. Even Fox News, which found nothing particularly strange in the detention policy at Abu Ghraib, faulted George W. Bush for mouthing empty can-doisms while the mainly black people of deluged New Orleans were gasping for breath and water. As the city was plunged into several sorts of darkness, and people without cars or gas or money or health care were abandoned for days at the city's Superdome, the president flew above in Air Force One. His symbolic fly-past offered a new perspective to those keen to know what America has become; for those in the filth and lawlessness of the Superdome, or those waiting on roofs for five days with no milk for their babies and no road on which to make good their escape, it was a vision of a president who could send 153,000 troops to the other side of the world at an official cost of $205 billion. That is what people know. They also know that if a category-five hurricane hit, say, the Hamptons, then Air Force One—to say nothing of every helicopter on the eastern seaboard, and every public servant—would be requisitioned to save lives.

Two paramedics, in New Orleans to attend a conference, were caught up in the hurricane. "Two days after it hit," Larry Bradshaw and Lorrie Beth Slonsky wrote in a piece that appeared on the web a week or so after the hurricane,

> the Walgreens store at the corner of Royal and Iberville streets remained locked. The dairy display case was clearly visible through the windows. It was now 48 hours without electricity, running water, plumbing. The milk, yogurt and cheeses were beginning to spoil in the 90° heat. The owners and managers had locked up the food, water, Pampers and prescriptions and fled the city. Outside Walgreens' windows, residents and tourists grew increasingly thirsty and hungry. The much promised aid never materialized and the

windows at Walgreens gave way to the looters. There was an alternative. The cops could have broken one small window and distributed the nuts, fruit juices and bottled water in an organized and systematic manner. But they did not. Instead they spent hours playing cat and mouse, temporarily chasing away the looters . . . We are willing to guess that there were no video images or front-page pictures of European or affluent white tourists looting the Walgreens in the French Quarter.

Eighty percent of New Orleans was underwater by the third day. Both the Superdome and the Convention Center were full and hellish, and the buses that were meant to evacuate people didn't come. Disaster relief became a matter of volunteers. In situations of panic and urban emergency—especially when those situations are comprehensively mismanaged—victims can come to seem like enemies to the authorities. FEMA exists to make sure that never happens, and yet, in New Orleans, this became the dominant theme. And the military, when it finally arrived, only compounded the problem. Any black person in a supermarket was assumed to be a looter. The devastation and chaos caused by the hurricane were understood—by FEMA, the government, the police and the military—as a threat not to life and limb but to law and order. People trying to set up camps on the freeway in order to survive were treated as insurgents.

Sam and Terry were nervous when they arrived on the fringe of New Orleans. They had seen the reports about roving gangs, so Sam checked his gun and placed the bag around his neck as the truck approached a checkpoint. The state troopers were asking for proof of residence and generally policing the traffic. The city was virtually empty by this point, and, off the record, troopers were saying that people remaining in New Orleans were to be treated with suspicion. "Hi, gentlemen," said Sam.

"We've driven here from North Carolina and we want to help. I've got a chain saw and a generator and plenty of water. Don't know where the hell to start."

"Straight on," said the cop.

The smell was immediate, bosky, swamp-like and dark-fumed. "You can smell death around here," Terry said.

"Look up," said Sam. "Chinooks everywhere. Look at that, man. Twin blades. Awesome." A lone buzzard flew underneath the choppers. Everybody kept talking about the trees. They had been damaged or destroyed for hundreds of miles. In New Orleans, they all inclined the same way, in rows, like a cheap painting of Hawaii in the breeze. The truck was covered in lovebugs, and they swarmed outside too. Mating flies, they copulate on the wing, and Sam was having trouble making room for them amid the war-movie excitement and his wish to get things done. "I hate these goddamn fuck-bugs," he said. He crushed a pair with a paper tissue. "Look," he said to Terry, "they died in each other's arms. Thought you'd like that."

Terry's greatest concern in life is sex. He says so all the time. In the hour before they arrived at the flooded end of Jefferson Highway, Terry said the word "pussy" twenty-six times. At one point, waiting for gas, he rolled down the window as a young woman passed with a clipboard. "Mmmm. Uh-huh. I like it like that," he said.

"Excuse me?" she said, walking into the gas station.

"I like its ass," he said in Sam's direction, but Sam was on the phone. "I'm going in there to see what I can say to her." When Terry came back, phone-numberless but not in the least dejected, Sam chucked him a walkie-talkie he got at Wal-Mart and started to speak into the voice piece.

"Come in," said Sam.

"Your mother," said Terry.

"Your mother's dick."

"And it's a big one."

"Your mother's a crack whore," Sam said.

Over the highway, the McDonald's giant yellow M was bent like a corkscrew. The power lines were down and the poles lay across the road or had crashed through houses. When their truck reached the first fully flooded area, Sam and Terry fell silent, as if awed by the scene or attending a church service. Sam kept his face close to the wheel as he drove the truck through the water. He stopped when he saw that to go further would mean getting stranded. Ahead of the truck, cars were floating or tipped on their sides against buildings.

The houses were cheaply built and quick to turn to papier-mâché. Yet it was obvious that not all the damage was nature's work: cars abandoned at the side of the road had back seats covered with clothes still on their hangers with price tags attached. One of them had a pile of unopened CDs on the passenger seat. Terry got out of the truck and walked into the water. He met a guy called Terence who worked for the city's road crew. He was wading though the water looking for relatives whose house was near Jefferson Highway. The man's friend and coworker was keeping him company. He said to Terry, out of Terence's earshot, that their supervisor had already been told that Terence's family were dead. Nobody could face telling him. Sam beckoned a policeman and asked him what was happening. "Tell you the truth," said the policeman, "we don't know ourselves. We don't have a clue." He said they had pulled some bodies out from under the rubble at the corner of Cicero and Jefferson.

The boys' help was refused at most places. They went to the Ochsner Clinic and were greeted by a crimson-faced FEMA worker who was supervising the building of MASH tents outside the hospital. "We have electricity but no water," the man said. "The hospital's full to capacity but we're expecting more injured, so that's the reason for the MASH tents. I don't know what to tell you. It's just so confusing." Someone else told Terry that in one of the hospitals the patients had been abandoned in their beds as the water rose and the staff were forced to flee. (Forty-five bodies were later found at the Memorial Medical Center.) There still were people in many houses. Sam was growing indignant. He felt he was answering a historic call for volunteers, and now that he was in the embattled zone no one knew how to make use of him. At one point, with a police escort, he drove the truck to the temporary headquarters of the fire department. On the way they passed many houses with signs outside saying You Loot, We Shoot. The person in charge at the fire department was not encouraging either. "We just had a fuckin' volunteer guy fall out of a fuckin' tree and land on a chain saw," he said.

In some of the graveyards the coffins had risen with the tide and popped out of the ground, returning the bones and dust of the dead to the glare of the Louisiana sun. The climate was shot to pieces, yet not so much that the night air could fail to carry the scent of magnolia, or the same breeze now and then to lap prettily on the devastating waters. Every inch of New Orleans was a warning from Faulkner or Carson McCullers. The old, bleached hotels, with rotten water seeping up through their boards and plasterwork, were a series of flashbacks from Tennessee Williams; the floating chandeliers tangled with Spanish moss were Truman Capote's; and the white-haired survivors, seeking a way out of town with their plastic bags of photo albums, were a tribute to Eudora Welty. It was the week Southern Gothic became a form of social realism, the grotesque and the biblical stepping out to fulfill an old legacy. But the aspect of New Orleans that will remain in the memory is the ghostliness:

every citizen an image stranded at the center of a civil rights mythology, a city of Boo Radleys, visible in half-light behind a series of splintered doors and broken windows, a thread of national prejudice traveling on the becalmed air and stinging the nostrils of those who once felt they truly belonged to the Big Easy.

Standing at the top of one flooded street, Terry noticed a glinting light at the far end where furniture and cars were floating among the fallen trees and a premature mud of autumn leaves. "It's a terrible smell," he said. The light was not a person flashing a torch, as first seemed possible. It was the sun glinting off a decapitated traffic sign.

"Everyone's gone, one way or another," said a man who came by with his wife. The man had owned a small post office behind the street. "It's well hidden now," he said, "which might be lucky." New Orleans had become the thing that geological memory knew it to be—a voluminous swamp, a lake of reeds and tangled boughs, except that television sets and teddy bears and living people had got in the way.

Sam wanted to be pulling people from the water: he saw himself as being part of American heroism, and the chaos he encountered, the lack of direction, left him stranded in doubt about the authorities and about himself. Depressed, he stayed in the truck as Terry inspected the street.

"Come back!" Sam shouted as a group of black men suddenly appeared from a house and started walking in his direction. They loitered at the edge of the water and eyed the truck. Terry walked calmly back, and when he climbed into the truck he saw that Sam had his gun out and was swearing over the steering wheel. "Let's get the fuck away from here," Sam said.

"The natives are restless," Terry said, opening a can of cold ravioli and eating it with a plastic spoon.

The military stopped the truck from entering another part of town. "There's a curfew," the soldier said. "It's not a good place to be."

"All right," Sam said.

Further down the road, an old man wearing a hospital wristband was islanded on a grass bank. "I need help getting across there," he said. But the water stretched out in every direction with cars submerged up past their windscreens. His house was over there, under the water. The Salvation Army office was submerged too. Sam couldn't do anything, so he tuned his walkie-talkie to listen in to the military.

"If civilians want to go in, they can go in," said the crackly voice. "But they should know they're not getting back here if they don't have a county resident's pass. Do you copy?"

"Yip," said the second soldier.

"Did you leave a copy of the evacuation route over there?"

"I don't know where it's at. The press are renting a boat from a guy over here and using this patch of water to get to people and their houses and stuff. Is that OK?"

"I don't think there's much we can do about that. Over."

Helicopters were grinding away over the flooded Shell Oil plant in Metairie. "Life is full of important choices," said a sign on the plant's gates. "Make safety yours." Sam's head was turned up to the sky and all the helicopter activity. "That's a Huey 204, man," he shouted. "They haven't used them since Vietnam. I'm tellin' ya."

Terry began laughing into his shirt as Sam hyperventilated trying to cross a bridge over the Mississippi. "This place has had it," Sam said. "It's a muthafuckin' cluster fuck, man. Nobody knows what's going on." After he'd made it onto a drivable part of the freeway — yellow school buses abandoned all the way down the route — he started shouting out the window at the military vehicles passing on their way into New Orleans. "Go home, you fuckin' losers! You dumb Yankee fucks. Why don't you go back and do somethin' useful, like play paintball, you bitches!"

"They're crazy about looters," said Terry. "The troops shot one of them last night, and they put a sign on him that said, 'A thief died here.'"

"He wasn't white," said Sam. "I haven't seen a single white person looting."

"You haven't seen anyone looting," said Terry.

"But it's blacks, Terry. About two hundred of them."

"I done seen none," said Terry.

As the truck disappeared over the broken freeway and New Orleans receded in its soup of chemicals, Mayor Ray Nagin came on the radio. His only song was about the failure of Washington. He had no plans of his own, nothing to propose. Blaming Washington was the only thing that mattered. There was an almost delighted tone to his self-exculpating voice. "Mosquitoes that are biting dead people are starting to fly," he announced.

Sam combed his hair in the whiteness of his rear-view mirror. "We're needed in Mississippi," he said. "Gulfport, Biloxi. Those folks need what we've got. I just wanna help some people."

Terry Harper had reckoned that a good way to get away from the trouble of school was to join the air force. He forged the date on his birth certificate and gained entry that way, leaving North Carolina on October 31, 1973. He was sent to Montana, where, he says, there was a lot of racism on the base. "The base commander threatened to have me shipped to Iceland," he said, "because I was fucking his daughter. I mean, there were only four black girls on the base and 140 black men, and those girls charged for pussy." He got out of the air force after ten months and went to college to study mental health technology. "That was a fun time," he said. "Pussy for days, a different bitch every day if I wanted one. Me and this white guy, we had an apartment at the country club and we took women there." But he was married by then and his wife couldn't stand his philandering, so she asked him to leave. "She threw all the furniture I'd bought out in the street, man," he said. "It was all just lying there in the snow."

Terry went to live in a mobile home. "It was a good thing AIDS wasn't poppin' back then," he says, "because I'd be some dead muthafucker. This stinky-assed bitch—she's a preacher now—she lied and said I was fucking her, and her husband came around with a shotgun in his hand and told me he'd shoot me if I fucked around with his wife anymore. I took the bitch out into a field the next day and said, 'Bitch, you tried to get me killed today,' and I put a gun to her face and she was scared, man."

Eventually, he went to graduate school in Atlanta. He got a Woodrow Wilson fellowship for $39,000 but dropped out because, he says, in a class of sixty-six people he was the only black. "I had no voice," he says. "I just felt I was in the wrong place. This was America and I had a God-given right to be heard, but if you spit on me, goddammit, I go directly to your ass. Things have stayed the same in a lot of ways. A whole lot of white muthafuckers, they think they can talk to you any old way they like." He ended up working with deprived kids. "Hard-assed kids," he said. "But you can make a difference to kids like that. One of them I worked with is now a district manager for Taco Bell. He runs three Taco Bells. He's one of the most respected people I know."

Terry has had problems with drugs and women. That's what he says. He lost a good job as a drug and alcohol counselor because of cocaine (he was using on the job), then he lost his career as a photographer for the same reason. "My mother was killed by alcohol," he said. "From an early age I felt I had to compete with my brother. He always got everything. My sister, too. Back in the day, complexion was everything, and she was whiter than me. Until recently, you couldn't get anywhere near elected office unless you were light-skinned, and that's what I grew up with."

Terry paused often when talking about his life. He wants to get things right. He wants to be honest. "I wanna get out of the Waffle House by next February," he said. "Back to Atlanta. Back to photography. I'm good at that." When he said this he hesitated and stared into the near future, then he smiled, as if there was something more essential about himself that he had not brought out. "I once fucked fifty-eight women in one year," he said. "I had a contest with some guy—who could fuck the most women. And man, I even fucked his regular girlfriend. It isn't that hard if you know how to go about it. We used to strip for wedding showers. It was a good thing, you know. Two hundred dollars a pop, plus tips."

We couldn't find a motel in Mississippi, so Sam parked the car in Hammond and we spent the night in the truck. A neon sign—ALL YOU CAN EAT CATFISH—rasped through the early hours, and Sam occasionally woke up and bathed his face in the blue light of his laptop, typing furiously, attempting to figure out how best to reach the poor Americans who needed him. Terry propped his bad leg up on the dashboard. "Goddammit," he said at first light, "I might have to get me to an emergency room."

"Looks like we won't be taking a bath today," Sam said, pouring talcum powder down the front of his shorts. "Mmm," he said, "feels like gittin' a whole new pair of drawers on, man."

A woman walked by with her dog on a lead. "She's got some ass, man," Sam said. "Lookit, Terry. She's your color."

"Hot damn!" said Terry. "She's got one of them be-donk-e-donk asses. It goes all the way down, baby. She's fine."

"Go on, dawg! She make yo jump up and slap yo mama."

Sam and Terry decided they might need more equipment to help the people of the Mississippi Delta, so they joined the dawn chorus at the nearest Wal-Mart, touring the near-empty aisles in a couple of electric-powered buggies, the ones intended for the old and the infirm. It was the calmest they had been for days, the store's Muzak dimming all anxiety as they threaded through the aisles. They chucked insults across the gaps, and eventually Terry pulled up at one of the checkouts with a basketful of cheap toys. "A dollar each, right?" he said. The girl looked at him strangely, but Terry was sure there would be children in Mississippi who had lost all their toys.

Beside the front doors, an overweight pensioner was talking to her neighbor. "What if the Great Man Upstairs says, 'You haven't learned your lesson yet, you need some more'?" she said.

"God praise the volunteers," said the neighbor. "That's all I can say. The volunteers are the salt of the earth."

On the Mississippi coast, the morning seems to arrive not out of the sky but out of the trees, a golden show coming slowly until the day is bright and firmly begun. "We're gonna do good today," Sam said.

"We already did good," said Terry. "We's offering. That's all we can do, and if the people wants help, they'll get it."

"Today," said Sam. "I'm serious as a heart attack."

As the truck entered Gulfport, a holiday town that had taken the full force of the hurricane the Sunday before, some of Sam's general edginess was beginning to influence Terry's view of the situation. "I wish some of them TV news stations would inter-view me," he said. "CBS, NBC, CNN, all those muthafuckers. I'd tell them like it is. They're saying, 'This is needed, that is needed.' Everything is here, man, they've just got to use it right. These utility people, man. They're tellin' like they're working round the clock. That's complete bullshit, straight-out lies. They're not leaving their motels until ten in the morning."

"They oughta be organized just like the military," Sam said.

"You don't know jack shit," said Terry.

"Don't tell me what I don't know. I work with television. I know about cable. Them boys care about people. You just got a goddamn chip on your muthafuckin' shoulder, Terry." The two argued often, but they would always retreat from any serious confrontation by hooking onto some shared joke, usually about a passing woman. "I could grunge-fuck that bitch," Sam said of a woman walking past a convenience store in Gulfport. "She's just the way I like 'em." On the other side of the road, a sixteen-wheeler full of hearses was being unloaded, hearse by hearse, in the forecourt of a gas station that had no gas.

Gulfport was struck by winds of 160 miles per hour. The morning had started out very blue and very calm, but dark clouds broiled in the sky and Hurricane Katrina ripped over the Gulf and slammed through all the towns and villages on the Mississippi coast. The casinos that stood at the oceanfront in Gulfport were gutted, and several of them had ended up on top of the freeway. The devastation was still spectacularly obvious: lorries piled on top of one another; hotels pulped, with glass and mud and trees and bathroom products scattered over a massive area. Concrete had been blown apart. Metal was twisted. And for five or more streets back from the ocean, people's houses were splintered.

By the time we reached Gulfport, soldiers were very much in evidence, though nobody knew what to do with them. A lot of saluting took place, a lot of standing before maps of the devastated areas. As in all military zones, a great deal of attention was taken up with the troops themselves — transporting them, feeding them, briefing them, guarding them. Only sporadically were they put to work. Some people concluded that they were there to provide a show of force, a warning to looters and evidence that the federal government now cared. Yet the real stuff of the Mississippi relief effort was being run by agencies and volunteers. It might be said that the salient characteristic of modern American soldiers is that they always appear homesick, they always seem alienated, and they always look bored. This may be true of any military force in any part of the world, but it was certainly true of the troops who came to serve in the American South.

The Volunteer Command Post was in a school just outside the town, and much of the military was stationed there. As Sam drove up he was flagged down by four young men in uniform. Three of them appeared to be seventeen years old, and the one who stepped forward to speak, the one with authority, was no more than nineteen. Sam rolled down the window.

"Morning, zug-zug," said the officer.

"Hi," said Sam.

"Have you any weapons, zug-zug?"

"Sorry?"

"In the truck, sir. Do you have any weapons in the truck? Zug-zug."

Sam looked at Terry and shrugged. "A handgun," he said.

"I have to check that, zug-zug," said the officer.

He walked off to speak to a superior, and Sam turned with

his mouth open. "What in fuck's name is he saying? What's this 'zug-zug'?"

"Fucked if I know," said Terry.

The young officer came back shaking his close-shaved head. "I'm afraid we can't allow any guns on the facility. Zug-zug." The men behind the officer were smiling now.

"What is this 'zug-zug' shit?" asked Sam. The officer broke into a broad smile and his men cracked up behind him.

"It's just a joke we've got going, sir," he said. "Things are a bit slow out here, so he dared me to say 'zug-zug' after everything I said."

"Oh, cool," said Sam, "I got ya. What I'll do is, I'll go and bury this gun and then come back. Is that all right with you?"

"Do what you have to do, sir." Sam drove along the road and buried the gun as he said he would, right in an old pile of dirt next to an abandoned house. When he drove back the soldiers searched the car and then waved us through.

Nothing fazed Adam, the co-coordinator, nothing excited him, nothing moved him: he was a disaster professional, a young man hardened by too much experience, practical to the point of insolence. "The thing about this situation," he said, "many people downtown who look like they need help, who've suffered a lot of devastation, they can afford to pay for having trees cleared and cars towed. You don't have to do it for them. It's the poor and vulnerable ones you have to look out for. If I drive down there and I see generators outside people's houses, I just drive on. That's the way it is. There are folks who need help who would be happy to see you guys. Be choosy about who you help."

Sam had nodded through this speech, but he did not take any of its detail to heart. He had come from North Carolina because he had watched television and felt Hurricane Katrina presented a challenge to ordinary people as well as an opportunity for self-definition. He didn't mind whom he helped. New Orleans had been too murky and unreal, too spooky, too inaccessible, but here in Mississippi Sam was going to do his bit for America. On the back roads of Gulfport he drove the truck and kept his eyes open. Power lines had collapsed, and every house had something shattered or crippled about it. In one of the nicer ones, Sam spotted an old white man and his wife trying to lift a generator down from the back of a pickup truck. He hit the brakes and swerved into their driveway.

Eli Myrick has lived and worked in Mississippi all his life. That day, it being hot, he was wearing light-colored shorts, a polo shirt and a straw hat, with white socks climbing up his weak legs in a style both senior and fresh. Sam and Terry got to work lifting down the Myricks' new generator. Their house had lost power and one of the walls had caved in with the force of the hurricane. They were well-off, though, and had a second house out of state, so this was all just a pest. Sam was kneeling on their patio dealing with the transfer of gas from the old generator, and Mr. Myrick leaned against the kitchen door, pleased but also not pleased, the eclipse of his competence almost too evident in the words of his wife. "Oh, let them do it, Eli. You'll only hurt your back. Oh, honey, let them go ahead. Step back. That's right. They know what they're doing. This young man's an engineer, Eli."

Mrs. Myrick brought pink lemonade and Spam sandwiches for the boys and told them about her years as a history teacher. "Well," she said, "I was just saying to my friends the other day: with all this terrible business happening to us here in the South, it proves that the Civil War will never be over. God save us from the North."

Terry was leaning against the truck when Sam came out. "That sandwich she gave us sure was salty," he said.

Sam drove on and parked the truck on the oceanfront, where Chiquita banana lorries lay about like crumpled toys. People who ignored the warnings and remained on this stretch died instantly when the hurricane hit the shore. Terry walked into the shell of an old employment center: there was nothing left, not a paper clip or an office chair; a spout of toxic water bubbled up from a hole in the concrete floor. In the car park outside, where huge trees lay snapped in two, a tennis ball was pushed softly by the remaining wind. Terry saw a wheelchair abandoned in the middle of the highway. Earlier, he had wondered why so much of this destruction was somehow familiar, and he realized he had seen it before, like every other person in America, in *War of the Worlds*.

The streets behind the ocean were no-go areas. The army was discouraging people from entering. But Sam and Terry drove around, looking for people to save or simply to help in their struggle with the collapsing buildings. Where the houses had doors, many of them were marked with orange paint and a number, which indicated how many had died there. The sight of the devastation had affected the two men differently. It made Sam more practical, calling out to people he saw to ask if they needed help with the rubble, had enough cold water or were OK inside. But with Terry the dreadful sights of Mississippi brought him further into contact with his militant past. He saw the effects of inequality in the mud around him. At one point, someone said something about Jesus, and Terry just shifted his bloodshot eyes. "Let me tell you about this country," he said. "The Catholic Church is filled with the worst racists of them all. Some priest, he sucked two hundred little dicks, and you know what happened to him? He got a raise, man. They made him goddamn archbishop. And any black priests who commit adultery get kicked out the diocese. That's it."

"Well," said Sam, surveying the ruins from behind the wheel, "I ain't helping no black people. I just wanna see how bad they live." Then he sang a few bars of "God Bless America." He saw a woman on a porch. "Man," he said into his dead walkie-talkie, "you're so ugly you'd have to wear a pork chop around yo neck to get the dogs to play with you." Terry sniggered into life.

"You're so ugly you would scare a glass of water," he said.

The Red Cross had warned Sam and Terry that it was dangerous to drive in those areas without a military escort. One of the Humvees had been shot at earlier that day. But the military men up at the command center didn't want to escort the boys: they didn't think it was their job. It appeared that no one had bothered to establish a chain of command between the Red Cross and the military, so the people, such as Sam and Terry, who were delivering aid were expected to take their own risks and only help people they felt they could trust.

That night, the dark in Gulfport seemed darker than the dark of anywhere else. Electricity was still only minimally available, and the stars looked down with keen eyes. Terry's gouty ankle had grown to the size of a small planet, and he slept out in the open air at the back of the truck, stretched out on a long toolbox, his leg hoisted higher than the rest of him and pointing at the stars. Sam fell asleep in the driver's seat with the broken walkie-talkie tight in his hand.

When he was a child, Sam was committed several times to Cherry Hospital, a place for children with problems. "I've always wanted my friends to come with me," he said. "But they never have. They never will. I don't really have any friends, to tell the truth."

He had attention deficit disorder and the doctors put him

on Ritalin. "I was always puking in the afternoon," he said. "I was like a zombie, but that stuff works in some way. I could rush through my lessons no problem, but by four-thirty in the afternoon I'd be so angry. I've always been angry, but that was too much even for me." Sam's grandmother, who tried to look after him, turned to alcohol just as his mother had, and she spent a lot of his childhood in rehab. As a way of avoiding reform school, Sam went as a teenager to a place called Camp E-Ku-Sumee, in Candor, North Carolina. It gave him a way of transcending danger and fear. "You had daily chores," he said. "Latrines. Powwow. Making kindling wood for the fire. All that. I cried like a bitch when I had to leave that place. They were like family — you woke up with them every day. I loved it there. I used to climb trees just to breathe, man. You could see for miles up there. The hills and everything."

Sam said he's always wanted a bigger purpose. "I also wanted a true friend," he said. He had two friends when he was young, Algernon and Moo-Moo, two black kids who died after being shot in separate incidents, but he always felt Cherry Hospital ruined his chances, because people thought he was retarded. "Everybody always told me I'd be in prison by the time I was twenty-one. Well, I've proved them wrong, haven't I?" Sam has made his work and his children and his truck the center of his bid for renewal. And he always wants to make good the past. "One day I was talking with my father," he said. "We were talking about education and stuff, why I'd been passed over so much and had failed so badly. He told me that the whole time I was being sent off to the mental place, they were saying, 'The son will be fine, save the mother.'"

Sam's story, he indicated, even asleep with the walkie-talkie in his hand, is the story of how a person might overturn anger with usefulness, if not goodness. He isn't sure that this will work, but he hopes so. "I've always had this feeling," he said, "that there was something for me to do that was important and the whole world would know about it. I suppose this whole trip has been about that feeling."

At the Orange Grove Elementary School, a gymnasium was piled halfway up the bleachers with donated clothes. Some of them had tags indicating they had come from Utah, from the Church of Jesus Christ of Latter-day Saints, and others were from people in Canada, Mexico or New York. Sam and Terry stood in the middle of the gym trying to separate the great heap into women's, men's, boys', girls' and babies'. Terry found *A Bible Promise Book* in a box of tangled T-shirts. He opened the book at random and saw a quote from Jeremiah: "I will rejoice in doing them good and will assuredly plant them in this land with all my heart and soul." Many of the T-shirts in the box had Coca-Cola logos on the front or American flags or Disney characters. A man walked past who had lost his house in Biloxi. His name was Leroy. His girlfriend and his mother had disappeared in the flood. "The walls of the house opened up like a zipper," he said. "The tide dragged me out and then threw me back in again, just sucking me out with all the furniture and then back again, and eventually I held on to a tree. Held on to that tree for fourteen hours, just waiting for the storm to pass and someone to come get me." He looked down at the pile of skirts and bras and women's jeans. His arms were badly burned where he'd hugged the tree.

A woman in her fifties came in and lifted some clothes out of the heap. Her name was Charlene. "All my memories floated out on that filthy water the day of the hurricane," she said. "Everything. I'm just gonna make a little pile here of clothes to take away." A Red Cross coordinator asked the boys if they'd load up their truck and take emergency supplies to some of the outlying towns, Long Beach and Pass Christian, that had been badly hit and were not getting enough help.

"Let's get to it!" Sam said. "They're desperate for food out there."

They loaded up the truck with water, pasta sauce, baby food, assorted tins and military MREs — meals ready to eat. Long Beach was weirdly quiet except for the sound of gas-fueled generators. We stopped at a Conoco gas station and the woman who ran it clapped her hands and got her husband to help the boys unload. No sooner was the food on the ground than people were moving in to take it to their cars. "This is great," said the woman. Sam was like a field commander by this point: he found out what else they needed and arranged with the woman to bring further supplies, while calling Yolande in North Carolina to tell her what was happening.

"He's like a goddamn reporter," said Terry.

Many of the doors in Pass Christian were daubed with orange paint. A terrible, plague-like atmosphere existed among the shattered houses. It didn't seem as if the hurricane had come in from the Gulf at all but instead had risen from the center of the earth. Houses had simply been split down the middle or had exploded in a thousand flaws. Sam drove the truck to a dropoff point in the worst area and then felt excited. It was part of their camaraderie: whenever Sam was feeling pleased with himself he'd immediately start feeding Terry's appetite for sexual repartee and girl talk. A young woman and her boyfriend were holding hands under a battered bridge. Sam stopped the truck to ask if they were OK and then turned to Terry as he drove away. They did it in the style of an elaborate hip-hop-style joke.

"I'd rape the fuck out of that pussy. You?"

"All the way," said Terry.

"We could mangle the boyfriend fucker," said Sam. "I'd hold her down for you. Would you hold her down for me?"

"Nope," said Terry.

"You wouldn't hold her down for me?"

"Nope. I don't do that shit."

"Well, fuck you," said Sam. "There's been a lot of fuckin' rapin' down here with this disaster shit."

A woman called Audrey asked the boys if they'd put some of the supplies into the trunk of her car. She was seventy-three years old, wearing a polka-dot shirt and flowery shorts and carrying a bottle of water. She had a tumor on her neck. "I have terminal cancer," she said. "And my husband here, Mickey, he is on dialysis. We're going to New Jersey so's he can get his treatment." Audrey began to cry when someone brought up the subject of New Orleans. "I come from there," she said. "It's too terrible. I think people should just get out of there and never go back. It can never be the old way again."

That night was Sam and Terry's last night in Mississippi. They had borrowed fold-down beds from the Red Cross and had set them up beside those of the refugees in the school library at Orange Grove. A Hispanic man had lost his identification and was worried about being able to get the $2,000 relief package that FEMA was offering to hurricane victims. He sat on the edge of his bed in the library with a copy of *The Adventures of Huckleberry Finn* on his lap. "I found this on the shelf," he said. The front of the book had a page with children's names written out beside the date of borrowing. The man's name was Carlos A. Garcia and he was thirty-three years old. "That Sunday morning," he said, "it started raining and there was a little wind. I lived in the apartment block at 601 Josephine in Pass Christian. The block had a lot of Hispanic people living there. Not everybody speaks English. The storm got up and the trees were breaking like crackers. The trees were bent over like people praying. The cars flew past the window, man, and then the stairs of the apartment got ripped off. We ended up on the roof. We put the old people up first. The water got so high that people were swept off the roof and some of them jumped in. Twenty-four people from the apartment are lost, and I just know they died."

The shelter at the Orange Grove School had a Stars and Stripes and a Confederate flag outside, rippling in the breeze. The night was ripe with the sound of crickets, and some old men sat smoking and tapping ash into a bare tin can. The red sky had turned dark, and the men were worrying about a new hurricane that was said to be gathering force outside Florida. A weeping woman came wandering across the car park and stopped a state trooper. Her child was clinging to the backs of her legs and seemed frightened. "We're here in a shelter and he's drunk. He's over in that truck drinking beer and he's drunk." She asked the officer to give her husband a Breathalyzer test but he demurred. The husband walked over and the woman pulled at her hair and shouted past him into the school windows: "If you can drink when we're homeless! If you can do that! What's the use?"

One of the old men tapped his ash several times and stared through the smoke at the other men. "Everybody's got problems," he said.

Sam and Terry were bonding with the local boys. "We thought we could ride it out," said George McCraw. "We ended up running to the Gates Avenue Baptist Church two miles from the beach. Man, the roof was caving in and the children were screaming. The wind was poppin' so bad and it was like rotor blades going over there. The steeple was coming off the church and the light poles were scattered across the road. Sparks flyin' everywhere. You could feel the force of the hurricane move you, man. It was like someone had dropped a bomb. You'd never think water could do that damage. It was bad, man. We had just got on our feet down there. We found this little place and a good job and we had a car. We weren't insured, though. Everything's gone. It's just toothpicks. But the Good Lord was with us the whole time. We looked hell straight in the eye. That's what we did. We looked at hell."

George's younger brother wondered if there was any liquor to be had in Gulfport that night. "Not with the curfew," Sam said.

"There's a garage up by the freeway," George said.

Sam and Terry were told to load up as much of the supplies as they cared to take back to North Carolina. "You guys have earned it," said the Red Cross coordinator, shaking their hands. "I wanna thank you guys. You guys are patriots."

They loaded up the truck and looked over at the homeless young guys pushing and joking under the white light above Orange Grove. "That bitch, woooo," said George's younger brother. "She comes out here, eyes poppin' like a frog."

"I'd bend her over and fuck her like a dog," George said.

"That's right," Sam said. "I hear you."

Terry disappeared into the library to find a book and lie down with it. "Some drivin' to be done tomorrow," he said. "I hope we can stop off in Atlanta. I wanna go and speak to that son of mine."

"He's just an old dog lookin' for a bone," said Sam. When

most people had gone to bed, he walked across the car park and lingered there with a cigarette. He'd given his mobile phone to people who needed to make calls and he stood there thinking about friendship and looking into the trees. Sam looked to the very tops of the trees and then turned back to the school. There was laughter inside. "I'm going to miss you guys," he said.

*October 2005*

# Brothers

*When lilacs last in the dooryard bloom'd,*
*And the great star early droop'd in the western sky in the*
*night,*
*I mourn'd, and yet shall mourn with ever-returning spring.*

*Ever-returning spring, trinity sure to me you bring,*
*Lilac blooming perennial and drooping star in the west,*
*And thought of him I love.*

— Walt Whitman, "When Lilacs Last
in the Dooryard Bloom'd"

EVERY TIME YOU BLINK there are ten flashes of lightning in the earth's atmosphere. If you were to look down from a vantage point at the edge of near space, you would see constant flashes from deep inside the earth's cloud cover—red, white, red, white, blue—a fugue of lights that might seem to warn of emergencies down below. Had you been looking on May 2, 2005, you might also have seen phenomena that were new to the planet's history. In the Atlantic Ocean, icebergs larger than Manhattan were floating away from the coast of Antarctica. A hurricane season was brewing that would break all records: Hurricanes Cindy, Dennis and Emily were gathering their elements, preceding Hurricane Katrina, which would hit America's Gulf Coast and become the costliest disaster in that country's history. But on May 2 the trouble was merely stirring while US aircraft carriers traveled east through the curiously cold waters of the Atlantic.

In southern Iraq, just south of Al-Amarah, the main city of Maysan province, the British military base at Camp Abu Naji was preparing for the night. Set at the northern end of the marshlands between the Tigris and the Euphrates, the camp is now abandoned and looted, but in May 2005 it was a busy center of military operations. Al-Amarah has seen many reversals of fortune and opinion: it was once a hideout for anti-Saddam insurgents, whom he punished by draining the marshes. He also killed many of them, and buried their bodies in mass graves around the city. But by the time the 1st Battalion of the Coldstream Guards was operating out of Camp Abu Naji, it was the British army that had become the enemy of the people. Mortar attacks on the base were just part of the general grief, a handful of dust to be thrown regularly in the face of the occupying forces.

Anthony Wakefield, aged twenty-four, had a long memory of nighttime patrols. He had done any number of them in Northern Ireland. On the evening of May 1, 2005, he was talking about his children and making jokes while assembling his kit to attend a briefing by the company commander, Major Coughlin. The plan that night was to leave Camp Abu Naji and travel in a northwesterly direction, seeking to prevent the enemy's retreat from an area under Coalition control. Guardsman Wakefield was told to provide top cover in the second of two "snatches"—a

V8 Land Rover, lightly armored—which would travel the road out of Al-Amarah in the dark. Sergeant Ian Blackett was in the patrol's first vehicle and had known Wakefield for five months. There were fourteen men in the patrol, and Wakefield was one of the most experienced. "He was a professional soldier," says Blackett. Some soldiers don't seem to do much except cheer up other soldiers, yet they surprise everyone with their readiness. "A good lad, who was definitely up to it."

Guardsman Gregory Shaw says they left camp at 10 p.m. Wakefield's head and shoulders were protruding from the top of the second snatch, the usual position for a soldier doing top cover. "Everybody was fatigued," says Shaw. "You know it's going to be a long, hot night. A lot of people are shy of work and want to do as little as possible, but he [Wakefield] was always one to muck in." The patrol could hear bursts of small-arms fire as they made their way along the road. Over the course of the next hour or so they met other patrol groups from the company. "We then did a U-turn on Green 9 and Green 12 [combat zones] and turned into an area known to us as 'India,'" says Lance Sergeant Stephen Phipps. "We then made our way through the Al-Mukatil al-Araby district. I'm not sure if we drove to Green 5—the streets were getting quieter." The patrol was about forty kilometers from Camp Abu Naji and the vehicles trundled over a dimly lit road. "It was a sort of urban area but with a lot of waste ground," says Blackett. "A few buildings on the road, a few shops, and very dark. Very few people. It was one of the roads leading out of town."

"He was happy. He seemed cheerful," says Guardsman Gary Alderson, who was next to Wakefield in the snatch. "Seemed happy all the way round. I was facing rearwards, he was facing forwards." Two hundred meters short of the zone called Green 6 there was a loud explosion and what some of the soldiers describe as a fireball at the right side of the second vehicle. "Wakefield fell inside the snatch," says Alderson. "I went down inside as well. I was very disorientated and can't remember much." Lance Sergeant Phipps's immediate impulse was to get the patrol out of the "killing zone." He instructed the driver to power ahead, but the vehicle was damaged and broke down after fifty meters. "I could see Wakefield lying across Lance Sergeant Newton's lap," says Phipps. "Guardsman Alderson was injured. Wakefield had a pulse but was not breathing." The stranded occupants just stared into the blackness at the retreating lights of the snatch in front.

In the first vehicle, Blackett saw a flash and sparks at 2337 hours, and told the driver to put his foot down and get out of there. Then he realized the second snatch wasn't following them and went back to help. They radioed headquarters as their snatch rumbled back to the stricken vehicle.

The regimental medical officer at Camp Abu Naji, Captain Vickers, was woken before midnight and told to come to the operations room. "A contact had been made and we had a casualty." The blast had come from an explosive device at the side of the road, concealed in a mound of dirt with an infrared trip set in front of the charge. The device installed in every vehicle, intended to detect and short-circuit such devices, had in this instance failed.

Guardsman Wakefield was wearing standard body armor at the time of the blast, which provides protection to the front and back of the torso. Projectiles entered his neck and upper chest, the latter through the unprotected side area of his vest. A forensic pathologist later said the neck injury severed one of four main arteries to the brain. The material passing through his chest hit a lung and the heart, causing massive internal bleeding. He had no chance of survival. Captain Andrew Cox dispatched a helicopter to pick up the injured man and take him back to base. The helicopter carried him to Camp Abu Naji, where he was ventilated, but his pupils became fixed and at 0050 hours on May 2, 2005, surrounded by medical officers, Guardsman Wakefield was declared dead.

The last day of Anthony Wakefield's life was a deadly one in many parts of Iraq. At a Kurdish funeral near Mosul, two dozen people were killed by a car bomb. American soldiers handing out sweets to children were targeted by a bomber in Baghdad. As the new Iraqi government debated the Sunni cabinet positions, homemade bombs went off all over the country in a spree that saw 120 dead. It was two years exactly since George W. Bush had announced that "major combat operations" in Iraq were over, an anniversary marked with seventeen coordinated bombings in Baghdad.

Scholars of human chronology might have noticed several other anniversaries that day. It is the date of Joseph McCarthy's death and J. Edgar Hoover's. It is the date of Tony Blair's 1997 election victory and the day in 1982 on which a British navy submarine torpedoed the *General Belgrano*. Soon after colleagues at Camp Abu Naji woke up to news of Anthony Wakefield's death, Lynndie England would appear in a Texas court that day to plead guilty to charges of maltreating Iraqi prisoners.

Many servicemen, British and American, were expressing disgust that day about the crimes of England and her associated military reprobates. One who did so was Lieutenant Colonel John C. Spahr, an executive officer with Marine Fighter Attack Squadron 323, based at Marine Corps Air Station Miramar in San Diego; he had served during the spring of 2005 in the Persian Gulf, on the USS *Carl Vinson*. Lieutenant Colonel Spahr was six feet three inches tall and did a memorable impression of John Wayne, which lent him his call sign, "Dukes." His sister Kelly told me he wasn't motivated by politics, but was driven by a keen sense of right and wrong. "Those top pilots are all alike," she said. "They are not available. That's why a lot of them are single or marry late. They never really talked about what they did: there are things John did in the line of duty that I knew he would never talk about. But he said that being in the jet was like being inside his own skin."

At 7 p.m. — eighteen hours after Guardsman Anthony Wakefield was pronounced dead — John C. Spahr climbed the ladder onto the flight deck of the *Carl Vinson* and walked to his F/A-18 Hornet. Lance Corporal Lindsay, who did final checks on Spahr's jet that evening, said he came out onto the flight deck smiling and joking with his fellow Marines. The ship is more than 1,000 feet long and can carry 5,500 personnel; its motto is *Vis per mare,* "Strength from the sea." A major carrier is more like a floating town, often surrounded with smaller ships serving as warehouses. Lieutenant Colonel Spahr and his colleague Marine Captain Kelly Hinz had their orders: they would fly into south-central Baghdad and support the Marines on the ground, many of whom were fighting insurgents and taking sniper fire. Lieutenant Colonel Spahr was more than familiar with the journey. He had been the first pilot to fly into Baghdad on the night of March 21, 2003 — the first of 1,700 sorties flown by the US Air Force — at the beginning of the campaign called Shock and Awe. Launching from the aircraft carrier, "you go from about zero to one hundred fifty miles an hour in less than two seconds," says Captain Daron Youngberg, a colleague of Spahr and Hinz. The pilots left behind a series of signalmen scurrying on deck as each rose and tilted their $55 million plane over the empty horizon. Other pilots watched the pair ascend from the *Carl Vinson:* "There goes Dukes," said one of them, whom I later spoke to.

"He was the best Top Gun pilot of his generation and what I would call a complete man," he told me.

I had seen hundreds of pictures of John Spahr over the months I spent looking for his story. Many of them showed him in the cockpit of his fighter plane: one with his visor down and his thumb aloft as he waited to launch from the carrier; another in the blue sky as he saw off some Russian jets; and yet another, looking focused and fit, under a message which said, "Do One Thing Every Day That Scares You." On May 2 the two pilots were flying at 26,000 feet, high over fawn-colored houses south of the Tigris, the river that stretches towards Al-Amarah. Lieutenant Colonel Hunter Hobson, who had been with Spahr at flight school and later ended up in the same fighter squadron, the famous 323 Death Rattlers, told me Spahr had what few people have: "an amazing ability in the airplane." When I spoke to Hobson he was at the Miramar base at San Diego. "When you're flying complex, multimillion-dollar aircraft, hand-eye coordination is crucial," he said. "You have to know how to use that machine lethally. The tangible difference with John Spahr was his athletic ability. And you know, being in charge of that machine — it's exactly where people like John and me need to be. All the training is for that moment. If you had to choose one place for it to end, it wouldn't be in a hospital, it would be up there."

Hobson had been flying the same course as Spahr and Hinz that night, but he was called back and the others went on to refuel in the air. The conditions were terrible, an ugly sandstorm, low visibility, though Hobson says the weather was better in Basra. "There was lightning," said Hobson, "and after the refueling John and Kelly lost sight of each other." It seems that Lieutenant Colonel Spahr was behind and below Captain Hinz when Hinz's plane suddenly dropped fifty feet and slowed, at which point the planes collided. Both men were killed. Hobson and others believe that the pilots ejected, but an F/A-18 parachute was unlikely to deploy effectively at that height and in those stormy conditions. Lieutenant Colonel Spahr's life may have ended at the moment of collision, but there are signs he died on impact with the ground. He fell more than 25,000 feet to the desert, where his body lay, still strapped into his ejector seat, until it was recovered the following day. "That night will never leave my mind," said his sister Sabrina when I met her in Philadelphia. "I feel I need to know exactly what happened to John so I can properly empathize with him in those final moments over Iraq."

At the bus stop in Newcastle, people stood with damp hair and stared into space. The buses going east, in the direction of Heaton, were half full in the morning and nobody spoke. When I arrived at the house of Paul Wakefield, I immediately saw a picture of his handsome younger brother on the coffee table. "He was my bodyguard," said Paul. "He was always quite tough, but brave. He was my hero and he always will be." Paul answered the door in his pajamas and went off to grill some bacon. "He was too good for most people," he said from the kitchen. "I don't think I'll ever meet anyone who could compete with my brother."

*The Jeremy Kyle Show* was blaring on television. "You Abandoned Your Baby When He Was Two Years Old," it said on the screen, and all the people, audience and guests, looked angrily compliant or defiant. Paul's sitting room smelled of fresh ironing, and there were plastic bags from Primark and Iceland along one wall, with Misty the cat easing around them and pawing the legs of his pajama trousers. Paul threw a dismayed look at the TV and stroked the cat. "It would be the best thing they ever did if they left their children alone," he said. On the pale wooden mantelpiece there was a Girls Aloud CD and a photograph of Paul and Anthony's late grandmother standing outside her house with a birthday cake.

"My epilepsy started when my grandmother died," he said. The doctor gave him carbamazepine, an anticonvulsant, but Paul is reluctant to take it because he thinks it will aggravate his weight problem. He is twenty-eight and gay, with a part-time job in Marks & Spencer. "Anthony lived with me here when he split up with his wife," he said. "And it was a happy time, d'yer know what I mean? When my brother died in Iraq I think I just fell to pieces, to be quite honest. I had to take antidepressants. It kills me to think that someone as strong and beautiful as Anthony could lose his life just like that. The army's after-care service is rubbish. At the time, they say they're going to give you the world, but they don't."

The last thing Anthony Wakefield saw in life was dimly lit waste ground, a road going out of town at the edge of Al-Amarah. But the sight could not have been unfamiliar to him: he grew up in a similar place in the north of England, in the depressed area of Walker, where he was born on August 20, 1980. Paul was almost exactly a year older, and the brothers were always "the boys." Their father, Jimmy Wakefield, died of a heart attack when Anthony was four; he'd been beaten up in the street one day and died in the armchair of their house in Walker Road, aged forty. Paul says their mother abandoned them at that time, and that things have never really been right between them since. She still lives in the area. "Anthony and I went to live with my grandparents," he said. "My grandmother was from Greenock in Scotland, and my grandfather, he was from a mining village in Durham." But they were really brought up by their aunt Emily and uncle Danny. When I went to see Emily, her house in Apple

Tree Gardens was teeming with porcelain cats. "Anthony really loved army films," she said. "He watched *Platoon* every other day and he kept army films under his bed. My husband, Danny, bought him combat trousers when he was about seven—him and Paul—and you couldn't get them off him to wash them. When Anthony wore his out, he stole Paul's to wear."

Emily showed me photographs of the boys at that age. I could see from the photos the ubiquity of the combat trousers, and a certain fearfulness in Anthony's face. "When his mam left and their dad died," said Emily, "I think Anthony was left with the feeling that if he got too close to people, they would leave him."

The boys were "injured-seeming" when they first arrived, said a teacher at their old school. Anthony was the more outgoing, but he was clearly troubled when his grandfather died suddenly in 1987, while queuing for unemployment benefits. Anthony liked football and was always easy and popular with everyone. The boys didn't see much of their mother (she had another family), and as the years passed their grandmother's people, whom Paul calls "my family," were estranged from her. Paul was initially keen to steer me away from her, which wasn't hard, as she carefully steered away herself.

Anthony was always very good-looking, and in childhood pictures is often jumping or running. On a trip to Holy Island, Anthony is casting himself about, seeming to look for adventure or entertainment, while Paul always appears to be retiring from the scene. "It was like he was the older brother," said Paul. "And eventually, telling him I was gay was just like borrowing a cup of sugar. Anthony just said, 'I know. I used to share a room with you, Paul. I don't care.' When Anthony was next to me I felt about twenty feet tall, d'yer know what I mean?"

Sister Josepha, the headmistress of St. Vincent's Primary

School, can still remember the boys coming to the gate for the first time. "Anthony was so neat and tidy," she said. "Walking up with their grandmother, you could feel the pain. I just wanted to bring them in and look after them; they seemed so small and so tentative. Anthony wasn't strong educationally. You know the way some children are . . . not shell-shocked, but frozen somehow."

St. Vincent's was built in 1932 as a result of the voluntary efforts of local Catholics. It is a small school in a difficult area, and according to prideful lore, workingmen were known to have stolen building materials from the Tyneside shipyards to help with its construction. The day I went to see her, Sister Josepha was wearing sandals and a black wimple, and her eyes smiled through gold-rimmed spectacles. Behind her stood a large print of the Virgin and Child. "There was an awakening with Anthony," she said. "He developed into a bit of a monkey and people wanted to be with him. It was just too sad. When I heard Anthony had gone into the army I said, 'No!' His whole physique was so thin and I couldn't imagine him in that macho world."

Sister Josepha showed me some old registers and school photographs of Anthony. His hair was light brown and the headmistress remembered the way he suddenly burst out of his shell and became popular. "But he wasn't the sort of boy you had to check," she said. Listening to her talk of her fears about Iraq and compare the loss of young men to the devastations of the First World War, my eye fell on an open Bible next to her. The passage was from Luke: "Many have undertaken to draw up an account of the things that have been fulfilled among us, just as they were handed down to us by those who from the first were eyewitnesses and servants of the Word."

Memory was the issue for Mr. Simpson. A former math

teacher at the school, he now suffers from Parkinson's disease and said he found it difficult to settle and remember things. Mr. Simpson sat in a high-backed chair wearing purple pajamas. His living room was small but it housed a great many Bibles, which he sat in front of, his arms flailing and his legs jerking as he tried to clean his glasses and speak to me about Anthony. It seemed an incredible effort, and I asked him if he'd like to take a rest. "No," he said. "They were great dancers, the girls in Anthony's year. He never fought at school or anything like that. I think I had him as a fullback on the football team."

Paul leaned in to Mr. Simpson's chair. "Can I ask you a question?" he said. "Can I ask you what you thought of me when I was a kid?"

"Nice," said Mr. Simpson, rocking. "A quiet boy."

Brian Simpson's sister looks after him. She brought us tea and a plastic tub of biscuits. "I remember," he said. "I remember" — and his hands beat a semaphore, as if guiding the words into the room — "that Anthony would walk up at the end of the day and stand at my classroom door, showing his big smile. I remember several times he came up like that and I drew, with chalk, three stripes on the sleeve of his blazer. He seemed to like that, the stripes."

John C. Spahr was born on January 9, 1963, at Our Lady of Lourdes Hospital in Camden, New Jersey. His mother, Eileen, is the eldest of her Irish family, the Kellys, who came to Boston from Ireland before the Second World War. Eileen married Ronald Charles Spahr of Philadelphia, the son of German immigrants, and in the late 1950s the couple moved to a three-bedroom colonial house in Cherry Hill, New Jersey, which is fairly close to Philadelphia. Everyone you ask speaks of the Spahrs as a classic American postwar family, moderately affluent and natively tough, putting great stock in education, sports, meal-times, prayers, memories and earning money. It is the kind of American family that knows its European origins, each genera-tion doing a little better than the one before, while remembering where they came from. The Spahrs could always dilute conven-tionality with a few drinks, but overall they gleam with a sense of family duty, a common purpose, which might sometimes have chimed with the national mood.

It was obvious from babyhood that John Spahr was going to be big. He filled the crib and was often irate at first, but before he was three years old his gentleness had begun to assert itself. He was Ronnie and Eileen's first boy — their fourth child — and in all the pictures he appears placid and willing to be charm-ing. Yet there always appears to have been something reticent about him; on his first day at kindergarten, as he left his mother and faced the new doors, he turned and said to her, "What's my name?"

"We were the house in the neighborhood that all the kids would gravitate to," says his sister Sabrina. "I guess being the house on the street with the largest number of kids was the reason, but if you ask us, even today, we'd say it was because we were the most fun." Dinner always happened at 5:30 p.m., and everybody remembers Eileen laying out the food on seven plates. They all said "please" — always twice, "Mother, may I please be excused from the table, please?" — and their father would never say much. Before the children left for the bus every day, the whole family would kneel in a circle in the middle of the carpet. "In the name of the Father and of the Son and of the Holy Spirit," they said, "good morning, dear God, thank you for another lovely, happy day. God bless Mommy and Daddy and all my brothers and sisters. Amen." Then off they would go down the path with their satchels and lunches in brown paper bags, each with his or her name marked on them: Kelly, Sabrina, Tracy, John, and Stephen. They liked to build a snow wall in the yard at Christmas, to battle the Burcher boys across the street. And they had Easter outfits and lots of swimming at the beach in summer and every kind of sport you can imagine. It sounds like the world of the Kennedys, and not just because of their Irishness. It's that American open-air life, that instinctive response to conditions outside.

Early on, it became obvious that John was gifted at sports. He was peaceful but determined. When he was trying to learn to ride a bike, he just fell off and got on, fell off and got on, until finally he mastered it. For John's father, the great hope was that his son might become an athlete. Some of the siblings feel today that the pressure to succeed was almost too much, but Ronnie would get up with John at five in the morning and drive him down to the boathouse, to see him row. It was Ronnie's dream that his eldest son prove his specialness that way, perhaps exceeding hopes he once had for himself.

When I turned up in Cherry Hill, the lawns were already twinkling for Christmas. It was not so much a matter of keeping up with the Joneses as showing the Joneses that some values were held in common, the wire Santas and flashing sleighs a signal of consistency. Eileen Spahr answered the door in a Chanel suit and a beautiful silk blouse; there was something rather resplendent about her looks and her Irish sense of rules. She appeared to aim for correctness — or perfection, to judge by her hair and her nails, her teeth and her sense of manners — but a merry air of devilment occasionally rises as if from her genes. Mrs. Spahr made tea and set it down in a green cup. She has lived in that house for almost fifty years, and the bustle has gone. Her husband and her elder son are dead, and the others are out there prospecting for happiness, while Mrs. Spahr maintains a sense of style among the lonely hours.

"Ronnie was passionate about sports," she said. "My husband was an intense person." Mrs. Spahr is a keen reader, and she asked me several questions about books I had written and pieces I'd done. She had never allowed a writer into the house before and wanted to be sure she could handle it. She is intelligent enough to know that other people's writing can offer disclosures that may be a little difficult to bear if you are close to the subject, but the Irish in her wanted to speak and pack up her troubles. "Oh, yeah," she said when I asked her if John was fixated on pleasing his parents. "And it wasn't a burden for him. He wanted to be a good guy. He said to his brother once, 'Don't you want to be all right for them?' From a young age John was focused."

"Well, he had no choice but to be successful," his sister Kelly said to me later, "because my dad was always pushing. Dad was always torturing himself. But he didn't have to worry about John, because John always liked to be doing something at a high level."

When he was about twelve, John was always out on the street shouting orders at the other kids. He had that leadership thing and all the kids respected him. "Then suddenly," says his mother, "he just stopped all that. I asked him why he wasn't shouting anymore. He said, 'I just don't wanna be that way.' When, in junior high school, he was called out and had a fistfight, he had to tell his mother about it. She was simply pleased he had won. "I thought it was always my job to keep them safe and on track," she said. The boys spent a lot of the summer holidays cutting grass for money around the neighborhood.

"That's the smell I remember," said Sabrina. "The boys'

room always smelled like old, grassy, preteen sneakers. I remember opening their closet and looking down to a mound of sneakers and thinking, Why are there so many?" And when I spoke to her in a bar at the top of a tall hotel in Philadelphia, Sabrina kept turning over the pages of old photo albums as if they held a mystery. She'd been putting the albums together ever since John died, wanting to bind the material of his life and all their lives together. "Ever since he was young," she said, "he had a coach's mentality. The kids in the street wanted to be like him. And, you know, the motto of the Marines is *Semper fidelis,* Always faithful. That was him and always was him. Even before he was flying, he loved to fly at things. We had a great childhood."

Mrs. Spahr wanted to show me around the house before we continued talking. The boys' room had an American flag above the desk. The trees outside seemed frozen and watchful while Mrs. Spahr recounted how the boys would play games up here once upon a time, and share stories and laughs. It was hard not to think of soldiers all over the world who started off in small bedrooms like the one in Cherry Hill: as I looked at the placid walls and the tidy small space, a certain dream seemed to rise for a moment and take hold, a very domestic dream of glory. Motivations are perhaps the greatest mystery of all.

"You know, his father hated to fly," said Mrs. Spahr. It seemed he would do anything to avoid going on a plane, including driving across the country to see John when he lived in San Diego. "Ronnie wanted John to be a football coach and that was that. He didn't want him to join the Marines, and thank God he wasn't around to see what happened to John, because it would have killed him, too." Mrs. Spahr was dabbing her eyes with kitchen napkins as she spoke; they were brightly colored, with the words "Happy Holidays" printed the same on each one.

When I caught up with Sabrina again, it seemed as if she had been thinking about significant things in the meantime. "Even at a young age," she said, "he wanted to bring out the best in people and teach you what he knew. That was his gift. For my father, it was all about family. We went to church and it was always the front pew. It was a house where they would have parties, cocktails and cigarettes. It was that time, right?" Sabrina is different from the other members of her family: she worries a lot and tends to be an organizer. She will say, in quiet moments, that there is something missing in her life and that what happened to John stopped her in her tracks. Like her sister Kelly, she often starts sentences with the phrase "I said to my husband . . . ," and she gives off a feeling of hope that family can answer all of life's demands.

Mrs. Spahr played down the influence of her husband's anxieties on John's chosen path, but others felt the influence was pretty decisive. "Not a lot of fathers in New Jersey would get up at five in the morning to drive their son to the river," said Sabrina. I thought about that, and wondered at Ronnie's overall effect on his son's inner life. Sabrina's voice is quiet, even quieter when she's discussing their father, as if he might be listening, as if she were speaking in church, as if she were being disloyal. "He didn't talk about much," she said. "My mom talked. I always wished that he had talked more."

In May 1981 there was a story in the *Philadelphia Inquirer*: "Spahr Is New Jersey's Gift to St. Joseph's Prep Rowing," said the headline. "In America, those kinds of young men are a breed apart," said a friend of the family, "and they're treated like gods in certain schools." The photograph accompanying the article is of a tousle-haired, clean-limbed and smiling John Spahr, looking like a tragic hero out of F. Scott Fitzgerald.

Why does one of the very best scholastic rowers in the United States go to school in North Philadelphia—when he lives in Cherry Hill? "It was just word of mouth," said John Spahr, who won the Junior National Singles championship last summer, rowing for St. Joseph's Prep . . . Spahr, who gets up at 5 a.m. daily so that he can start practicing on the Schuylkill at 6, isn't just an oarsman. He started at quarterback for the Prep this fall, and started for the private school stars in the City All-Star Game in April.

The newspaper spread also included a picture of Mrs. Spahr, elegant as ever, a believing mother, midlife, pre-crisis and far from the vexations of a poor Irish childhood, shouting encouragement to her American boy from the bank of the river.

St. Joseph's Prep is a Jesuit school. Past a hall of portraits showing successive principals since 1966, the head rowing coach, Bill Lamb, sat in a room under an overactive air-conditioning system. "To educate mind, body and spirit," he said, "and show how these three components make a complete person, that is the Jesuit mantra." Mr. Lamb had a habit shared by many of the people I spoke to about John Spahr: he talked about him in the present tense. I wondered as I listened to the coach's tough statements what effect the death of a young man had on the lives of people who lived for the vitality of youth. But Mr. Lamb was circumspect: one imagines he feels, somewhere, that sacrifice is a known and regrettable part of the game. "John is the perfect model," continued Mr. Lamb. "To turn the skill and the confidence you learn in athletics and use that to develop as a person—and John, in a heroic way, took that complete person and recognized how he could best be of service to others. He dedicated his life to that."

His star pupil wanted to lead and change things. He was

popular and athletic, and the rowing team needed that very badly at the time, because it was feared the school might lose its position in the league. "If we could get John to row, the rest of the kids in the school would look at rowing as something cool to do. When this started we had nine guys, and by the end we had over a hundred. The best marketing is when the kids tell other kids there's value in what they're doing. He was successful at everything he ever did. But even when he was at the top level, John acted as if he was at the bottom. Out of any year, you can see there are two or three who will do outstanding things."

I imagined Mr. Lamb was a lot like Mr. Tothero, the coach in the first of John Updike's *Rabbit* novels:

> The coach is concerned with developing the three tools we are given in life: the head, the body, and the heart . . . "All those years, all those boys [says Tothero], they pass through your hands and into the blue. And never come back, Harry; they never come back . . . Give the boys the will to achieve. I've always liked that better than the will to win, for there can be achievement even in defeat. Make them feel the, yes, I think the word is good, the *sacredness* of achievement, in the form of giving our best."

"Some talented guys can sit back a little," said Bill Lamb, "but John was working as hard as the weakest guy on the team. He didn't want to risk the privilege by getting involved in some of the things that teenagers get involved in."

"And what about his father?" I asked. "Some people have suggested the influence was strong."

"His father was a very, very conservative, strict disciplinarian," he said. "He raised all his daughters as if they were boys. It was his way or the highway."

"Isn't there a danger in the American system," I said, "in creating such a platform for sterling brilliance at school that the rest of life is a struggle to maintain it?"

"Absolutely," said Bill Lamb. "That's our greatest challenge. We have a lot of kids who never leave high school. They're thirty years old and they're still operating as if it was St. Joe's Prep, and the real world isn't like that. Some of them have a problem in applying the lessons they learned here to their daily lives. But it's about hard work. Pick up the sports pages, I'll show you five of those guys. But with John it was almost as if he didn't really exist. He was the model of success, and you couldn't have drawn it any better."

Down at the boathouse it was dark and the town's lights were reflected in the black ripples of the river. Al Zimmerman, another of John's teachers, showed me the boat that was named after John, and the memorial plaque. Mr. Zimmerman used to teach Latin and Greek at the school, and he wrote the words for the plaque; he skirted around them when I was there, as if shy of what he had produced. The boathouse was full of expired energy and prolonged ideals. Al talked of what they tried to give John and about what he gave them. His voice lapped gently and kindly at my back as I looked out at the river, and beyond that to the merging borders of Pennsylvania and Delaware and New Jersey, wondering how many of the people out there once knew a young man called John Spahr. And what did his life say about theirs? About ours? About the lives of nations? "He liked to roll his sleeves up and get the job done," said Al Zimmerman. "And that's what you really need in a crew. He applied those same principles elsewhere."

The river Tyne is a place where famous industry appears to have given way to infamous leisure. The only ship I passed as

I made my way to visit Anthony Wakefield's wife and children was one called *Tuxedo Princess,* a former liner now converted into a nightclub. Along the quay the flashing lights spoke of concert halls and happy-hours, while the shipyard cranes stood still against the dark. Among them, once upon a time, battle cruisers were built to order and the Gatling gun was made by W. Armstrong & Co.

As he came to the end of his schooldays, Anthony kept saying he wanted to be a soldier. Living with his grandparents, he always enjoyed the stories his grandfather would tell about surviving the Normandy landings. Anthony's guardians made a rule that no toy guns were allowed in the house. But at secondary school Anthony got in with a rowdy crowd and was expelled. His childhood was transformed in that period by an adult accusation: some girls said he'd got rough with them in a park. "It wasn't true," said his brother, "but it shocked him. Anthony was dyslexic and was never going to sit exams anyhow."

The Army Careers Office in Northumberland Street turned Anthony away the first time. They said he was too small and too thin, so he got a job stocking shelves at a discount supermarket; the second time they let him have the forms. His uncle Dan says he didn't think Anthony would pass the interview for the army because he was a little bowlegged and had high arches. Anthony accepted another job, at the twenty-four-hour Tesco in Kingston Park near the airport—where many of the staff go round on roller skates—but right away the letter came from the army saying he was in. Anthony and Paul's beloved grandmother was dying, but she said she wanted to hold on to hear Anthony's news, "Just to make sure the boys were all right," said Paul.

Anthony's choice of regiment, the Coldstream Guards, was made on the basis, he said, that all the best-looking guys joined the Guards. (The regiment performs many ceremonial duties:

the queen's birthday parade, trooping the color, the changing of the guard.) He did his training at Catterick and Aldershot and then Pirbright, where he passed out in 1998 on St. George's Day. "We had to stand in a line for four hours," wrote Anthony to his aunt Emily during his training. "All our legs hurt and we are all very tired and we are starving. The only thing I've had is a Murray Mint off one of the lads. We are going to get our hair cuts tomorrow."

Once he got going, Anthony was earning about £250 a week, serving first in Belize and then in Northern Ireland. When he came home on leave, he would sometimes go out with Paul and his friends to clubs in Newcastle. Anthony loved tanning parlors and dancing, so he was as comfortable in his brother's preferred gay haunts as anywhere else. "If anyone had come near him I would probably have killed them," said Paul when I asked him about it.

"Was there anything about Anthony you didn't like?"

"I didn't like it that he smoked," said Paul, "or that he had tattoos. The tattoos came with the army."

On the left side of his chest Anthony had a fairly large tattoo of a ripped flag—a Coldstream Guards staple—and he also had a tattoo of a kneeling girl in fishnet stockings. During his second tour in Northern Ireland, a young Catholic pulled a gun on him but he didn't fire, and Anthony was commended for standing his ground. Before that he'd already got married to Ann Toward, a girl he'd met in the Global Video shop on Shields Road. "He was just dead nice," says Ann. "He took care of himself and he was a laugh."

Ann already had a little girl, Stacey, when she met Anthony. She had the baby when she was about sixteen, and she has never had a job. (She is thirty-three.) She and Anthony went on to have two more children, Scott and Corey, who are aged ten and five. Anthony's aunt Emily told me Anthony "totally loved" having a house of his own. "He would love making dinners," she said. "And he'd want everybody round. When he did that, he'd clean the house from top to bottom. It was as if he just loved the idea of making a proper family himself."

Paul has few good words to say about Anthony's widow, and she knows it. I tried to steer him away from saying too much. I told him I was writing everything down, but he said that didn't bother him. The circumstances of his childhood and his brother's loss have made Paul self-absorbed, understandably so, perhaps, but he doesn't see how difficult it must be for Ann, bringing up three children on her own. Paul and Anthony's difficulties with their own mother may lie behind some of this confusion. Paul was boiling with rage about his mother one night when I drove him round Newcastle. At that stage, his mother hadn't wanted to speak to me, and Paul couldn't understand why. He couldn't work out why other people didn't see the point of the story — as if it meant they didn't see the point of Anthony — and he considered his mother's refusal to be yet another rejection.

This had all been part of the chaos of Anthony's life, not just his childhood but also the time before he died, when he and Ann had split up and he was going out with a local hairdresser called Kym. The Byker estate complex was pitch-black the night I called on Ann, and her house seemed overexcited and overpopulated, children rushing in and out of the bright kitchen. She is a pretty woman with a nice smile and a bad cough. She was looking for her inhaler, but she held a pack of cigarettes in her hand the whole time I was there. I was told Scott had attention deficit hyperactivity disorder, and he certainly whirled around a fair amount, crashing into the fridge and clearly finding it hard to settle.

"My dad and me went to the lighthouse museum," Scott said, wrapping himself around my arm. "On my birthday my dad hided all the presents behind the settee and in the cupboards. I found five and then he told me where the other ones were. There was a hundred stairs at the lighthouse museum."

"He died," said Corey.

"I went in me dad's car with me friend," said Scott, "and we ate chewing gum and we asked Dad if we could put music on and that, and he say 'Aye.'"

I asked Scott what he would like to do when he grows up. "I want to be a high court judge and work with horses," he said. The whole family spoke with singsong Geordie accents, the words pouring into one another.

Stacey came down the stairs wearing a Playgirl T-shirt and with her hair in bunches. She is fourteen. A neighbor told me that Anthony doted on Stacey. "When he got home on leave," she said, "he was always taking her up the town to buy her phones and trainers, whatever she wanted." By the time Stacey began to speak—it took her a while to stop chewing the ends of her hair and giggling—the living room had turned into a corner of Bedlam. Scott was thumping the Formica kitchen top with a giant stick and shooting us all with a plastic gun, and Corey was blowing a whistle. "My dad was nice," said Stacey. "He told jokes and he didn't shout at you. We went to the Metro Center on my birthday. He bought us a Girls Aloud CD and jeans and everything, then we went to KFC."

When Anthony Wakefield died, his loss animated a series of hurts and complications that might never end. "Every Christmas, every birthday, every memory," said Ann, "the death of Anthony affects the kids. To Corey his father is just in heaven. Stacey goes off on her own to her bedroom and broods about it and has her own thoughts. With Scott's problems, he often just doesn't understand. At the time of Anthony's death, Stacey would blame me, saying, 'It should have been you,' and things like that."

I asked her if they had enough to live on.

"We have eight hundred pounds a month," she said. "Four hundred and sixteen of that goes on rent for this house, and there's another hundred a month for council tax."

"So you and the kids have seventy pounds a week left to live off?"

"Aye," she said. "You've just got to get on with it."

It was hard to speak to Ann while Paul was there: resentment made him vigilant, and he felt angry when she spent a few moments with me in the kitchen alone, "forcing you to hear her side of the story," he said.

"There needn't be sides," I said to him later. But I felt sorry for Paul and thought his possessiveness about his brother's memory could only be part of his grief.

"I've got these kids and I get the pension and that's what bothers him," Ann said. "He never comes here. Neither does their mother, the kids' grandmother. She hasn't seen the children since the day of Anthony's funeral. There's been a lot of nasty stuff, but I'm not bothered, really. People might think I stole Anthony away too young and made him have kids. But it wasn't like that. We did it together, and now he's gone we have to make it the best way we can."

When I asked her, Ann said that Anthony really loved being in the army. That was his first love. "We probably married too young," she said. "He only had two days' leave when Corey was born, then it was on to Iraq. It was hard and things just fell apart. But I don't think the dislike will ever end with Paul and his family. It's sad for the kids, but you've just got to get on with it."

One of Ann's neighbors in Byker is called Angela Cairns. As I walked to her house there was a crack of lightning over the estate and a roll of thunder. Angela knew Anthony and Ann when they first met. "He had a huge picture of the singer George Michael above his bed," said Angela. "Everybody teased him about it, but he said, 'One day I'll be famous like him.'" Angela was wearing huge hoop earrings and slippers covered in hearts. Whenever she got excited she kicked an Argos catalogue that was sitting on the floor beside the front door. "One night, when he was home from the army," she said, "Anthony went out on the town with my son Stephen. They went to Buffalo Joe's on the Gateside quays—Steve was Gothic then—and they were drunk and coming across the swing bridge. Stephen was really pissed up, and he climbed onto the side of the bridge and lost his footing. He fell all that way down into the Tyne, and he was struggling in the water 'cause his Gothic gear was dragging him down. Anthony dived in. The tide is strong down there, and Stephen was losing consciousness, but Anthony pulled him to the side by the hair and then insisted on giving him artificial respiration. He saved Stephen's life, and then Anthony was up all night crying."

When he was leaving for Iraq that last time, it was a Sunday and he went with Paul and Kym to have lunch and then began packing his bags. "Don't be a hero," said Paul. And when his truck back to Aldershot broke down, Paul and Kym decided to drive him and another young squaddie all the way down in Kym's car. "We were exhausted by the time we got there," said Paul, "and we all fell asleep in the one bed in his living quarters, me and Kym with Anthony in the middle. In the morning all the soldiers were pleased to see him. He had a shower and then he gave me a microwave oven to take home and a DVD player. When it was time to go he grabbed me and gave me a big hug. It was usually me that instigated that, but this time it was Anthony, and it meant a lot. That was the last time I ever saw him. He just looked spotless. We were always like that when we were kids, always spotless." We were in a restaurant at Newcastle quayside when Paul said this, and he sat back in his chair. "We didn't have much as kids," he said, "and . . . that's it. We didn't have much."

Ann and the children were asleep on May 2, 2005, when the knock came at the door. Ann was shaking as the children went down the stairs, Scott saying, "When my daddy comes home I'm going to ask him to buy me a backpack." Ann took all the children into the kitchen and told them there had been an accident. "Daddy's gone to heaven," she said. The children were screaming and Ann phoned her neighbor Angela in a terrible state—"heartbroken," Angela said—and everyone was bewildered and disbelieving at four in the morning, the children crying and trying to imagine how it could happen. Paul says when he heard the knock on his door he thought it would be Anthony. "He must be home." But through the spy hole he saw it was Ann and Stephen. "I was so stunned," Paul says, "that they thought I was going to smash the place up. I remember walking around the house putting pictures of Anthony in my pocket." Then the three of them went to tell Anthony's mother. "It's all my fault" is what Paul remembers her saying. "She was throwing up her hands," says Paul, "shouting 'Jimmy, Jimmy' . . . shouting for her husband. She said she thought it was all her own fault because of what happened when we were little."

Months after my first visit to Newcastle, I went back when the opportunity arose, very suddenly, to spend a little time with Anthony's mother, Sylvia Grieve. Her house on Finsbury Avenue is very neat and modest, with a sign on the side facing the street that says NO BALL GAMES. Mrs. Grieve was wearing black trousers and a black top; she is a small, easily embarrassed woman, wearing a bracelet covered in gold hearts, and with eyes that seem to show some experience of what the world is like—her world, at least. "Anthony had been a very happy baby and daft as a brush," she said. "I lost them when they were very young because of marriage difficulties. I was too young when I had kids. My own family background wasn't very nice, so you rush into things to get a house of your own. It was mainly worries with money and his dad liked a drink. When I got the news about him I felt guilty and wondered why it wasn't me that died."

Mrs. Grieve has photographs of Anthony on several of her walls, and she appears to live a lot of her life between the gas fire and the television set.

"And did you worry about him?" I asked.

"You always have this thing in the back of your mind," she said. "But you could tell he was frightened the last time I saw him, before he went off. I says to him, 'Just tell them your mam says you have to come back or else I'll come looking for them and I'll bash them.' And when they came with the news that he'd died, I just kept hearing Anthony's voice saying to me, 'Come on, Mam. You've got to say something.' That's what I imagined him saying."

Mrs. Grieve was quoted later as saying that she blamed Tony Blair for her son's death. (Paul puts it differently: he says George Bush murdered Anthony.) You can tell Anthony's mother isn't actually very interested in politics, but she wishes her son had come home, and she says she feels the Americans are taking all the glory. "But I suppose Anthony wanted to go," she said. "He was eager. From the beginning, from the very beginning, Anthony always wanted a little limelight on him."

• • •

As evening approached in Cherry Hill, Eileen Spahr began to tell me her own story. She has the kind of faith in comfort and progress that comes from not having known enough of either in childhood. When it comes to her children, she points out that she may not always have got things right — too much pressure, perhaps, on Stephen, the younger son, who was more rebellious; too much emphasis, perhaps, on her husband's hopes — but with all that she has a basic certainty about the values she sees her family as having tried to live by. "You've got to have testicles," she said to John when he was dithering at college. "Go full force and take advantage of the opportunities in life. John was my best friend — he had this beautifulness of spirit — and we could talk about pretty much anything."

Under his photograph in John Spahr's high school yearbook, he chose the motto "Good company on a journey makes the way seem shorter." He got his degree from the University of Delaware, and he met and fell in love with Diane, who later became his wife. "He was affable," said his sister Tracy, "and he had a real soft side. At Delaware he did a lot of growing up." He went to university trailing high expectations, and he lost his football scholarship, which people say was part of the bigger job of getting to know himself. "I think he was quite shaken up by not quite knowing what to do," says Tracy.

After that, he worked for a while teaching physical fitness. He also spent time teaching sports to handicapped children. "I knew he wanted a large life," said his mother. "So I went down there to have lunch with him. I said, 'John, what do you want to do?' And he said he wanted to fly jets, so I said, 'Go do it.' Ronnie had totally figured out what John should do with his life — he should go to the Naval Academy and coach football: that's the life my husband would have wanted. I don't want to be disloyal to my husband, but he knew he was right. He became more and more German every day of his life. My father was domineering, you know, and my mother's policy was appeasement."

Three times that summer, John came home to tell his father he had joined the Marines, but three times he left Cherry Hill having failed to tell him. In any event, he had entered a five-year program to become a pilot. On August 6, 1991, Mrs. Spahr wrote about John in her journal: "On this day John called in the middle of the afternoon. And I said 'why?' and he said 'jets' and I said 'happy?' and he said 'yes.'" A couple of years later, there's another entry in Mrs. Spahr's diary: "John called a few minutes ago. 'I am alive and I am happy—the best day of my life, winged in the Marines . . . Whatever happens, I am content. I did my best.'" Mrs. Spahr says that from that point on, no man was ever so proud of his son as Ronnie was of John.

"I met John as he followed his dream of becoming a Marine jet pilot at the basic school in Quantico, Virginia," said his friend Kevin Wolfe. They went on from there to further training at Kingsville, Texas. "Dukes stood out," said Wolfe. "He had the classic good looks and swagger of a Marine—he carried himself with confidence, and right away you wanted to follow him and you didn't know why. He had an unparalleled work ethic: he lived in our tactical manuals, perfecting his briefing and debriefing skills. John wanted to be a Top Gun instructor, and because he had performed so well in the navy's premier strike fighter course, he accepted their invitation. It was there that Dukes would have an indelible impact on pilots throughout the navy and Marine Corps. He was funny too. My wife Heather and I were there when his daughter Chandler was born in San Diego. I remember as we all anxiously waited to know his or her arrival, John came out with a sheepish grin and said, 'Well, she's a Republican!'"

John Spahr and his wife Diane worked hard at their marriage, but in the end, like so many military marriages, it didn't work out. In trying to give an account of a life fully lived, a writer wonders what is most essential and most true. In the end, what we write is not merely an account of the bare facts, but an account of our choices and of other people's: the Spahrs are a family who care about family, and they speak of John's endless affection for his daughter. "He was married to flying anyhow," said his sister Kelly. "It's like a vocation, and that's that."

Lieutenant Colonel D. A. Robinson was an instructor on the Top Gun staff with John Spahr. This is the elite training school for fighter pilots in Fallon, Nevada. "A number of his commanding officers said he was the best officer that has ever served under them," he said. "And a number of his own staff said he was the best officer they'd ever served under. He always had a special faith in the underdog." At the Top Gun school, instructors would be expected to debrief rookie pilots when they returned from a training exercise. This would normally take twenty minutes or so, but Spahr's were famous for their length. Major Tim Golden remembers "a debriefing of John's that took six hours. Nobody could believe it. The poor guy was in there for six hours, and John would go over everything in detail."

I met Major Tim "Nugs" Golden and Major Dan "Knuckles" Shipley in an Irish bar in Washington, only a few minutes' walk from Capitol Hill. There was a game on television as we entered, and Rich Gannon was commentating on the Miami Dolphins' performance as we ordered. "Gannon played behind John Spahr in school," said Nugs. "There was always this competition between them, and many people felt that John was better than Gannon." This is the world these men live in—a universe of professional self-improvement and ceaseless competition, where being better than the next guy is a survival instinct. "John was the guy everybody listened to," added Nugs. "He was the best instructor by far—a coach, really. And he was so competitive. We were all out there in 2003 in the Gulf and John would be involved in the most stressful things, then he would stay up all night playing Xbox. I remember we all played and then turned in for the night, and we kept calling him to get some sleep, but whenever I woke up, all the way to six a.m., he was still playing that damn thing, trying to get to the next level. He was up all night."

"And he had natural flying ability," said Knuckles. (I noticed these pilots liked me to use their call signs; anything else seems too formal to them.) "He had flown more dogfights than anybody else and was so far ahead of the action."

"That was it," said Nugs. "His only fault was to push and push, and you'd say, 'Hey, dude—relax, friggin' relax.' But he always wanted to do more and more, which was a pressure on him and on others as well."

"He chose the toughest route," said Knuckles. "It's much more intense being a Marine fighter pilot—six months' infantry training, then two years' flight school. You gotta learn how to land that thing on an aircraft carrier. Then they ask him to come back as an instructor, and he comes back and he's the best. God, man, you wanna kick him in the nuts. But he had humility. There were people who were as good pilots as he was but none of them had his humility."

In training videos, you see how John Spahr would explain to groups of elite pilots all the things that could happen while flying his particular jet, but he kept it mainly technical. He could draw on three thousand hours of flying experience, but he was discreet about his missions. In the 1990s and early 2000s, Spahr had in fact spent a great deal of time in military combat, flying sorties in Bosnia and supporting the no-fly zone in southern Iraq. In 2003, he was aboard the USS *Constellation*, a veteran carrier made famous during Vietnam, and it was from here that he would lead a bombing campaign in Iraq that would exceed the might and devastation of all that conflict's previous campaigns.

On March 20, 2003, the CIA received reports from Iraqi spies that Saddam Hussein would spend the night at a farm on the banks of the Tigris in eastern Baghdad. The Shock and Awe air campaign was launched at 9 p.m. local time on the following day, involving, according to William Arkin of the *Washington Post,*

> 1,700 aircraft flying 830 strike sorties plus 505 cruise missiles attacking 1,500 aimpoints at several hundred targets: palaces, homes, guard headquarters, government buildings, military bases. More targets were attacked in Baghdad in the span of one hour on March 21 than we hit in the entire 43-day air campaign in 1991, and airpower followed up reliably every day with hundreds more strikes. When the sandstorm came, when the Fedayeen arrived, when ground commanders got nervous that Iraq was not the country that the U.S. had wargamed against, when the Red Line was crossed, when the public got equally nervous, airpower continued in the background, bombing, bombing, bombing.

According to Jon Lee Anderson's account in his book *The Fall of Baghdad,* "The sheer power and scale and precision of the attacks were at once terrible and awe-inspiring and placed us in a state of mind in which almost anything seemed possible."

John Spahr was the first pilot over Baghdad on March 21, and the first to deliver bombs. His sister Kelly said he would never talk about what happened. "That's what John said," remembers Kelly. "There are things he did that I knew he would never talk about. But John wasn't political in the way some people are: he believed in the commander in chief and he followed orders. That's what he did." John told his friends that if his commanding officer said "Go," he'd go, and personal opinion had nothing to do with it. At the end of that first mission in Baghdad, as the sun was coming up, John had his photograph taken in midair by one of his colleagues. For the photograph, John tilted up the bottom of the jet, to show the camera that his bombs were gone.

Knuckles, another member of the Death Rattlers on those missions, told me what it's like up there in a fighter plane during a mission. "There's antiaircraft stuff coming at you," he said, "and you're working via night goggles. Your mouth goes dry and it ain't funny anymore. This is what happens when you're in-country. Time slows down to an incredible level and everything is deliberate. And you're making sure you're getting precision in the bombing. You're taking information like drinking from a fire hose. You've got to be aware of your altitude; you're looking at your wingman. You're worried if you can make it back. It's literally overwhelming. It's such a frickin' challenge and you know it's a son of a bitch. And then at the end you have to land this thing on a ship in the middle of the ocean in the middle of the night." Nugs was a mission commander that night. "You're saying, 'Please, God, don't let me mess this up,'" he said. "It's as confusing as hell out there."

"I loved to fly with Dukes," said David Peeler, another pilot who served with Spahr in Marine Fighter Attack Squadron 323. "John and I had something in common in our childhoods that prepared us very well for that business. It was not a game to him. He understood that to 'go to the show,' as he put it, was what we all aspired to do — that is, lead in combat."

Anthony Wakefield and John Spahr were, at whatever remove, brothers in arms, but they also had brothers back home who would have to live with the glory they had sought and found. John Spahr's brother Stephen wears his own duty with a smile: he is proud of his older brother, and perfectly silent on the pressure that must always have existed for him to live up to his example. But, whatever he says or doesn't say, his burden multiplied after that fatal flight on May 2, 2005.

Their mother says Stephen was always different. She remembers him, as a boy, pouring water down from the top of the stairs onto the carpet below, an act of gleeful destruction that would never have occurred to the solid John. Stephen got into drinking and girls pretty early, and his freedoms were never squeezed by his father's dislikes. He was his own man and he still is, while knowing that his brother's example is now not only an alternative to his own life, but a hallowed ground that surrounds him. "We stayed up late, John and I, at my sister's house one time," said Stephen. "We'd had a few cocktails together and were pretty drunk, and John said we were different in a way that he did what was important to make my parents happy . . . going to St. Joe's Prep, a steppingstone to a good career and all that. Whereas I did what made *me* happy. John was more focused. He didn't want to share the glory, neither would I — if you're gonna play baseball, you wanna be the pitcher. If you're gonna do crew, you want to be in a single shell. He wanted to make my parents proud."

Stephen will always remember the boys' bedroom at Cherry Hill, the trees outside, the brothers' customary whispers and laughter, and the bus journeys to school in the morning after they'd been to the boathouse. But his abiding memory of John might be one of his last, when he visited his brother on the aircraft carrier in Honolulu. "I was looking down and looking for his plane," said Stephen. "And suddenly I saw it taxiing up from the end of the carrier. He's got the full facemask on and his uniform, but I knew it was him just by his mannerisms. He gave me the thumbs-up and then I saw him holding on to the dashboard — then, *phweeeewo,* he was off. He said to me one time, just before that last tour, that he was a little bit disgusted with what was going on with the war. He was getting a little frustrated with the military — I think he didn't like killing people — and it started to get to him a little bit."

I was later briefed on a report written by the Pentagon, and it seems that John Spahr probably died instantly. It is unlikely that he ejected at the point of collision, but even if he did, it appears that his parachute did not deploy, and, falling five miles in a sandstorm, he would not have been conscious. He suffered a severe injury to his head, and he was later found in the desert a great distance from the jet fragments, a great distance from the floating city he knew as his temporary home, and a great distance, too, from his daughter in San Diego and from the boys' room at Cherry Hill, where he once stared into the dark and dreamed of glory in the miles that were said to exist above the trees and beyond the shores.

On that day in May, two Marines came to the door at Cherry Hill and found that Mrs. Spahr was in Florida. The neighbor across the road saw them and called Sabrina, who was already panicking when she saw the television news, which spoke of two pilots assigned to the USS *Carl Vinson* having gone down. "No," said Sabrina, "please don't say it's John."

In Florida, Mrs. Spahr was staying with a friend, and she was in the back of the house when her host shouted that two of her friends were at the door. Mrs. Spahr came through and nearly passed out: she knew the meaning of two Marines standing at the door of a house containing the mother of a Marine. "I had always planned," Mrs. Spahr told me, "that if I saw those Marines come to the door, I would just go out the back door and I would run until I disappeared into the earth. That was my plan. I went to the Tomb of the Unknown Soldier with John and Chandler one time. He wanted her to see it, and he loved it there. He was such a peaceful man. That's what you would say about him. I've been there a bunch of times, but I'm not going to that place again. I just can't go there anymore. When I was in Florida that time, I took a drive up to the Gulf Coast. I felt so peaceful and everything was so beautiful — for about an hour there was just this exquisite peace."

When a soldier was clearing out Anthony Wakefield's quarters at Camp Abu Naji, he found a collection of posters stuck above his bed, and they too were sent home to Newcastle, the Blu-Tack still on the back of them. They included posters of John Lennon, the Sex Pistols, Adam Ant and Bruce Lee. Anthony had filled in standard MOD Form 106 — a soldier's will — saying that the contents of his savings account should be split among the three children and that all his personal belongings should go to his girlfriend, Kym. These belongings made for three small boxes, and included a sandwich toaster, a gold ring engraved DAD, various CDs, civilian clothes and a Gucci money clip, along with cash totaling £27.76. His collection of papers was not voluminous, either: some legal things, vehicle documents, a booklet from the Guild of International Songwriters and Composers and a membership card for Blockbuster Video.

A letter came to the home of Anthony's aunt Emily, the woman who had brought him up, from Lieutenant Colonel Nicholas Henderson. "Such was his, and their professionalism," he wrote, "they were chosen to look after the most demanding and dangerous part of the city — in order that real progress could be made. They were having a positive effect on the Iraqis, who are desperate for peace and security, and we will continue in the same manner, partly to fulfill our mission here, but also, and most importantly, to honor the memory of Anthony."

Anthony Wakefield's body was flown back to RAF Brize Norton, and from there to Newcastle. The funeral took place at St. Gabriel's Church in Heaton. Before the service, the hearse drove past his old house, and his son Scott looked out the window and wondered what the car and the box inside it had to do with his dad. There was a large crowd on the streets around the church that day, and the coffin, covered in yellow tulips, was taken up the aisle to "Ave Maria." Paul put a card in beside his brother, saying all the things he wished he had said before; it went down into the ground with Anthony, and Paul feels pleased that nobody will ever know exactly what it said.

The Benton Road graveyard was empty the day I went there with Paul. It had the look of so many English urban cemeteries, neglected in the evening traffic, more a place of forgetting than a garden of remembrance. Vandals had made their presence felt, gravestones pushed over, lager cans strewn in several areas, the remains of small fires. You could see the buses lighting up on the main road as Paul took me first to see his father's grave, and then past rows of civilians, the local people of Newcastle who had died where they were born and whose arguments had come to rest in the same place as the people they were arguing with. "Everybody ends up here," said Paul, except he hoped that he would not, and that a job entertaining on a cruise ship would come up before the end of the year. We stood in front of Anthony's headstone, a simple gray one paid for by the Coldstream Guards, and I thought of Paul's letter moldering in the local soil. There wasn't much light left at the end of the day, but enough to see other headstones just like Anthony's further along the line. "There was nobody like him," said Paul as we turned to go.

• • •

Lieutenant Colonel John Spahr was buried with full military ceremony, the occasion marked by the first fly-past in Washington since the events of 9/11. John's sister Tracy was involved in the second term of the Reagan-Bush administration, working as an assistant press secretary. She later campaigned for the vice president and had several posts in his administration. "My friends at the White House had always wanted to know about John," she told me. "It was awesome to think of him up in that plane. Everybody was impressed with him, but to him it was just his calling. He accepted it, and he made the sacrifice. I know that, had he survived, John would have gone on to very great things. The Pentagon was certainly on his list." A few days after his death, a letter came to the house from her old boss George H. W. Bush. "Dear Tracy," it said. "I am so sorry that your brother was KIA. Perhaps it is of some comfort to know that this truly good man gave his life serving our great country. May God bless him as he holds John in his loving arms. Please convey to all your family my most sincere condolences. To you I send my love." Two hundred family and friends, and his beloved daughter Chandler, accompanied John Spahr's coffin to Arlington National Cemetery, where he was buried in a low plain reserved for the American dead of Iraq.

John's sister Kelly picked me up in Baltimore and we drove to Arlington from there. "John was timing his retirement to be when Chandler was in high school," she said. "Just to be with her." As we got closer to Washington, I began to notice how many of her mannerisms were just like her mother's. "What's my point?" she would say if she got lost in talking about John. "We went to our boys' school," she said, "and there was this sign hanging up and it was a kind of American motto—MEN FOR OTHERS. I turned to my husband and said, 'I think we've had enough of Men for Others, don't you?'" She told me about their beach house, where one day a few years ago, when they knew John was going to be flying past that way, they went down onto the sand and wrote in big letters, HELLO JOHN.

In Arlington Cemetery there were red-ribboned wreaths in front of every grave, stretching in each direction as far as the eye could see, along a vast slope to the higher points commemorating the Union dead. When we reached the part where John is buried, Kelly's voice changed and she lay down on the ground and cried there, as if the earth were merely a barrier between her and her brother. I put my hand on her back and thought of the miles, the entire oceans that spanned one human loss and another. In some ways, after searching out these lives in Britain and America, I had arrived at the simplest truth, but I felt that I tasted the complications of the Atlantic that day, as a young woman sobbed into the earth for her dead brother. Kelly stood up and gestured with her arm at the rows of graves. "When will all this madness end?" she said. "The last time I was here, John's row was at the end of the field, and now look." She moved her arm over the many new rows of young men and women who had died in the fight for Iraq. Many of the graves were those of servicemen born in the late 1980s.

At the other end of the field the stones were more weathered, the beginning of the past: Vietnam, Korea, the Second World War, and on to Fredericksburg, Bull Run, Antietam. Then we left John Spahr and went to look for the Tomb of the Unknown Soldier. Anthony Wakefield and John Spahr were as different as land and air. One saw his life in epic terms, the other was more pragmatic, but their ends were the same, and they each served as part of a special relationship between their two countries, a relationship that, in its dreams and in its undoing, may be seen to mark the end of a period that started, not with Churchill and Roosevelt, but with Thatcher and Reagan. As I climbed up over the manicured lawns in company with John's sister Kelly, I remembered a letter Margaret Thatcher once wrote to her dear American friend. "Your achievements in restoring America's pride and confidence and in giving the West the leadership it needs are far too substantial to suffer any lasting damage. The message I give to everyone is that anything which weakens you, weakens America; and anything that weakens America, weakens the whole free world."

Before us at Arlington, a uniformed soldier marched up and down and we looked beyond the tombs and the urban parks to see the Washington Monument, stark as a compass needle in the distance. It seemed that summer must exist in a place behind the sky. It wouldn't be long before the smell of cut grass was back in the air, the smell of John's childhood returning, as fresh-seeming as the taste of Anthony's Murray Mint, to show the world that something was truly lost in all this human struggle for gain.

*February 2008*

# Racing Against Reality

LET US TAKE AN ordinary man from that terrible day. His name is Kevin Michael Cosgrove. If you put his name into Google, it takes exactly .12 second to discover that he was born on January 6, 1955. It takes no longer than it is taking you to read this sentence to discover that Mr. Cosgrove lived in West Islip, New York, and worked as a claims vice president of the Aon Corporation, based on the 105th floor of the South Tower. From Wikipedia you will find that he is buried in St. Patrick's Cemetery in Huntington. If you have another ten seconds to spare, you will be able to click to an image of the South Tower moments before its collapse, and hear a recording of Mr. Cosgrove speaking his last words to an operator. "I got young kids," he says. "We're young men." "We're not ready to die." "Please hurry." And at the building's collapse, he says, "Oh, God."

Dying in full public view has been a theme of Don DeLillo's since the time when September 11 was still a nothing day in the average American calendar, a zone of postvacation humdrum shortly before the beginning of Ramadan and just after Grandparents Day. In *Libra,* his novel about the killing of JFK, we find the image of a king mown down in his Cadillac in broad daylight, his death fixed in the gaze of his courtiers and his subjects. It was a scene to play forever in the public mind, and the exact moment of impact, as filmed on an eight-millimeter home movie camera by Abraham Zapruder, is understood in that book to represent a turning point in our relationship with the mass media, though not even DeLillo, writing in 1988, could have guessed that within two decades we would be able to download our worst nightmares in .12 second. In a relatively recent introduction to *Libra,* DeLillo outlines something he calls "Assassination Aura," giving a notion of how the events of history might come to find themselves in the weave of fiction. "Some stories never end," he writes.

> Even in our time, in the sightlines of living history, in the retrieved instancy of film and videotape, there are stories waiting to be finished, open to the thrust of reasoned analysis and haunted speculation. These stories, some of them, also undergo a kind of condensation, seeping into the texture of everyday life, barely separable from the ten thousand little excitations that define a routine day of visual and aural static processed by the case-hardened consumer brain.

It is his interest in the conjunction of visual technology and terrorism that really sets DeLillo's mentality apart — a setting-apart which also put him on the road to having September 11 as his subject long before the events of that day happened. His 1977 novel *Players* features Pammy and Lyle, a Wall Street couple who get tangled up with a bunch of terrorists. Pammy works in a new building called the World Trade Center; she feels that "the towers didn't seem permanent. They remained concepts, no less transient for all their bulk than some routine distortion of light." When DeLillo was writing that novel, a nine-year-old boy called Mohamed Atta was studying English in the bedroom of his parents' house in Giza, outside Cairo.

Many of DeLillo's novels are propelled by an acute sense of communal dread — of crowds, of surveillance, of the desperate "creativity" of the terrorist, of an "airborne toxic event" — and long before living history affirmed a number of his paranoid presumptions, his novels were making the case for America as a place where nothing very much was reliably innocent or safe. Here's Jack Gladney in *White Noise,* head of Hitler Studies at the College-on-the-Hill:

> The discussion moved to plots in general. I found myself saying to the assembled heads, "All plots tend to move death-ward. This is the nature of plots. Political plots, terrorist plots, lovers' plots, narrative plots, plots that are part of children's games. We edge nearer death every time we plot. It is like a contract that all must sign, the plotters as well as those who are the targets of the plot."

Later, we find Gladney trying to have a conversation with one of his colleagues, Alfonse Stompanato, who is trying to establish an Elvis Presley power base in the Department of American Environments. DeLillo wrote these lines in the year Mohamed Atta turned fifteen — though at that time Atta may have called himself Mohamed El Sayed and his telegenic flight into the World Trade Center was half a life away.

> "Why is it, Alfonse, that decent, well-meaning and responsible people find themselves intrigued by catastrophe when they see it on television?"
> I told him about the recent evening of lava, mud and raging water that the children and I had found so entertaining.
> "We wanted more, more."

"It's natural, it's normal," he said, with a reassuring nod. "It happens to everybody."

"Why?"

"Because we're suffering from brain fade. We need an occasional catastrophe to break up the incessant bombardment of information . . . The cameras are right there. They're standing by. Nothing terrible escapes their scrutiny."

"You're saying it's more or less universal, to be fascinated by TV disasters?"

"For most people there are only two places in the world. Where they live and their TV set. If a thing happens on television, we have every right to find it fascinating, whatever it is."

"I don't know whether to feel good or bad about learning that my experience is widely shared."

"Feel bad," he said.


That was a key flavor of DeLillo's earlier work, that we were all waiting for something terrible to happen, something that might blow us apart but which might also bring us together. It might be shopping or marketing. It might be a killing gas in the subway. But most likely it would be something that partook of the energies of each of these things: American capitalism and the toxic waste residing at the other end of it. In 1997, when the novelist wrote the following wonderful passage in *Underworld,* Mohamed Atta was living in Germany and had just been recruited by al Qaeda. *Underworld*'s Brian Glassic works at Waste Containment, and he is standing next to a mountain of trash at the Fresh Kills landfill site on Staten Island:[1]

---

1. According to the writer John Coyle, Fresh Kills was closed in the spring of 2001. "It was reopened on the 13th September of that year to receive debris from Ground Zero," he writes, and "Fresh Kills is currently being developed as a redemptive nature sanctuary."

He imagined he was watching the construction of the Great Pyramid at Giza—only this was twenty-five times bigger, with tanker trucks spraying perfumed water on the approach roads. He found the sight inspiring. All this ingenuity and labor, this delicate effort to fit maximum waste into diminishing space. The towers of the World Trade Center were visible in the distance and he sensed a poetic balance between that idea and this one . . . He looked at all that soaring garbage and knew for the first time what his job was all about . . . He dealt in human behavior, people's habits and impulses, their uncontrollable needs and innocent wishes, maybe their passions, certainly their excesses and indulgences but their kindness too, their generosity, and the question was how to keep this mass metabolism from overwhelming us.

These were high-flying sentiments, written, to great effect, in DeLillo's increasingly jokeless prose. He's a writer who has become less funny as he gets older, perhaps more serious as he moves towards the presentation of his darker purpose. Not that he was ever light, mind you. In any event, it is part of his genius to have engaged with the discomfiting strangeness of our period, and by the time he published *The Body Artist,* in 2001, DeLillo's writing had entered a style of passionate numbness. The prose was cautious and drained and none of it seemed funny anymore. Meanwhile, Mohamed Atta, the man of many aliases, had developed a hatred of American habits that bordered on the messianic. As DeLillo pressed the keys (and returned the carriage) to create the following passage, Atta was on American soil and in daily contact with his fellow conspirators while training on flight simulators at a rented house in Florida:

His future is not under construction. It is already there, susceptible to entry.

She had it on tape.

She did not want to believe this was the case. It was her future too. It is her future too.

She played the tape a dozen times.

It means your life and death are set in place, just waiting for you to keep the appointments.

All these passages, written over the course of a career, could be understood to evoke something very like a terrorist's trajectory towards an encounter with the twin towers, but they also describe the journey made by a singular American novelist towards the day of days for his preoccupations as an artist and his brio as a stylist. If the twin towers could be said to have stood in wait for the Mohamed Attas of the world, then the Mohamed Attas of the world were standing in wait for Don DeLillo. To have something exist as your subject before it happens is not unprecedented in the world of literature — consider Kafka and the Nazis, Fitzgerald and the Jazz Age — but the meeting of September 11 and Don DeLillo is not so much a conjunction as a point of arrival, and a connection so powerful in imaginative terms that it instantly blows DeLillo's lamps out.

"In a repressive society," the novelist said in an interview published around the time of his novel *Mao II*, "a writer can be deeply influential, but in a society that's filled with glut and repetition and endless consumption, the act of terror may be the only meaningful act . . . People who are powerless make an open theater of violence. True terror is a language and a vision. There is a deep narrative structure to terrorist acts and they infiltrate and alter consciousness in ways that writers used to aspire to."

So there you have it: the writer and the terrorist have something in common, and so it feels like something of a consummation when a person called Mohamed Mohamed el Amir el Sayed Atta appears on page 80 of DeLillo's novel *Falling Man*. The novelist seems to recognize Atta's impulses as if they were old friends: "This was Amir," he writes, "his mind was in the upper skies, making sense of things, drawing things together." Yet Atta has little narrative reality in DeLillo's book. He is the ghost in the machine, flying so fast he is barely separable from the surrounding ether, and the reader indeed will find himself knowing Atta only as a distinguished absence, present everywhere but visible nowhere, like Flaubert's idea of the perfect novelist.

The main character in *Falling Man* is a youngish lawyer called Keith Neudecker, whom we meet at the book's opening as he walks north in lower Manhattan on the morning of September 11, 2001, his face covered in ash and blood and his hair full of glass splinters. He carries somebody else's briefcase, and for reasons he might never fathom he heads directly from the rubble of Ground Zero to the apartment of his estranged wife, Lianne, and their son, Justin. Keith and Lianne had been together for eight years before "the eventual extended grimness called their marriage" ended in a well-educated state of suspended resignation. Now he is back—and back in her bed—though there is no telling for how long.

Lianne's mother, Nina Bartos, is an aged, recently retired professor—"the So-and-So Professor of Such-and-Such," says Keith in a burst of the old DeLillo humor—and she has a lover named Martin. The women scrutinize each other as mothers and daughters often do, harboring special, harsh feelings about the other's motivations and choices. To Nina, Lianne married Keith only to be close to someone whose potential for inflicting emotional damage made her feel "dangerously alive"—Nina tells Lianne that "this was a quality you associated with your father." But Lianne knows her mother would forgive Keith all his faults if he happened to be a raging artist.

The child Justin has two friends whom they call the Siblings and who live ten blocks away. The children talk in code, and they are always standing at the window of the Siblings' apartment, looking at the sky through binoculars and whispering about a man called "Bill Lawton." Like children in a science-fiction movie, the Siblings and Justin seem connected in some unspoken way to a much bigger picture, but we don't get to hear a great deal from them. (DeLillo is not good on children: they always exist as runes foretelling the bad weather of adulthood.) In any event, *Falling Man* is, to say the least, a book in pursuit of adult vexations on an international scale.

Keith survives the planes owing to a piece of luck, so he spends much of the novel embroiled in poker, the game that is a dramatization of luck. Before the planes, he used to play it on Wednesdays with six men at his apartment: "the one anticipation," DeLillo writes, "that was not marked by the bloodguilt tracings of severed connections." The poker evenings ended when the towers came down, but he thinks about the game a lot. He is interested in the meaning of good fortune, and we find in time that he is also a cheat, whatever that means.

In the course of the novel he goes to see another survivor, Florence Givens, the owner of the briefcase he took from the North Tower; he visits her more than once, and he goes to look at his old, frozen apartment, the one he rented when he split up with his wife. Apart from this, there is only recovery, if that is what you'd call it. Keith does a little homework duty with his son and walks the boy to school, "going slow, easing inward . . . drifting into spells of reflection."

Lianne is doing some work for a university press, editing a book about ancient alphabets. Her hobby survives the attacks: it involves conducting "storyline sessions" in East Harlem, which take place in the company of half a dozen or so people with Alzheimer's. Apart from some calmness it perhaps brings to her — and aside from a kind of Manhattan midlife ennui — it is not clear why Lianne spends so much time with these forgetful narrative makers in East Harlem. They write about the planes. We also know that her father, Jack, had the beginning of senile dementia; not able to face it, he killed himself with a sporting rifle.

Lianne is therefore a victim of violence, with a mother now messing around with an art dealer. Though DeLillo keeps it pretty spare, we feel we understand Lianne as one of his types. At some level she is surrounded by death — even her husband, when finally he comes home, walks in from the most famous American death trap in history — and she is ripe for some sort of urban epiphany to set her heart in motion. The closest she comes to such an experience is to see a performance artist known as Falling Man — he dangles upside down from a structure in Pershing Square, reminding people of the jumpers who chose air over fire on September 11: "It held the gaze of the world, she thought. There was the awful openness of it, something we'd not seen, the single falling figure that trails a collective dread, body come down among us all. And now, she thought, this little theater piece, disturbing enough to stop traffic."

Don DeLillo has always been good at male dissociation, especially the kind that can thrive in certain domestic environments, and he can be as forensic as Saul Bellow when it comes to showing the way married couples might go about dismantling one another's powers and confidence. On this occasion, he treats Keith like a male archetype. "This was the period, not long before the separation," he writes,

> when he took the simplest question as a form of hostile in-
> terrogation. He seemed to walk in the door waiting for her
> questions . . . She understood by this time that it wasn't the

drinking, or not that alone, and probably not some sport with a woman. He'd hide it better, she told herself. It was who he was, his native face, without the leveling element, the claims of social code.

Those nights, sometimes, he seemed on the verge of saying something, a sentence fragment, that was all, and it would end everything between them, all discourse, every form of stated arrangement, whatever drifts of love still lingered.

These descriptions are the best things in the book: they have the force of felt life, and through them we begin purely to understand what estrangement really means with this Manhattan couple. They each have known a little hate. But how can they relate to each other now that hatred means something else, now that it means flying planes into public buildings? How are their own feelings changed now that hatred means terrorists and victims shouting in their final moments to different gods?

Yet such inquiries, however acute, however felt, cannot make up for DeLillo's failure in *Falling Man* to imagine September 11. The hallmark of those novelists who have tried to write about the attacks is a sort of austere plangency — or a quivering bathos — that has been in evidence almost from the moment the planes hit. Those authors who published journalistic accounts immediately after the event failed to see how their metaphors fell dead from their mouths before the astonishing live pictures. It did not help us to be told by imaginative writers that the second plane was like someone posting a letter. No, it wasn't. It was like a passenger jet crashing into an office building. It gave us nothing to be told that the South Tower came down like an elevator at full speed. No, it didn't. It collapsed like a building that could no longer hold itself up.

Metaphor failed to do anything but make one feel that those

keen to deploy it had not been watching enough television. After the "nonfiction novel," after the New Journalism, after several decades in which some of America's most vivid writing about real events was seen to be in thrall to the techniques of novelists, September 11 offered a few hours when American novelists could only sit at home while journalism taught them fierce lessons in multivocality, point of view, the structure of plot, interior monologue, the pressure of history, the force of silence, and the uncanny. Actuality showed its own naked art that day.

DeLillo the novelist prepared us for September 11, but he did not prepare himself for how such an episode might, in the way of denouements, instantly fly beyond the reach of his own powers. In a moment, the reality of the occasion seems to have burst the ripeness of his style, and he truly struggles in this book to say anything that doesn't sound in a small way like a warning that comes too late. Reading *Falling Man,* one feels that September 11 is an event that is suddenly far ahead of him, far beyond what he knows, and so an air of tentative rehearsal resounds in an empty hall. What is a prophet once his fiery word becomes deed? What does he have to say? What is left of the paranoid style when all its suspicions come true? Of course, a first-rate literary intelligence can eventually meet a world where reality acknowledges the properties of his style by turning them into parody, and in these circumstances, which are DeLillo's with this particular novel, the original novelist may be said to be a person quietened by his own genius. This is another American story — the story of Ernest Hemingway and Orson Welles — and it gives us a clue to the weakness of *Falling Man.*

But the novel itself is packed with clues, the first and most obvious being the author's inability to conjure his usual exciting prose. In his best novels, DeLillo is pretty much incapable of writing unexcitingly — but September 11 vanquishes the power of his sentences before he can make them linger. Good prose in a novel depends on its ability to exhale a secret knowledge, to have the exact weight of magic in relation to the material, the true moral rhythm. DeLillo had all of that in many of the novels he published before September 11 — so much magic, indeed, that it was initially difficult to absorb the events of that day without thinking of his writing. On September 11, however, novelists of his sort ceded all secret knowledge to the four winds: to CNN, to the website of the *New York Times,* to CCTV and to the widespread availability of video cameras in Manhattan, each of which captured the event in real time.[2]

Reading *Falling Man,* one often feels that DeLillo's formerly superlative intuition has become a form of ignorance: he dangles uncertainly between what he knows of that day from pictures and what of it he predicted in his novels. But the current book is merely blank with shock, as if his sense of awe and disbelief may express itself only in a fetish with the obvious:

> She was awake, middle of the night, eyes closed, mind running, and she felt time pressing in, and threat, a kind of beat in her head.
>
> She read everything they wrote about the attacks.
>
> She thought of her father. She saw him coming down an escalator, in an airport maybe.
>
> Keith stopped shaving for a time, whatever that means. Everything seemed to mean something. Their lives were in transition and she looked for signs. Even when she was barely aware of an incident it came to mind later, with meaning attached, in sleepless episodes that lasted minutes or hours, she wasn't sure . . .

2. The only novel so far to capture, in a private way, the strange public horror of the event is Claire Messud's *The Emperor's Children* (2006). You'll have to read it to see how she does it, but suffice to say that she meets the glare of the day with subtlety.

But things were ordinary as well. Things were ordinary in all the ways they were always ordinary.

This most assuredly is not the DeLillo of *Libra* or *White Noise.* In the first of those novels, the author enacted wonders the Warren Commission could never have imagined. He had readers in the corner of that room at the Book Depository, practically squeezing the trigger with Oswald, feeling the press of his eye on the scope. But *Falling Man* is a distillation of fear and grief over real-life drama next to which the 9/11 Commission Report reads serenely and beautifully. Open that report at any page and you will find a breathtaking, second-by-second account of that morning, and of the hijackers' backgrounds, that will make DeLillo's novel seem merely incapacitated.

The author might know the nature of his trouble. He might see it. At one point, we hear of a book written by someone called the Unaflyer that predicted all the events: "A book that's so enormously immersed, going back on it, leading up to it . . . it seems to predict what happened . . . It's badly written." People still speak of the anxiety of influence, but what of a novelist's anxiety about his past work's influence on himself? *Falling Man,* it seems to me, is about a brilliant writer's free-falling anxiety of that sort, and most of it comes to be expressed in this novel through ruminations on art and terror.

This is old DeLillo stuff: who can forget Klara Sax from *Underworld,* the lady who once studied the twin towers as they were being built, later to find fame as an artist who paints B-52 bombers, the kind that once carried nuclear weapons. She displays these objets d'art in the desert with their innards ripped out and their shells coated in beautiful color. ("This is an art object," she says, "not a peace project. This is a landscape painting in which we use the landscape itself.") Later in that novel, we discover that Klara and her contemporaries had been fascinated by the nearness of art to violence, fans of a near-invisible graffiti kid called Moonman 157 who paints subway trains. DeLillo has always favored showing the art world as a place where cultural anxieties are made compact and fashionable, but his repeat of this ploy in *Falling Man* pushes the book towards silliness.

Martin, the boyfriend of Keith's mother-in-law, is a German art dealer — apartment in Berlin, liking for inscrutable works — who we learn was once a member of a 1960s antifascist collective called Kommune One. Martin, it seems, was a kind of terrorist, living with people whose faces would one day end up on posters. "We're all sick of America and Americans," he says at one point. "The subject nauseates us." But Martin is a nullity: Who could care about him and his little European pieties on the state of the world and the politics of art? Is he a terrorist? Who cares, he's a goon. Meanwhile, people are holding hands and jumping from the 102nd floor of the North Tower, the novelist's imagination nowhere in attendance. When Martin speaks we sometimes imagine he could be speaking for DeLillo. "Nothing seems exaggerated anymore," he says. "Nothing amazes me."

In this book, the events aren't enough, or they are too much, which amounts to the same thing for a novelist. There appear to be few writers in America now who could bring us to know what might have been going through the minds of those people as they fell from the building — or going through the minds of the hijackers as they met their targets — but there is no shortage of those who would do what DeLillo does, which is to show us an anxious, educated woman watching a performance artist hanging upside down from a metal beam in Pershing Square. It is a form of intellectual escapism. The oddity of the art world can easily be made to stand in for the profundity of life and death, but none of us who lived through the morning of September 11,

2001, could easily believe that the antics of a performance artist, no matter how uncanny, would suffice to denote the scale and depth of our encounter with dread. The Falling Man, the artist, can do no better than constitute some figurative account of the author himself, suspended in free fall, frozen in time, subject to both the threat of gravity and the indwelling disbelief of the spectators below.

DeLillo's novel was inspired by a photograph of a real person — most agree that he is Jonathan Briley, who seemed at a certain point in his descent from the North Tower to plummet straight, upside down, one leg bent, his shirt flying off in the ferocious breeze, his head scorched, "The Falling Man" whose image became a token of horror and a mass-media legend. And the things pertaining to his image are what interest Don DeLillo. Yet the person inside the legend was a man from Mount Vernon who worked in the North Tower restaurant, Windows on the World. He was flesh and blood, not just an idea. He was born on March 5, 1958. He was six feet five. His father was a preacher. He suffered from asthma and had a wife called Hilary. He died sixty-five minutes twenty seconds after Mohamed Atta, and is currently awaiting a writer sufficiently uncoerced by the politics of art to tell his story.

*June 2007*

# Guilt: A Memoir

MY GRANDMOTHER'S HOUSE in Millroad Street existed to remind us that we had probably done something wrong. The Glasgow habit of calling it a house has survived with me, but it was really a tenement flat across the road from the fish shop where my grandmother worked. The flat had a plastic holy-water font by the front door and the three rooms smelled of vegetable soup. I can still see the green wallpaper in the bedroom, with its slanted rain of tiny yellow flowers. I see her spectacles case, a tumbler for the false teeth she preferred not to wear. An oval mirror hung on a chain and a black-and-white photograph was pressed into the frame. It was of her husband, Michael, dead for thirty-five years by then and sorely missed.

My education in guilt began there. It was where I first heard the words "the bad fire," a place for boys who didn't finish their soup or failed to close the door of the outside loo. I don't think I ever saw my grandmother not wearing a plaid apron, a uniform then worn by Glasgow women of all ages, as if to show their readiness to scrub and clean and generally get on. Over in the fish shop, which was staffed entirely by women, the white tiles were bare except for a sign saying no tick — no credit — along with a framed picture of Jesus wearing a crown of thorns. My father told me that my auntie Jeanie once pointed at the Jesus and then pointed at him. "Mind yersel'," she said. "That's what happened to Jesus for being good. Imagine that." Years later, at the time my brothers and I were growing up and looking for trouble, the picture of Jesus was still there and so was my granny's outside toilet. Old Glasgow seemed dark, the East End in particular a place of unsettled scores splashed with vinegar.

My grandmother could gut a herring in four seconds. She went to mass at St. Mary's every morning. Occasionally she smiled at one of the priest's wee jokes, and she was brave and stoic, but the thing that seemed most to excite her was suffering. Not just her own but the suffering of the whole world. In her painfully restrained Glaswegian remarks, it was clear that she found our failings, and her own, to be more interesting than our virtues. A person was the sum of his sins, and his character was an ongoing expression of his guilt. It was often said that she "wouldn't say a word against" my father, her son, though she never had a good word for him either. In truth she was frightened of him, and her actions spoke against him in ways that were louder than words. I don't think it would ever have occurred to her, or to her supporters (her three daughters), that her attitude towards him would condition not only his life but much of our lives as well. It was clear that he was more or less a bad man in her eyes, and that gave me a certain amount of pity for him as well as a wish to give him the benefit of the doubt. Loyalty works weirdly in families like mine. My granny felt loyal to the memory of her husband, lost at sea, but that didn't mean she spread the good word about him. She was loyal to God, obviously, and to those who served God, but she wasn't loyal to those who chose to serve him differently from her. Not long ago, when I tried to ask my father what kind of person she was, he looked right through me. "She was just a lovely, lovely person," he said.

In 1959, just before she married him, my mother was taken into the bedroom by my grandmother. I imagine it was one of those gray Glasgow evenings around teatime, when everybody could seem in such a busy state of belonging. Apparently my grandmother pulled back the curtain and showed my mother a broken window. "That was him," she said. (He was always "him.") "We were having an argument and he threw a ginger bottle at the window." My mother was nineteen years old. "I just want you to know what you're marrying," my grandmother said.

So, at an early age, I felt guilty not only for what my father had done and failed to do, but also for not instantly forgiving my granny for the guilt she imposed. It all felt very nicely regulated, as if this were how life was supposed to be, and there wasn't really much room for childhood. I enjoyed myself, but my enjoyments were in my own mind and they always involved the transporting of adult worries and adult concerns. My three elder brothers and I had no childhood that could proclaim itself: childhood was untidy, and untidiness was banned; childhood was loud, and silence was demanded at all times; childhood was riddled with needs, but the adults in our lives were always too needy themselves to contemplate the needs of their children. So you grow up fast, and you grow up guilty about almost everything.

In my school days, the sentence I remember uttering most often was "Please don't tell my mum." My mother was busy coping with my father and she had four part-time jobs, starting at six in the morning, when she would leave the house to clean at one of the local primary schools. My three brothers and I would get ourselves dressed and would often walk to see her at eight-thirty, by which time she was on to her second job, clean-ing a chip shop. It was all a bit thrilling to be among the peelings and the mops. My mother did her best to look after us, and at the time we didn't feel the lack of anything, but there were no storybooks and no pancakes. And we always had a keen sense of our parents' difficulties, so much so that it made us feel guilty about expressing any of our own. I worked out quite early that life could offer ways of attracting attention. In my second year at primary school, for instance, the class was doing a project called Home and Shopping. The teacher had us all in a semicircle and she placed a cake on a table. The cake was very pink and very glossy with a large cherry. Later, Mrs. Nugent said I had been like a sleepwalker. She said I stood up from my place and walked over to the table, lifted the cake and took a large bite out of it before sitting down again. Nobody else did. Mrs. Nugent kept me back after the class and asked if I was hungry.

"Naw," I said.

"Did you have breakfast this morning?"

"Aye."

"What did you have?"

"Please don't tell my mummy."

A lot of the fathers were working on the oil rigs. Mine wasn't: word would come from building sites in Liverpool or Birming-ham, and I would try to imagine those places, the traffic on the streets and the different sense of busy belonging that must pre-vail there. I often daydreamed about being in a lorry, and a vi-sion of orange lights on a motorway worked its way far into my psyche: still, when I see those sodium lamps I feel excited by an idea of what life has to offer. At the same time, missing my father always seemed like an indulgence. We felt guilty for run-ning to him when he came through the door, and eventually we stopped. Only my brother Charlie would run to him, and he set his course that way. When my parents eventually split up, Charlie went with my dad.

There was music at a house three doors up. It was accordion music and sometimes pipes, played by a couple of wild creatures from the north called Hazel and Sandy. I felt at home there, and also felt guilty for feeling so much at home. I remember thinking that music and things like that—intelligence, I don't know, capability in general, the achievements of art—might make my family happy and keep them together. But the truth is I was already slipping away. Hazel and Sandy were the beginning of a bid for freedom, accompanied by Strathspey reels that seemed to proclaim independence. I was always looking to cuckoo in other people's nests, and I felt at home in that house with all the noises, the mess and the childhood atmosphere. I was only ten but I often wore a suit, as if I were turning up for something formal and life-changing. There are very few photographs of me as a child, but I have one here as I write. It was taken in the square of the housing estate where we lived. I am standing on the rocks the council laid for the children to play on, holding the hand of Sandy and Hazel's daughter, Jill. I am wearing a suit that my mother bought me in Saltcoats. I'm standing there in the suit and a tie like someone about to step into a meeting.

There's always a danger with childhoods that weren't perfect: trying to tell the story truthfully can feel like an exercise in sentiment. (And sentiment is certainly part of what prevailed and what remains.) Yet I began to feel, even in the middle of those years, that art made you a kind of aristocrat, and that deprivation and elevation had a more comical relationship than I had hitherto suspected. As a result, my childhood was OK. It was a kind of psychological joke. Not that I'm always able to see it that way. I regret not having had any *Swallows and Amazons,* and I open up to one of the lesser literary attributes, self-pity, when I think of some of the things we were exposed to so young. But it was quite common. The most popular picture round our way — every family had one, usually above a three-bar fire — was a commercial painting called *The Weeping Boy*. There were several versions of it, but they all showed a child in distress. I believe it helped us to visualize our self-pity, and to accept a certain amount of kitsch. I spent hours looking at that picture, thinking it odd, thinking it mawkish, but feeling it must be social realism.

It always seemed like a betrayal to love both your parents at the same time. It felt wrong to need them equally. When my parents began the long slide towards separation, they made arrangements to accommodate their resentments, the main one being to move me out of the bedroom I shared with my brother Charlie and into the double bed beside my mother. It was a cold winter, and I can see the patterns of frost on the bedroom window, my mother asleep and my father and Charlie talking in the next room. A certain amount of excitement and dread mingled in the small hours: the Cold War had entered the house, and it crept through my mind like an intruder in the dark. My mother felt warm against my back in the strange guilty wrongness of the room. She only ever had one book by the bedside, a blue, sensible self-help book published by Al-Anon called *One Day at a Time*. I had bought it for her with my pocket money, and my mother read a page of it every day.

It was hard to know the difference between guilt and ordinary awareness. We were Catholics, of course, and so a certain institutional comedy of shame was set in plaster. Freud didn't get a look in, but Our Lady did, and we all lived as if the turmoil of life were ordained by higher beings. Priests were sometimes engaged to preside over pledges and to maintain the status quo in a bad marriage, but I found it hard — even harder, I think, than my brothers did — to understand how relationships could be sustained with so much anger and mental cruelty. In families like that, the most outlandish behavior can come to seem normal: my father always worked, yet my mother would be forced to stand with us in queues at the Social Security, as it then was, hoping for funds to tide us over until my father was sober. You'd feel guilty for taking up space in the queue. Likewise, we were expected to claim free dinners at school. The administrator gave you a special green ticket, but in our case my parents hadn't even filled in the means-tested application form. We would have to make a case every term and have our names written down in ink at the end of the typed list, as if our parents were completely absent from all decisions and all procedures.

You felt guilty at both ends of the argument: guilty for not having the form and guilty for resenting your parents for not having what it took to complete the form. I suppose I was less good at taking life on the chin, always believing, in my airy way, that this wasn't life as it had to be, that this was something we had chosen. In her sadness, my mother took to me as an inspirational speaker. She thought I could magic her doubts away with words. I tried my best, and so did Michael, my eldest brother, who became, at sixteen, the man of the house and someone whose own life appeared to be temporarily suspended. Yet none of us wanted to blame our parents. Establishing the right target for blame might make you feel better, but it doesn't make you feel less guilty. Guilt is impervious to justice. Guilt feasts on irrationality.

Yet a writer can gain his feet that way. A writer romances the truth and invents his own freedom. My childhood can never let me down as a guide to human complication. But I sometimes wonder how my brothers survived it. Partly, I guess, by trying to be better parents, happier people. In many ways that is the greatest task of them all. My brothers have invested their hopes for renewal in family life, a good place but also the most difficult one, like employing yourself as the clean-up guy at the scene of a crime. It is a daily struggle to establish the sovereignty of your own story over that of your parents. At every turn, there is the endlessly repeated narrative of your mum and dad, the old wounds and the litany of blame, the bad decisions and the failure to protect the innocent parties. And everybody wants to win the battle of the more-done-to-than-doing. If you come from that kind of family, you spend years in a defenseless state over your parents' woes, and then, when your defenses are sound, you discover they are rusted with guilt. Despite what Tolstoy says, all unhappy families have in common a dreadful inability to let the past sleep and let the future sing.

When I was eleven years old, I decided the only way to cope with my parents was to teach them a lesson in how to seek freedom through humiliation. My brother Gerry had tried a similar trick a few years before by becoming a punk. He spiked up his hair and put posters of the Sex Pistols all over his bedroom wall. My father came back from one of his adventures and hit the room like a tornado: the posters were ripped down and replaced with a crucifix. My own bid followed a few years later, and it involved joining the local ballet class. No boy on that parcel of land had ever done ballet. Reader: Billy Elliot, c'est moi. The local paper got involved and wrote a story about me, though I wouldn't allow them to take a picture. (I was too guilty at the sheer scale of the humiliation.) My father's complexion actually changed forever to a deep, alarmed red.

I turned out to be rather good at the old *battement frappé*, but my main purpose had been achieved when I saw the size of my parents' fears. Ballet seemed quite natural to me, but it was really the extremity of the choice that felt so very natural. It soon gave way to other choices, editing a fanzine, being in a band, going to university, each of which was extreme in its own way, bringing a new language into the house and using our social stuckness as a platform for do-it-yourself deliverance. Music gave me the lift I needed. Not Strathspey reels in the long run, but all those punky bands who seemed to constitute, for so many of us, the soul of the north in the first days of Thatcher. And who, more important, seemed to give youth back to kids who didn't have one. They did it ironically, too: those fresh-faced, postindustrial boys who dyed their hair gray and wore a gold stud in their ears were full of androgyny and working-class escapism. We listened to Joy Division and wondered if Ian Curtis, the band's singer, hadn't died from too much guilt and too little time to put it right. When I hear their album *Closer*, I think of the Winter of Discontent and the layers of frost on the bedroom window.

Some people imagine that when you try to talk about guilt what you're really talking about is blame. But in discussing my early years I don't feel like blaming my parents: to me, they were the greater victims of our circumstances. They hadn't had childhoods either. One time my mother was ill and I wondered how long it would take her to ask her mother for help. She never did, and her mother, my "happy" granny, was allowed to imagine her youngest child was just good at coping. So much happened during those years that I can only really glance at them for now, knowing that we all, with more or less equal fault and merit, passed through a season of derangement. I feel guilty for describing it that way, but there you have it. My life was made out of my parents' chaos, but I wanted them to know that I could take that chaos further. I was too young to understand that a child's bid for personhood can actually come to renew his parents' hopes. Even after the last waltz — or the last pirouette — when writing became my favorite task, those same parents were to be found cheering from their separate sidelines, glad at last to hear a story being told that wasn't the one they told themselves.

*November 2009*

# The Boy Who Mistook His Life
# for a Crime

I'VE BEEN THINKING all week about Jon Venables. In some way, I find it too distressing to write down what the case means to me, when so many people believe the young man is simply a lost cause, a person in the grip of evil. The papers have been ringing asking for comment: the messages go to voicemail. Outside, buses pass in quick succession, the passengers reading their newspapers and seeming very sure of something: "Once Evil, Always Evil," says the *Mirror*. I keep thinking of Meursault, who didn't know why he did it, who didn't see the size of the damage, who wasn't able to opt for survival, with the sun beating down and explaining nothing.

When I first wrote about the killing of James Bulger, in the *London Review of Books* in March 1993, I was in my early twenties and it was the first proper piece I'd written for publication. The nation was in an uproar, and something about the boys on the CCTV footage made me uneasy about myself. The editor sent me home to think about it, and over that day and long night I came to see my unease was to do with familiarity. Venables and Thompson were not only like the boys I knew, but like the boy I had been, and their crime was an extreme version, different in degree but not in essence, of things we had done on the housing estate outside Glasgow where I grew up. The amoral meandering of the boys was something I recognized.

When I wrote that piece, my childhood was still close enough for me to enjoy the surprise of having escaped it. Now, at this distance, I realize Venables is nearly thirty. I find the confluence, if that's the word, of his ruination and my visibility disturbing. At some level, I will always feel I could have been Venables, and the more opportunity I get to make myself understood, the more it becomes obvious that he will never escape condemnation, the thing John Major called for more of in his statement at the time of the trial. I have dreams about the boys, and sometimes dream I am the person in the CCTV footage who walks past them with a shopping bag at the exact moment they abducted James. I can see the butcher's shop where James's mother is waiting for her change; I see the floor tiles reflecting shadows and hear the mall's Muzak bending sinister as the shoppers go about their business. I hear the echoing swimming-pool clamor of the ordinary day about to go wrong.

Sometimes I stop in front of the boys and catch something I would rather not see in their eyes. And I am frozen there, sure my face is the only one facing the cameras. I imagine I can rescue all three of them by reaching in and whisking the toddler free, that I can send Venables and Thompson on their way, to find lives that might turn out like mine, in the sense of having a childhood they can shrug off, and children whom they can look after, in rooms they have taken to house their sanity. All this happens in the dream, and I wake up shouting. Those who've heard it say that what I think is a shout is actually a moan; when I'm asked what the dream was about, I can never bring myself to say: "It's really about me."

I had hoped at least that Venables and Thompson might

have succeeded in wiping out their childhoods and starting again. The news in the past few days that Venables would stop people in the street to tell them who he really was, tell them he was Jon and he was one of the pair who had murdered the little boy in Liverpool, leaves me forlorn. I always thought he might be out there somewhere, inventing himself.

Every growing writer has his shadows, and by middle age we know these counterlives are part of us. For some, it may be a dead father still stalking their prose. Forster spoke of his mother, standing in that house on the margins of Stevenage, surrounded by all her plates and her shawls, waiting for him. But the media age has brought those shades from places we haven't quite been: when I dream I am in the Strand Shopping Center, I am seeing a configuration both made and sustained by the public eye.

Back in 1993, I thought I could name something that wasn't being named, spell it out plainly, and that would be that. But what I didn't know was the depth of the panic caused by Venables and Thompson: not only a crisis in the right-wing press, but a small crisis of liberalism too. Nobody knew whether to blame videotapes or economic depravity, negligent mothers or state schools, but a fundamental loss of innocence was at issue. The British papers were in their favorite mode, evident again this week: mixing vengeance with sentiment, while exuding prurience and humbug. Denise Fergus, the mother of James Bulger, is being paraded as the proper arbiter of justice: as if the mother of a murdered child should call the shots, should be the one to decide what ought to be done with the killers. She is not to be challenged: Who in their right mind would seek to challenge a grieving parent?

Yet we need to challenge her, because that also means challenging the moral stupidity the media's use of her represents, the urge towards counterviolence that always seems to make sense to the mind of the average working-class Briton. Of course she wants the boys behind bars forever. She wants their rights taken away. Which of us, given the horror, would never be tempted down that road? No matter what the law says, a sense of entitlement nowadays devolves to the families of murder victims. The tabloids, and not just the tabloids, like it that way. Among the tabloids I include the *Today* program.

This case has, from the beginning, involved the need to say that grief is not an achievement, doesn't confer power, and Denise Fergus should have no say at all in the fate of the boys who killed her son. She speaks contemptuously of the justice system, feels she should be consulted on every aspect of the case, and the media eggs her on because her words claim attention and sell papers. She, too, is one of the shades haunting the Strand Shopping Center. We want to listen to her, but to act on what we hear would be criminal. She says she won't rest until those boys are truly punished for what they did: she wants them incarcerated under their original names—a death sentence.[1] Meanwhile, the justice secretary feels he must pay lip service to her status in all of this.

In 1993 there was no liberal orthodoxy to apply to the case, and there isn't now. Yet we should still think about Boy A and Boy B, who became known to us as Robert Thompson and Jon

---

1. A vast number of people in the UK find this reasonable. Since Venables was taken back into custody, a text has been sent round by troublemakers to millions of mobile phones. The text claims to reveal Venables's adopted identity, David Calvert, which is, in fact, a name with no connection at all to Jon Venables. Mob tactics of this sort have found the Internet to be a valuable friend: it allows numbskulls to publish their banter quickly and at no cost. There are several Facebook sites devoted to hating or hanging Venables, and some football fan sites are involved in trying to unmask the man who used to be Venables. Some of this is not new: certain Liverpool pubs at one time carried posters of the two boys with their faces aged by computer imaging. Patrons spoke of a reward for information leading to the men, and all said they were doing it "for Jamie's family."

Venables only when the judge in the original trial proved over-zealous in meeting press demands that the boys be named and their likenesses published. There isn't another country in Europe where two ten-year-olds in trouble would have been exposed like that, and it led directly to their requiring new identities and protected lives. It now looks as if Boy B was unable to cope with that in the long term, and his new criminal activity, however sexual and however violent, will be horrifying to the same degree that it is consistent in a man with his experience. If he has been looking at child pornography, as alleged, or getting into knife fights, as also alleged, then we might acknowledge that this is what routinely happens in the lives of adults who lost their childhoods, who were abused themselves, who can't go home again, and who might be condemned to spend their lives in a cycle of harm and rescue. The question, therefore, is as much "What else did you expect?" as "How could he?" You can't magic his kind of trouble away.

The *Guardian* columnist Jill Tweedie called me after my first piece appeared. I didn't know her, but she was crying on the phone, saying there were things that she'd done in her past, childhood cruelties, that she had never recovered from, never even told her husband about. Another phone call came from a writer who said the case had drawn him back to a terrible incident at Eton when he stabbed a boy with a penknife. We might think about the steps people take to reimagine or redress their early lives when they know they were blighted by their own wrongdoing and by the wrongdoing that surrounded them before they could oppose it. With Venables and Thompson, we allowed ourselves to think that rehabilitation had put the past out of play, and that eight years of sterling effort by social workers had "fixed them," filled their minds with gratitude, canceled their anguish. But it was always possible that one or another of these boys would fall, as if for the first time, possibly by reaching for a childhood his circumstances now denied him.

It's said you can't unmake your childhood. But you can. You can unmake it every day of your adult life. I think I would say that every fictional character I've created has lived with that dream. But perhaps nobody can have lived with it as complicatedly as Jon Venables. In recent years, he has been drawn remorselessly back to the Liverpool of his youth, despite his license making such visits illegal. He worked as a bouncer at a club and he did some of the things other twentysomethings do: he drank cider and took ecstasy tablets and he found he had no balance, he had no story, he had no standing as a person beyond his own horrible myth. He had shown good form at the beginning of his "rehabilitation": he was the first of the pair to break down and admit what had happened; he was the first to express remorse and wish that the victim's family could know he was sorry. Under questioning, he was the wrecked and emotional one, failing to grasp the legal terms that were being spoken to him. At the trial, I was shocked at how little the defense did to try to explain the boys' lives.

To this day, I feel that Venables, especially, was unable fully to understand what he was doing the day they killed James. He knew what killing was, but in the same way that many children know what flying is: a thing that some people can do quite effectively and excitingly in films. After watching the film *Halloween,* about a series of frenzied murders, Venables made a drawing of a person wielding two knives and stabbing two smaller people. The killer had breasts. He called the drawing "My Dad's House." In the days before abducting James Bulger, the pals watched the movie *Child's Play 3,* about plastic dolls that are inhabited by the souls of "bad-guy" dolls. The bad-guy doll, Chucky, is spattered with paint and cut to ribbons. James

Bulger, it should pain us to recall, was spattered with paint on the road to his death. And beside his body on the railway line lay stolen batteries, suggesting the boys may have been confused between a real life and a toy.

The attempt to make sense of these things might be doomed to failure. In a very direct way, a "senseless killing" is more bearable, because it saves us the trouble of having to ask any questions of ourselves. But for me the Bulger case will always mean asking questions of myself: asking why we undid the belts supporting young trees and used them to beat a boy until his legs were raw, or why the cats on the estate were never safe from our excursions. Luck played its part in rescuing me from all that, but I had friends who were not so lucky, and I know their names and sometimes I see their faces in my dreams too. In some way I am tied to Venables and Thompson, and it feels very natural to me to have believed that writing could be a way of speaking up for all of us.

*March 2010*

# E. M. Forster:
## The Story of Affection

THE BEHAVIOR OF THE English in their gardens, at their dining tables, in their train compartments and in their bedrooms was to obsess E. M. Forster from the start of his vocation, at King's College, Cambridge, when he was amazed to discover he had the "special and unusual apparatus" to be a writer. In our time, his genteel, often picturesque take on these English things would make his novels very filmable, and one simply has to say the words "Merchant Ivory" to conjure a world of literary Edwardiana, a twilight world where ruby-cheeked girls in bonnets sit among aunts and reverends, often in foreign places, enduring their "barbed civilities." There is always a train, a few noble rustics, a nice young man and a muddle, but standing behind it all are Forster's vastly personal hopes for a binding of the realistic and the mystical.

Forster's quest, from the beginning, was for self-transformation and magic, for a prose that would carry the secret yearning of the heart into the bustle of the everyday. He succeeded that way, up to a point, but the questions arising from Wendy Moffat's meticulous biography (*A Great Unrecorded History: A New Life of E. M. Forster*) remain very powerful for those interested in Forster: To what extent did the man's privacy make the novelist's work possible, make it beautiful, and, conversely, to what extent did he feel that public avowals of desire might murder his talent? Even allowing for P. N. Furbank's magisterial two-volume biography of 1978, Moffat's is the first one to see the sex with an inviting degree of clarity. And what it sees is a man who was neither ashamed nor in hiding, but one, possibly, who understood that the mystery of literary creation, for him at least, was of a love that made a better choice in not speaking its name.

He early got into the habit of fully inhabiting his privacy, a fact that might seem strange today, or even underhand, but which was nevertheless a crucial engine of his imagination. Though as a teenager and young adult Forster was perfectly attuned to his desire for men, his romantic life consisted mostly of intense but chaste friendships with his cohorts at Cambridge, and of vivid homosexual fantasies. It wasn't until the age of thirty-seven, with four novels behind him — *Where Angels Fear to Tread, The Longest Journey, A Room with a View,* and *Howards End* — that he entered into his first sexual relationship, and even then, it was more of an encounter than a relationship, a lusty tryst on the beach in Egypt with a recuperating soldier. In middle age, Forster began to live an active gay life — cultivating numerous lovers and an affectionate circle of gay friends. He learned from Lytton Strachey, J. R. Ackerley and W. H. Auden how to be more himself, joining a group that defied English rigidities about class, embracing men from differing backgrounds.

In 1930 he met Bob Buckingham, a solidly built, very gentle policeman, and the two men commenced an affair that, over a period of forty years, settled into a kind of cozy, unorthodox partnership. Bob eventually married a woman called May Hockey, but his relationship with the writer continued with her tacit permission, while she and Forster slowly developed a loving connection of their own. But despite the unusual arrangements — the mutually sustaining ones — that governed his private life, Forster's public persona was resolutely conventional. It wasn't until 1971, a year after his death, that his novel *Maurice,* featuring a homosexual affair, was published, sixty years after it was written.

For Forster's artistic conscience, the novels succeeded where the voice sounded inwardly. He had his life, but his sexual activity was steeped in silence, or the kind of silence that opens up in diaries. With Forster you're essentially dealing with a novelist who stopped writing novels in order to succeed as a man who could love without inflection. This, admittedly, is not the triumphant note sounded by queer studies, but it is nevertheless the best Forster could hope for, and perhaps the best Oscar Wilde or Siegfried Sassoon could hope for, too. Their writing was built for the perfect articulation of privacy, and one man's imprisonment is another man's freedom. The achievement of Wendy Moffat's biography is that it shows us one kind of artist's life as it goes about itself, drawing sweet, personal air from a certain social stagnancy. Forster's life, so pitied by many, was on this account an admirable one: he moved through his times, breathing and loving and keeping his counsel, forever aware, I suspect, that literary talent might cleave to its mysteries.

Mind you, it didn't always seem sweet to Forster, and this is a biography that knows how to dramatize the turmoil he felt. "I should have been a more famous writer if I had written or rather published more," he wrote in his diary on December 31, 1964, "but sex has prevented the latter." It is a nuance often overlooked in the story of a writer's life that he will, in some cases, stop publishing in order to preserve the legend of his gifts. The matter goes to the heart of Forster, and we can find fresh evidence both for and against him in the books about his art.

It was D. H. Lawrence, of all people at the time, who spotted Forster's trouble (and his opportunity). In a letter to Bertrand Russell, quoted by Christopher Lane in his essay in the *Cambridge Companion to E. M. Forster,* Lawrence identifies the difference between the mind of Forster and that of others. Forster knows, he wrote, "that self-realization is not his ultimate desire. His ultimate desire is for the continued action which has been called the social passion — the love for humanity — the desire to work for humanity." As early as 1922, Forster was putting his "indecent" short stories into the fire, "as many as the fire will take. Not a moral repentance, but [because] they clogged me artistically. They . . . were a wrong channel for my pen."

This will seem counterintuitive to many of the literary freedom fighters of today, and they may be right. There's no question that Forster's disavowal of sexual "content" eventually stopped him from writing novels. Yet there may be little to be gained in contemplating the novels he might have written when there's so much to be said about the ones he did write, and we can now begin to see the special forces that made them possible.

"What Forster wants to know about the human heart," wrote Lionel Trilling in his critical study, "must be caught by surprise, by what he calls the 'relaxed will' [and] what is so caught cannot be caught in any other way." It should probably interest us, as much as baffle us, that *Maurice,* the only one of Forster's novels to deal explicitly with homosexuality, is by far his least successful novel. In a sense — a sense that may be purely literary — *Maurice* is a book that just isn't personal enough. It wasn't a product of the "relaxed will" but of some other province, the forced will, the need to produce something uninflected and to name the unnamable. Not only embarrassment or self-censorship, but self-knowledge, I believe, kept the book out of sight for sixty years. Forster was anxious, no doubt, not to shame his mother, but more crucially, he may have been anxious not to shame the character of his art. For Forster, art was based, in his own words, "on an integrity in man's nature which is deeper than moral integrity," and—weirdly—it is that deeper integrity that is missing from *Maurice*. It is a novel that displays desire but does not inhabit it; a novel that "deals with" reality but does not increase upon it. The book is fine, but it has none of the metaphoric stamina of *A Passage to India*. It hasn't the pattern, the subtlety, the authentic shadows of life and death, or the ascending power to be found in the best of his novels. (This must be what Forster means when he later said the story of Maurice and Alec, especially the happy ending with its note of salvation, was "fake.")

Trilling, famously, managed to write a whole book about Forster without once mentioning his sexuality. In a letter he wrote to Cynthia Ozick many years later, he said that it wasn't until he had finished writing his Forster book that he came to "the explicit realization that he was homosexual." Trilling felt that it might have been due to a "particular obtuseness" on his part, but it didn't at first seem to him of crucial importance. As he was writing the book, Trilling simply (or not so simply) believed that Forster's mind was odd and unpredictable, his work drawing on political and moral questions bigger than the question of whom he was sleeping with.

To some biographers, the estimable Wendy Moffat included, there is no question bigger or more haunting than that one, and she leads you further and deeper into the forests of possibility when it comes to Forster's sexual motivations. He would conceal himself and reveal himself in unexpected ways. The codes of his Victorian childhood lay deep in him, Moffat proves, but she also shows how he could be queeny when he wanted to be, later on, when he was friends with Isherwood's crowd. In 1933 we find him writing a startled, dubious, rebuking letter to Siegfried Sassoon, who, despite his past gayness, had just fallen in love with a woman and decided to marry her. Forster, like many artists motivated towards having more than one life, was not always so keen on tolerating the multiple lives of others.

As a novelist and critic, Forster was a little civilization unto himself, but it is not his view of himself that keeps his work alive, but his larger view of humanity. His very famous motto, "Only connect the prose and the passion," did not apply in any straightforward way to himself. But it applies to our understanding of moral realism and the novel. As Trilling saw it, Forster was a product of the liberal imagination but also a writer "deeply at odds with the liberal mind, and while liberal readers can go a long way with Forster, they can seldom go all the way." When you look again at the novels you see a map of compassion disclosing dark continents. There are seas of philosophy and peopled villages; there are home truths and foreign parts. And it is Forster's genius that he can make us know each terrain intimately, without the impulse to turn each story too simply into a story about him.

Forster started early with the art of reticence. Monteriano, the Italian town in *Where Angels Fear to Tread,* floats "like some fantastic ship city of a dream." It was a place, unlike England, where the exotic may hold sway, where brute passion might serve to upbraid the world of parasols and lace. But if this is honesty—if Gino is some gracious, hulking warning against human pretension—then the dominion of English civility is also shown to be relentless. "Foreigners are a filthy nation," says Harriet Herriton, and the novel's dramatic charm lies in the way Forster slowly reveals, via the horribly bungled attempt to steal Gino's child, how the modern world has suffered greatly (as well as benefited) from England's good intentions. Italy is a culture as sophisticated as any, and in this novel, Forster's first, English arrogance begins to look like moral dullness.

Yet the good thing about the English, as viewed by Forster anyhow, is that looking down on foreigners is only a small part of the picture when it comes to the rites of superiority. They must also look down on each other. Forster always tries to resolve this snobbery in favor of true love, but the general impossibility of sex is seen mired in Forster's novels around questions of English class. No one is free to love and assume a place in the world so long as latent aggression (and defensiveness) about one's true station is allowed at every turn to foul the air of liberty. The ringing note in Forster, thankfully, is one of social comedy. Look at this passage from early in *A Room with a View,* where the forthright Mr. Emerson and his son George attempt the (one would have thought) simple business of offering the ladies their nicer rooms at the Pension Bertolini:

> "It's so obvious they should have the rooms," said the son. "There's nothing else to say."
>
> He did not look at the ladies as he spoke, but his voice was perplexed and sorrowful. Lucy, too, was perplexed; but she saw that they were in for what is known as "quite a scene," and she had an odd feeling that whenever these ill-bred tourists spoke the contest widened and deepened till it dealt, not with rooms and views, but with — well, with something quite different, whose existence she had not realized before. Now the old man attacked Miss Bartlett almost violently: Why should she not change? What possible objection had she? They would clear out in half an hour.
>
> Miss Bartlett, though skilled in the delicacies of conversation, was powerless in the presence of brutality. It was im-

possible to snub any one so gross. Her face reddened with displeasure. She looked around as much as to say, "Are you all like this?"

By "you all" she means, of course, the lower middle class, the say-as-I-find, commonsense, not quite delicate English. None of the foreigners in the book can deploy the almost mechanical disdain that Forster gives to these ladies. As characters, they have become perfectly solid in the public mind, not least because of Maggie Smith's and Judi Dench's punctilious embodiment of their little peccadilloes in the film adaptation. These are ladies who fear the violence of plain speaking even more than they fear the oily encroachments of the Italians, the snide intellections of the French or the dark opportunism of the Indians, as experienced or imagined by Adela Quested, to terrible effect, in *A Passage to India*. But it is really the English who undo each other with their narrow versions of life, and in his keen observation of this, with his comic gaze and his captivating prose, Forster is a lightning conductor.

Wendy Moffat is a lively and suggestive companion, alert, in her own ways, to what makes a writer's history and mentality. *Concerning E. M. Forster* by Frank Kermode, who died in August 2010, consists of the Clark Lectures he delivered at Cambridge in 2007, plus a spirited "causerie." It is a book that engages our hero at the level of the sentence. Kermode had what is sometimes called a perfect ear — not least, one suspects, for balancing praise with admonishment — and eight decades of reading made him English literature's perfect sonar, a sounding device for what is possible in the language. But a good critic must have a fruitful imagination as well as a sensitive ear, and in this capacity Kermode was among the very best. When it comes to

Forster, he not only detects the pulse of the author's secrets, but the persistent music of his creative understanding, and while he can be tough on Forster's snobberies and on his occasionally prideful stupidity—his disgust at the very poor, his dislike of study—Kermode knows how to read Forster in such a way as to give him, and us, the benefit of all his doubts.

Our attention is drawn to Forster's love of Beethoven's piano sonatas. The novelist, by his own admission, was not a good player, but he kept returning to the music, believing that "they teach me a little about construction. I see what becomes of a phrase, how it is transformed or returned, sometimes bottom upward, and get some notion of the relation of keys." It is the Fifth Symphony that makes Helen Schlegel so rapturous in *Howards End*—"Panic and emptiness! Panic and emptiness!"—and one of the sonatas, Opus 111, is played by Lucy Honeychurch in *A Room with a View*.

Kermode pursues single words and phrases from their social redoubts, chasing them through the stories and across the novels like an electrician following wires, leading from the source of power to the facts of connection. He does this with the word "faking": tracing its use in a critical passage of Forster's back to its musical meaning as a sort of improvisation, then on from there to its application in the plotting of *A Room with a View*. He hears the rhythms of Forster's mind, he identifies the struggles of his thinking, and, at all times, he seems to perceive some basic, possibly transferred need in Forster to address the question of authenticity. He sees how Forster is "playing." He hears the music and the silence, too:

> An inspired passage may be followed by one for which no claim to inspiration may be made, but it is unlikely that anybody will detect the seam where the inspired and the unin-

spired meet. "All a writer's faculties, including the valuable faculty of faking, do conspire together thus for the creative act, and often do contrive an even surface, one putting in a word here, another there." Among those words lurk the rhythms.

By the time he wrote the sentence quoted, Forster was already twenty-three years into his period of stagnation as a novelist, a period that would last until his death. And as Kermode suggests, it was clearly a musical understanding that lay behind Forster's notion of spiritual abundance and of silence. Beethoven's sonata Opus 111 was described by Alfred Brendel as "a last word leading into silence forever." We might say that silence was a creative act for Forster, allowing him to transfer his literary duty and let the music resound, while he tried to live. The "faculty of faking," so essential to his kind of art, had run into trouble with his wish to love.

In Kermode's "causerie," a welcome peroration on Forster's creative life, the critic discusses Edward Carpenter, the socialist, anarchist, free-living homosexual whom Forster would always admire and always know he could never be like.[1] "Carpenter," writes Kermode, "pretty exactly fits Forster's idea of one kind of creative person. He or she must be making something; it needn't be something of great value or beauty—his writing in both prose and verse was poor, but the point is that the work has involved the person concerned in a disinterested exercise of creative power, an achievement that has nothing to do with success."

For Forster, art was a state as much as a pursuit, a place

---

1. "Carpenter practiced a type of high-minded, fuzzy, ecumenical radicalism," according to Julian Bell ("The Elegant Optimist," *New York Review of Books,* October 22, 2009), and this was exactly the sort of selfhood Forster could scarcely imagine for himself.

where someone "is taken out of himself. He lets down as it were a bucket into his subconscious, and draws up something which is normally beyond his reach. He mixes this thing with his normal experiences, and out of the mixture he makes a work of art. [It] is a blend of realism and 'magic.'"

Forster was a supreme noticer, a quiet lord of the social nuance and the moral detail, but to deepen that, he was a king of the unseen. The mystic element positions his novels above himself and above the world in a way that makes them nicely celestial. (He chose a perfect title for his short stories, *The Celestial Omnibus*.) A great many novels, flat with accomplishment, are too much about what they're about, but *A Passage to India* and *Howards End* are also about something else, the hunt for metaphysical significance in the modern world, a significance that barely knows itself. We have to look again at Moffat's biography to see how the right stuff, the abundance of the faculty of faking, allowed Forster to write like that, and how the loss of that abundance, and the turn towards the possibilities of everyday experience, ended his willingness to sit down and write novels. Here is a man who spent the last forty years of his life not doing the thing he seemed born to do, and it was a silence born of choice, a cessation of music that now seems essential to his substance.

The refusal was knitted into his conscience. He could either write novels and make it his life, or have sex and make that his great "unrecorded history," but the two would never marry. Moffat reminds us that "when he was only four, he spent days earnestly studying an etiquette book for children. The book was titled *Don't!*" At school he was both Mousie and Cissy, and later, among the Cambridge Apostles, he joined his fellows in having an "idealistic attitude towards homosexual love." He yearned, like everyone, for "an honest connection with another human being," but knew that the soul of his writing might not wear it. It would wear the yearning, but not its gratification.

Moffat shrewdly makes note of his conviction "that passion was the key to redeeming the English soul," but she offsets that conviction with a quotation from Forster's diary, a part written as he set out to be a novelist, in which he captures in three sentences the entire matter of himself and his gifts: "I'd better eat my soul for I certainly shan't have it. I'm going to be a minority, if not a solitary, and I'd best make copy out of my position. There is nothing contemptible or cynical in this. I too have sweet waters though I shall never drink them. So I can understand the drought of others, though they will not understand my abstinence."

The sweet waters, of course, would have their day, but in consequence the novels dried up. After the warmth he enjoyed with his Indian lovers and the comfort of his policeman Bob Buckingham—a comfort that would last to the end of his life, despite and because of Buckingham's marriage—he could no longer dwell in the house of art as Henry James understood it. Forster couldn't stand James's novels—"disembodied" and "fastidious in their emotional control," with no carnality, reports Moffat. There is, of course, something self-defensive in this estimation. Forster wanted love more than he wanted fame as a novelist, and we must take it as an aspect of his kind of seriousness that he felt there was no chance of his having both.

Leonard Bast, the clerk in *Howards End* whose "cause" is taken up by the Schlegel sisters, is, consequently, a failed creation, and possibly an educative one for the man who made him. I think the key to Forster's later silence as a novelist may lie with Bast, the kind of lower-order man chasing after literacy and self-improvement whom Forster would happily have slept with but whom he could only fail to embody on the page.[2] The schism lies there, and it would lie, for different reasons, in D. H. Lawrence, and for several English novelists who could only mock up the workingman. They could support the underdog, many of them, love him, some of them, but none could render him in literature.

Leonard Bast was not possible for Forster because he loved his type, only knew him as a type, and such knowledge repulsed him. (Kermode: "To make a success of Bast and represent not the poor of the 'abyss' but the genteel squalor of the city-bound upper working class, Forster needed to know that culture and to be careful with it.") Life had intruded at last, and this novelist could no more write well about Bast than he could write well about gay men in *Maurice.* They sailed towards his desire and blotted out the sun. When his bodily experience began to take precedence, the novel writing was essentially over and the music was gone. Leonard Bast's death, for me, is the true advent of Forster's silence, the scene where a young, poor, self-educated half man suffers heart failure and is crushed under the weight of a falling bookcase.

His talent as a novelist had one more shout, and we hear its echo in the Marabar Caves, where desire is finally encoded as a dark enigma. Looking back on his trip to India, he said, "I didn't go there to govern . . . or to make money or to improve

---

2. Several contemporary reviewers of *Howards End* spotted the failure. "We venture to say," reports an unsigned review in the *Daily Telegraph,* "that Bart [*sic*], the most fascinating of all the characters, does not ring true." To the *Manchester Guardian* it was "a novel of high quality written with what appears to be a feminine brilliance of perception." The *World* considered Leonard to be "too shadowy." Frank Kermode brings the matter up to date, going further: "D. H. Lawrence thought Forster's effort with Leonard was 'a brave try'—a generous comment, but Forster thought he had done better than that and was ready to say he was satisfied with his rendering of the domestic life of Bast and his mistress. It would no longer be easy to find admirers devoted enough to agree with him."

people. I went there to see a friend." And he wrote a novel that would put the past — and England's colonial past, perhaps — behind him, opening up the possibility of newness for himself. In *A Passage to India* Forster says goodbye to all that, offering, near the end, a passage to himself as he might choose to live in the future, no longer the great excavator of human connection, his own passion transferred in the effort, but a man who can finally let beauty exist ephemerally. It is a description of sexuality among the lower orders:

> The Court was crowded and of course very hot, and the first person Adela noticed in it was the humblest of all who were present, a person who had no bearing officially upon the trial: the man who pulled the punkah. Almost naked, and splendidly formed, he sat on a raised platform near the back, in the middle of the central gangway, and he caught her attention as she came in, and he seemed to control the proceedings. He had the strength and beauty that sometimes come to flower in Indians of low birth. When that strange race nears the dust and is condemned as untouchable, then nature remembers the physical perfection that she accomplished elsewhere, and throws out a god — not many, but one here and there, to prove to society how little its categories impress her.

Not only society's categories, but Forster's, too, would be found unimpressive and open to change. Beauty will have its day. It will all pass on, and the beauty of the novel, his kind of novel, will rest there, pulsing with life and with Forster's particular sense of an ending. He would never love better than he wrote, but this connoisseur of the cautious arts, this protector of talent's wellsprings, very much wanted to believe that "happiness can come in one's natural growth." In January 1939, when

Auden and Isherwood departed England for America, Forster was the only person there to wave them off at Waterloo station. "I have myself to face a world which is tragic," wrote the one-time novelist, "without becoming tragic myself."

*October 2010*

# Styron's Choice

ONCE UPON A TIME in New York, a girl and her friends were away from boarding school for the weekend. The talented, youngest child of a famous American novelist, the girl decided that they should all go to see the movie *Sophie's Choice*. This wasn't the first time she had seen the movie: in fact, she had been at the premiere with her parents some months before, and had loved the whole evening, feeling dazzled to find herself so deeply planted in a world of adult accomplishment.

Like many children of the famous, however, our heroine became aware that night of there being a great deal to live up to; as the cameras flashed and the microphones were extended, she rightly recognized her overwhelming need to go from being the offspring of "someone" to being "someone" in her own right. Yet the later screening with her friends allowed Alexandra Styron to feel something simpler — something fleeced of doubt. Here is how she talks about it in her stirring memoir, *Reading My Father:*

> In front of us a woman sat alone, weeping quietly during the film's most wrenching scene and then openly sobbing

as the show ended and the credits rolled. When the house-lights came up, one of my schoolmates reached over, tapped the woman on the shoulder, and pointed at me. "Her father wrote that," he said. "He wrote the book." I blushed madly as the woman wiped her eyes and looked at me with astonishment. But the truth was I couldn't have been more proud if I'd written the book myself.

Though she doesn't refer to them, there are a number of psychologically taxing implications in that "wrenching scene." It might be the most famous scene in literature where a daughter is given away by a parent, unless we conclude that King Lear gives Cordelia away. Sophie's choice is to hand over her son to certain death in a Nazi camp or to give away her daughter, and it is the little girl, Eva Maria Zawistowska, who is delivered into the hands of a crazed commandant and seen to disappear into the distance holding her teddy bear and her flute. Alexandra remembered a question her father had asked her while driving her home from school one day. It resonates in the mind. She must have been about ten at the time.

> "What kind of instrument would a little girl your age play?" he asked.
> "Umm . . . a piano?" I answered, my hand out the window, tracing the arc of the power lines.
> "No, too big. How about a flute?"
> I figured he was asking for his work. I wanted to be a help. My friend Lili had a flute.
> "Maybe," I replied, leaping a tree with my fingers.

There is a sense in which William Styron struggled to hold on to his children just as he struggled to hold on to his mind. The two things cannot be disconnected, and the best of his writing choreographs the movement of inner turmoil and outward action — a thinking person's relation to history, or the play of the mind in the workings of families and nations — in ways that we might find to be convincing and beautiful. For my money, Styron was the purest stylist among the male writers who emerged, ruby-cheeked and ready to go, from World War II, a generation that would include Norman Mailer and Gore Vidal, James Baldwin and James Jones, Jack Kerouac and J. D. Salinger. Like many of them, Styron was born, in a literary sense, into the age of annihilation, and his prose sets a certain store by violence and lyricism, while maintaining dialogue with the three great American literary heroes of the previous generation: Faulkner, Fitzgerald and Hemingway.

Questions of power and bravery, of faith and refusal, would rise and fall graciously, momentously, in Styron's best work, making him an American existentialist with a new song to sing in those first years after the war. All his life, even long before his mental breakdown at the age of sixty, Styron struggled to find a fluency or a confidence to match his gifts. It was no easy journey, but it left us with a few masterpieces, and it must be time, long since time, to celebrate the story of his talent without succumbing to regrets over what else he might have done.

Styron was one of those novelists whose talent brought with it a knowledge of death. From the beginning, he gave his characters over to death, and sometimes to self-slaughter, long before he admitted to having any such thoughts about himself. The fate of daughters in his work should be borne in mind, too: even the most evenhanded procreator has to think twice about letting the young die on the page, but Styron never hesitated. *Lie Down in Darkness,* his first novel, opens with Milton Loftis waiting on the train that carries his daughter's coffin into town. There is a sense of personal breakdown everywhere in the book, and a fine, perfectly modulated account of parental ennui. A decade and a half before we had Sylvia Plath evoking her black-hearted daddy with the "Mein Kampf look" we have the daughter, Peyton Loftis, who grows up in a perfumed savannah of gothic rituals, a place where no person is simply one person, and where images of the good daddy give way to the feverish iconoclasm of "Daddy Faith," a local religious leader. "Oh, Daddy, I don't know what's wrong," writes Peyton in a letter to "Bunny," her father, "I've tried to grow up—to be a good little girl, as you would say, but everywhere I turn I seem to walk deeper and deeper into some terrible despair. What's wrong, Daddy? What's wrong?"

That debut novel is like nothing else, with characters suspended in a kind of liquid darkness. Camus loved it, as everyone else more or less did, because it took a classic, wan, Faulknerian mise en scène and transformed it into a universal outburst about the postwar family breakdown. Styron's love of battle was not yet a battle chiefly with himself, but one suspects the rudiments of that track were always in place. "Why is happiness such a precious thing?" asks Peyton, and indeed, she would find, as the author would in time, that happiness is a virtue best understood in the manner of its absence. From the start, in Styron, parents were giving away their children, societies were giving away their civilized values, history was giving up its certainties, and war was giving up its dead, and the writer could only attempt to capture this with honesty while he or she still had the strength. A sense of spiritual breakdown, however, lies not at the end of Styron's journey but at the beginning, when sleep and optimism were still possible and literary success came as proof that America was able to ask big questions of itself.

The fall from heroism is a story known not only to fathers but also to old soldiers, and Styron was both. In *The Long March*, a second, short novel, he wrote a pitch-perfect account of a generation that was no longer fit for heroism; a generation, Styron's own, that had shown its character in World War II but was sick of itself by the time of Korea, when many were called back to uniform. Domestic life and a new refrigerator had held out a promise to these men: they would never see such mire again, or so they thought, and their spirit would be tested by making their living, surviving the sex wars and excelling at the swimming hole. He writes of the leading character: "It was simply that after six years of an ordered and sympathetic life—made the more placid by the fact that he had assumed he had put the war behind him—it was a fact almost mystically horrifying, in its unreality, to find himself in this new world of frigid nights and blazing noons, of disorder and movement and fanciful pursuit."

If Hemingway's soldiers and hunters are always on the front foot, taking their lacerations for granted, Styron wrote of men who lived perpetually on their heels, teetering on the brink of collapse and spiritual dissolution. Captain Mannix, the diehard Marine in *The Long March,* walks ten miles straight with a nail sticking up on the inside of his boot. *The Suicide Run,* a posthumously published collection of fiction pieces from Styron's war, contributes something to our understanding of the fear of annihilation that ripped through his generation. Not just the fear, but the seeming inevitability that comes with mutually assured destruction. These are not men, as it happens, who really believe they can fight their way out of trouble. They are not supermen, but civilians stranded in uniform, arguing with their own nature, strung out in a no man's land, waiting for Godot or the Bomb to drop.

And yet the tone is not mere hopelessness, but something more interesting: Styron shows us a generation, his own postwar crowd, whose disappointment turned harsh, building a Cold War aggressiveness in the American story, instituting an element of corrupt policing in what would soon be called the military-industrial complex. One of the stories in *The Suicide Run* is called "Marriott, the Marine," and it captures all of this and something else: the growth of a depressive tendency in the life of its Styron-like narrator. "But whatever our situation," he writes, speaking for himself and his fellow Marines,

> we were all bound to each other by a single shocked awareness, and this was that for the second time in less than a decade we were faced with the prospect of an ugly death. In an abstract way it was possible to say that it was our own fault we were here. Yet suddenly, as my gaze wandered from face to face among this sullen, murmurous assembly of misplaced civilians — these store owners and office managers and personnel directors and salesmen — I was gripped by a foreboding about our presence in this swampy wilderness that at once transcended and made absurd each of our individual destinies, and even our collective fate. For it seemed to me that all of us were both exemplars and victims of some uncontrollable aggression, a hungry will for bloodshed creeping not only throughout America but the world, and I could not help but abruptly shiver in that knowledge.

Man's fate, we see from Styron, is no longer dependent on his personal morality, his judgment or his courage: in the end, it will unfold as part of a mechanical joke, a scientific event consequent to a moment's panic or a domino theory, and future man, we can begin to assume, will be married to extermination as much as he is committed to life.

This was the legacy of World War II — a legacy Styron would return to — but at this point in his career his take on the soldier's lot seemed to be not only a moral warning but a description of his own state of mind. Even at the height of his first success, he was embattled, making ready, one assumes from his writing, for new kinds of warfare on new fronts. No wonder the French loved Styron so much: they saw in his delicacy the vulnerability of the period, and they heard an existential lullaby beside the rocking cradle of Cold War strife. By the time he published his third novel, *Set This House on Fire,* the author had traveled into some of the central questions of his time. He asked just what depths of evil there might be in being a man.

You can argue with Styron's prose style — too frowsy for some, too sonorous, too full of statement — but at his best he could start the kind of fire in a reader's mind that never goes out. The mind of the slave rebel Nat Turner was brought to life and given moral lineaments in 1967 in *The Confessions of Nat Turner.* What caverns of the national psyche did Styron explore when writing that book, only to find himself, on publication day, beloved and derided in equal measure? He wrote like someone for whom style is not merely a question of this word or that word, this tone or that one, pitched *just so* to please the ear; Styron's style was a matter of moral compunction and creative tact, the manifestation of one man's struggle with the questions of how to live and what to do.

Which excellent American writer, in the secrecy of his own art, has not been trying to improve on the Constitution all along? And so many of them, among the best, have reached for the bottle, cracked up at four in the morning or lifted a gun. William Styron knew the stakes were high in his kind of truth-telling, and, though not all his novels are great, they are all great attempts, serious adornments bodying forth from a troubled soul, the kind of writing that enriches the culture at the points where the culture least knows itself.

In Styron we find a novelist scorched by his non-sentimental journey, but few are able, as he was, to revivify the form by putting not only himself into his books, but the reverse of himself, the things he could never have been. Junior novelists take note: Styron had the kind of style that puts its essence to the test, asking fresh things of his inventive power. For a white Southern gentleman to impersonate a black revolutionary leader and improve our understanding of both parties, and many parties in between, is an imaginative service not to be undervalued, not in his time, nor in ours either.

*The Confessions of Nat Turner* rang true as the shots rang out, which might be as much as can be said of a novel that wishes to enter its times. Styron looked at Nat Turner and asked a simple but profound question: What price blood? And the day has yet to come when that question could seem merely historical. But writer's lives are not theoretical: it hurt Styron to be accused of being a white Southern racist, and the book's bestsellerdom and its winning of the Pulitzer Prize did not ease his sense of ill omen. *The Confessions of Nat Turner,* though, is a very handy book in the age of Obama. The real drama of its argument is ongoing.[1]

It took Styron a long time to follow that book up. Only in 1979 was he finally ready to publish *Sophie's Choice,* and again

---

1. The historian Eugene D. Genovese captured the point well at the time in "The Nat Turner Case," *New York Review of Books,* September 12, 1968:

> *William Styron's Nat Turner: Ten Black Writers Respond* shows the extent to which the American intelligentsia is splitting along racial, rather than ideological, lines. As such, the book needs to be taken with alarmed seriousness, no matter how absurd most of the contributions are . . . Certainly, we need not probe the motives of these ten writers as they try to probe Styron's. But it is clear that the black intelligentsia faces a serious crisis. Its political affinities lie with the black-power movement, which increasingly demands conformity, mythmaking, and historical fabrication.
>
> No one need believe that any of these writers would resort to deliberate falsification – which they so readily accuse Styron of – but the intellectual history of popular and revolutionary movements has overflowed with just such crises, in which dedicated, politically committed intellectuals have talked themselves into believing many things they later have had to gag on. The black intellectuals seem to be going through what Marxist intellectuals went through in the 1930s and 1940s. Let us hope that they come out a good deal better.

he leapt headlong into unknowable troubles, artistic and political. It was a period when the Holocaust, as a subject, was surrounded by murmured exhortations about the maintenance of a dignity-conferring silence — as if any amount of silence could make those horrors quiescent — and a period when some held to the view that poetry after Auschwitz was a mockery of the suffering and a reminder of literature's numbest limits. In this atmosphere, Styron produced a book about the camps that runs to over six hundred pages. And he made the main protagonist a Catholic.[2]

But I will leave it to others to see spiritual defamation in the paragraph quoted below. I see only a kind of psychological beauty, the kind that few writers could raise from this well of sorrow. It is the work of a man who wished to taste the worst his century had to offer, and yet to show compassion in the telling. The eponymous Sophie opens this passage by telling Stingo, the book's narrator, about a recurring dream:

> "The one I've had all my life is about my father."
> "It's strange," I said. "Maybe. I don't know. Mothers and fathers — they're at the core of one's own life somehow. Or they can be."
> "When I was asleep a while ago I had this dream about my father that I've had many times."

Sophie goes on to tell Stingo the background to the dream. It involves an eighty-year-old friend of her father's, Princess Czartoryska, a rich Polish woman he met in the village of Ober-

---

2. The writer Evan Hughes has produced a spirited account of Brooklyn writers that makes sense of Styron's brave ambitions (*Literary Brooklyn: The Writers of Brooklyn and the Story of American City Life*, 2011): "The real Sophie upstairs on Caton Avenue had in fact been Catholic, but Styron's reasons for making the character Catholic were also aesthetic. Very few works of art had addressed the non-Jewish victims of Nazism. There were millions of them, and in Styron's view this unjustly was 'not in the public mind.'"

bozen, where they used to spend the summer. The princess and her father would have conversations in German about how to get rid of the Jews. The anti-Semitic princess had a phonograph and she loved music. Here's Sophie again:

> "So in the dream that has returned to me over and over I see Princess Czartoryska in her handsome gown go to the phonograph and she turns and always says, as if she were talking to me, 'Would you like to hear the Brahms *Lieder*?' And I always try to say yes. But just before I can say anything my father interrupts. He is standing next to the Princess and he is looking directly at me, and he says, 'Please don't play that music for the child. She is much too stupid to understand.' And then I wake up with this pain . . . Only this time it was even worse, Stingo. Because in the dream I had just now he seemed to be talking to the Princess not about the music but about . . ." Sophie hesitated, then murmured, "About my death. He wanted me to die, I think."

You will recall that the daughter given away by Sophie in the novel's most wrenching scene is a little musician: she goes off to the extermination camp holding her flute. And the man who wrote these characters and scenes—who wrote the line about parents somehow being at the core of one's life—was also the same man whose difficulty and remoteness as a father is captured so vividly by his daughter Alexandra in her book. The key, I would suggest, to these correspondences, and to much inertia, disorder and bad feeling both experienced and caused by William Styron, was the mental illness that later took over his life. We see its shadows in his work from the beginning, and it might be fair to suggest that people often missed these portents in their understandable urge to find a stable person to glorify or blame.

*Darkness Visible* is the long, beautiful essay Styron crafted from the terrible depression, a miasma of bottomless despair, that overcame him in 1985 after he gave up drinking. It never really lifted. Even by the standards of suicidal unipolar disorder, Styron's illness reduced him to a near-catatonic state, not merely brushed by Baudelaire's wings of madness but felled by them. He had, like some Miltonic precursor, been looking through the dark for so long that when it became visible it nearly blinded him.

The book has become famous for its description of a condition many people endure but from which few recover, and it turned out to be the miraculous account from the trenches that Styron had waited all his life to write. The book is dedicated to Rose, Styron's wife, whom he acknowledged as having been the person who saved his life, the woman who endured most and stood by him. Many writers enter, at a young age, a forest of dark enchantments, a place that has no exit and suffers no companionship. But Styron was lucky in his family. He always knew that death and nightmares lurked at the beautiful ends of the imagination, but he went on and produced books that speak to elements of human experience made new by his talent. Styron could ascend from these dark woods like a poet, and shine a light into his century. His work stands for the contentious passions of life, and that means love as well as war.

*September 2011*